A Gospel for the Cities

A Gospel for the Cities

A Socio-Theology of Urban Ministry

BENJAMIN TONNA

TRANSLATED FROM THE ITALIAN
BY WILLIAM E. JERMAN, ATA

Wipf & Stock
PUBLISHERS
Eugene, Oregon

Wipf and Stock Publishers
199 W 8th Ave, Suite 3
Eugene, OR 97401

Gospel for the Cities
A Socio-Theology of Urban Ministry
By Tonna, Benjamin
Copyright©1982 Orbis Books
ISBN: 1-59244-972-7
Publication date 10/28/2004
Previously published by Orbis Books, 1982

To my friend and urban missionary
Brian P. Hall
who introduced me to the value of urban life
and its place in God's plans.

CONTENTS

PREFACE TO THE SECOND EDITION

A fact can also be a sign to act. The fact of the Third World supercity is also a sign to act in certain ways—particularly for missionaries. It is a sign of God's plans for the contemporary world, and it invites missionaries to perform acts of faith which promote these plans.

Such an act of faith was the origin of this book. When I wrote it in 1975, I had a very practical purpose in mind, and it had to do with the missions. I was then secretary of SEDOS (Servizio di Documentazione e Studi), a service set up during Vatican II by missionary-sending institutes, the purpose of the service being to collect and analyze information which could help the membership respond to the challenges of the times. I was expected to provide those in charge with facts before they acted on the missions. I soon learned to run SEDOS as a discernment agency—gathering, sifting, scrutinizing data and then asking whether the facts could also be pointers to God's work. After all, the missions were an act of faith in God's work of salvation. And missionaries believed there was a plan of salvation.

But there were so many facts that I had to prioritize. Which facts showed more probability of being carriers of signs of God's plans? Much of the information I handled came directly from the field, as I interviewed and visited missionaries working at the grass roots and their superiors. I came to appreciate, in particular, what they were doing on their own initiative, aware that this was their creative and existential response to God's own proddings. After some time, I began to discern from my research a recurring message: human settlements tended to bring together the experiences and ideas of missionaries.

With my staff and my directors I was also investigating the major signs of the 1960s and 1970s: population pressures, independence movements, and cultural changes. The study of these trends converged with my own discovery: whatever the fact under scrutiny, it was inextricably linked with human settlements. The concept of human settlements was providing anchorage to most other facts. And working from this perspective, I began to see that most of the groundbreaking missionary action seemed to be happening in the cities. In urban settlements we could observe the phenomenon of more and larger masses as they emerged and concentrated in fewer and smaller places, with far-reaching social and cultural consequences.

It was the same discovery that in the 1970s had led the major agencies of the United Nations to accept the fact of human settlements as a catalyst for their specializations, an approach neatly capsuled by the secretary general of HABITAT, the U.N. settlements center, in his preface to Barbara Ward's *The Home of Man*: "It is in human settlements that practically all persons spend their lives." Here was the principle for prioritization I had been looking for. The fact was there, very visible, and I only had to read it as a sign.

My faith told me that the supercity could be a sign pointing to the invisible reality of God's plans for our world. As such it could be pointing to the next phase of mission. I realized the fact of supercities had become so crucial to humanity that it showed more probability to constitute a sign of our times than did other facts. As such it could furnish precious indications about God's plans for us. When I proposed to read it, I understood that I had to begin by analyzing it on its own merits: I had to get "the facts of the fact" right before trying to interpret it as a sign of a faith-reality. Only after that reading would I be ready to derive the implications for missionaries.

The structure of the book reflects this state of mind formed by ten years of service with SEDOS, years which included liaison work with the World Council of Churches in Geneva, particularly with its urban mission desk. It is a book about the fact of the Third World supercity read as a sign which indicates the way ahead for the next act of the urban mission. By the time I handed in the Italian manuscript, I had come to the end of my term with SEDOS and had learned to read the facts in terms of the whole purpose of the missionary enterprise. Because mission makes no sense if it is not part of God's plans for the world, its specifics are valid only if they derive from a minimal knowledge of such plans.

The first part of the book (chaps. 1–6) attempts to put in a manageable form the benefits of my co-workers' and my experience. After a historical overview of the supercity (chap. 1), it provides a conceptual, sociological framework (chap. 2), the components of which are applied to analyze Third World urbanization in this order: population and territory (chap. 3), work and order (chap. 4), way of life (chap. 5), and collective response (chap. 6). The criteria used to interpret facts as signs of God's plans are derived from the Bible and from church history (chap. 7). The practical consequences of their application to the supercity are formulated in terms of attitudes required by urban missionaries (chaps. 8 and 9) and of orientations for urban churches (chap. 10). The concept of values plays a key role in the passage from fact to sign.

Ten years after writing the book, I can look at it in a fairly detached way; from my own "human settlement" where I am pastor, I can recheck the facts, the signs, and the acts discussed in the book.

Fact Finding. Today, part 1 betrays the times when it was written. In the early 1970s, the energy, ecology, and inflation crises had not yet reached their full magnitude. The hopes raised in the 1950s by the concept of economic development had already receded. But those raised by the political independence movements were still very much around. Though the situation today in the middle of the 1980s reflects the demographic projections and the geographic picture outlined in chapter 3, 1985 finds the cities in an economic plight much bleaker than that portrayed in chapter 4. Chapters 1–6 reveal the process that had brought me from the sociology of the parish to the exploration of the world which was emerging from the collapse of colonialism.

When I wrote the book, I was aware that industrialization, notwithstanding the efforts made in those years to foster economic growth in the nations of the southern hemisphere, had not produced there the same consequences as it had in the North Atlantic nations. I realized, of course, that momentous change was going on in the developing countries. I also realized that it was not driven, as in the North Atlantic countries, by economic forces but rather by political forces. During my study years in Louvain, Belgium, I had been privy to a minor uproar when a priest-journalist had dared to suggest that the then Belgian Congo should be given its independence by the 1970s. By the time I had finished my studies, in 1960, Zaire was already an independent nation! The movement for independence had made more rapid strides than expected. It was not too long after I had completed my studies that the documents of Vatican II, especially *Gaudium et Spes*, were written and employed political independence as a lens for viewing better the "signs of the times."

For expatriate missionaries at work in newly independent nations, such changes brought with them, in the first place, new relationships with local governments and peoples. I began to see the consequences of the nationalization of schools and hospitals, and of the indigenization of societies. These were changes of far-reaching significance and, from my base in Rome, I ran the risk of not getting the facts right and isolating myself in abstractions.

What was needed was a concretization that could be offered to the missionaries who were grappling with reality at the level of the cutting edge of the ongoing change. This would also be a means of aligning their course with the direction toward which the signs of the times were pointing. Where was the concretization to be found? I had already found it in the concept of human settlements. By studying them well—and in the spirit of the first sociologists of religion, who had pivoted everything on the distinction between rural and urban parishes—I could find a microcosm of the change in process. It was less a matter of a contraposition of the two realities of the old rural world and the new urban sphere than one of an interdependence of the two. The world of the young churches could, for that matter, continue to be rural, but by the 1970s it had become inextricably intertwined with the supercity. From there I came to the theme of urbanization. It was precisely when studying the urban phenomenon that the new elements introduced by the changes of the times began to come together. That was the message of the first part of the book.

Ten years after I finished the book, the demographic and geographic processes described in chapter 3 remain in motion. The following facts, taken from Arthur McCormack's recent (1984) study, substantiate this: In Africa, Lagos is now nearly 5 million, or four times the figure given in chapter 1, and it grows at the rate of 25,000 a month; Cairo has almost doubled. In Asia, Dacca has quadrupled since 1971 and could be over 10 million by the year

2000. In Latin America, Mexico City, with a population of 14 million, has become the largest supercity in the Third World. Its population stood at 8.6 million when this book was written. São Paulo, with a population of 10.7 million in 1975, is projected to top 20.8 million by the end of the century. As regards geography, the only novelty is that Nigeria is building a new supercity in Abuja, away from the coasts.

In terms of the economic and political factors analyzed in chapter 4, the picture in 1985 unfortunately appears darker, this as a result of the devastating impact of the energy and inflation crises. For example, in Jakarta nearly 7 million live in substandard housing and conditions. In Latin America 31 per cent of the urban households are not reached by piped water at all. The shantytowns of Bogotá, Seoul, and Calcutta hold up to 2 million each.

Chapter 5 looked to cultural analysis to provide new ideas to overcome the heavy odds against city planners and administrations. It was a hope expressed by Mr. Salas in 1980 at the Rome Conference on Population and the Urban Future: "There are bright signs for hope and enough reasons to believe that we can use our faculty of foresight and the vast banks of technological knowledge that have been opened to us to reconstruct a human world. . . . Together we shall make a finer edifice in international cooperation, plot a few lines on the drawing boards, outline the shape and mark of the guide post of values of a truly human city."

Between 1985 and 2005, the administration of each major Third World city will have to cope with up to ten million more urban dwellers. In terms of response, twenty-six of those cities faced the issue in an international symposium, Metropolis '84, held in Paris in October 1984. One recommendation was to establish a secretariat to help exchange information, a kind of SEDOS for the secular city. The challenge has also been taken up by the Futures Group (1029 Vermont Ave., Washington, D.C.), which has created Futurba, the great model city, for various U.N. agencies. By adjusting the fertility rate factor, the Futures Group generates three "futures": with a constant rate of 4.8 births per woman, a population of 4 million in 1980 would grow to 9.4 million by 2000 and to 14 million by 2010. If the rate were adjusted to 3, the population would become 7.9 million in 2000 and 10 million in 2010. Adjusted to 2, the population would be 7.1 million in 2000 and 8.3 million in 2010, all with due adjustments to migration rates. The corresponding labor forces would be 2.6, 2.2, and 1.9 million in 2010.

Sign Reading. It was my theology, inspired by Vatican II, that provided me with the criteria that I used in chapter 7 to read the supercity as a sign. In the years following Vatican II the church-communion concept began to take precedence over the church-institution model. The impact of this change upon me is revealed in part 2 of the book.

In the 1970s the idea of the local church as the existential meeting point of God and humanity was being developed to pin down the theology of communion. In the 1980s this idea has become a firmly established concept and has generated the model of the ecclesial base community as the operational unit of the local church. The Latin American bishops set their seal on it at the Medellín and Puebla conferences.

The concept of opting for the poor to incarnate God's saving action in the local church—a principle also approved by the Latin American bishops—has proved difficult to translate into patterns of action. But much work has been done, not least on liberation theology. In the process, the criteria developed in chapter 7 have been tested and proved valid.

No doubt, the supercity has more to tell us on how to be a local church which has opted for the poor. It already has its Christians and it has its poor, all on the same territory sharing the same culture. Urban mission will continue to bring them together in an ongoing response to God's plans for redemptive action.

Policy Making. All this certainly indicates that the era of discovery and exploration has not ended for missionaries. There were moments, during Vatican II, when I almost thought it had. Would it not be enough, I wondered, to consolidate the positions achieved by the younger mission churches, now established in almost all parts of the globe? After all, the methodology of consolidation, with appropriate modifications here and there, had been the one used from the time of the very first generation of missionaries. What still remained undone was to hand over the leadership of those churches to the local people, in line with the call of Pope Paul VI in Kampala, Uganda: "You Africans, be Africa's missionaries!" Such consolidation, however, assumed that the overall situation would remain stable and that, as a consequence, the "field" of those churches would continue to be predominantly rural.

The implications of all this were far-reaching. Missionaries, operating prior to Vatican II in a rural world largely immune to the impact of the urbanization, had adapted—and they were correct to do so—methods and structures suitable to a rural culture. Rarely did their people migrate to the city, or return home if they did. The media of communication, even of social communications, that could have conveyed urban values to rural homes simply were not there. But in the years following Vatican II this was no longer the case: the urban and rural worlds had interpenetrated. Methods and structures inherited by the churches ran the risk of being too closely bound to the rural world. Their anchorage was also reinforced by some of the older churches which continued to bank on and to export—through their missionaries—church life models that corresponded to the rural model.

Only rarely was the urban process explicitly treated in ecclesiastical documents. Even *Gaudium et Spes* showed scarce awareness of it. The bishops of Asia, Africa, and Latin America, in their conciliar addresses, did not go beyond a recognition of its existence. Only Pope Paul's *Octogesima Adveniens* made an analysis of it and drew some practical conclusions.

When I wrote this book, I was searching for a specifically Christian response to the phenomenon of the supercity. My quest was not for new people to evangelize but for the new life styles of the peoples our missionaries already knew. The urban way of life was generating one such new life style, if not a new version of what we used to call "natural law." It was here that I began to search for responses, in terms of urban mission policies, to the phenomenon of the supercities. I knew I had a long way to go: my sign was not yet act.

This situation has not changed much since I drafted the first manuscript. Even the usually prolific declarations of action principles of church authorities have not been very available when there was a question of the urban missions. But there was some improvement. One positive act came from SEDOS itself: after its major effort in its research seminar of March 1981 to face the issues of the missions of the third millennium, it dedicated its assembly, in 1984, to urban mission.

Fortunately, action continues to be present at the grass roots. Seen from afar, this can be bewildering, given its pluriformity. But this very fact of pluriformity reveals the values of interdependence and transcendence. As such it could be a sign to act on these two values both at the generic and specific levels of solidarity and mission outlined in chapters 8 and 9.

Today, in 1985, I can consider this book as my grass-roots act after reading the sign found in the fact of the supercity. The specific task I took on when I wrote the book was the reading of urbanization as a *locus theologicus* for mission in the final quarter of the twentieth century. Today, I dare to stretch the faith I mustered then to hope that this act now becomes a fact which prompts readers to interpret it as a sign for their acts. This could become a process: my act becomes your fact which you read as a sign for you to act. Your act then becomes a fact for others to read as a sign for them to act. . . .

ACRONYMS

ACPO	Asian Committee for People's Organizations
CIDSE	Centre International du Développement Socio-économique (International Center for Socioeconomic Development)
CODESCO	Companhia de Desenvolvimento Comunal (Community Development Company)
HABITAT	United National Habitat and Human Settlements Foundation; Human Settlements Centre
SEDOS	Servizio di Documentazione e Studi (Documentation and Study Service, a joint venture of Rome-based generalates)

Part I

The Process of Urbanization

1

MISSION TO THE CITIES OF THE THIRD WORLD

Urban mission is the confluence of two currents in God's plans for the contemporary city. Inasmuch as it is mission, its radical impulse comes from God—and this is the origin of the first current. Inasmuch as it is urban, it takes place in the setting of that part of humankind that lives in cities—and this is the origin of the second current. Convergence occurs at the point of encounter between God and this human being—in the city, the object and finality of God's plans. The three terms "mission," "urban," and "God's plans" must be defined at the outset.

Basic Concepts

Mission

"Mission" means primarily "something to be done." In this study it is a matter of the salvation that is offered to humankind. Inasmuch as this salvation is articulated in time and space, it would be more exact to speak of a "process" rather than "something to be done," because the term "process" implies a succession of events and actions that are repeated with a certain regularity, although in diverse modalities, and are oriented toward a precise finality. Mission would be the process that, repeated for the human persons of every generation and every geographical situation, guides them toward salvation.

Such a process will involve diverse types of persons. Mission can even mean that "one person" sends a "second person" to a "third person." In the present context, God is the one to whom the first instance of sending is attributed; mission has its origin in the inner life of the Trinity.

The persons sent by God form a "complex," a chain, in which we can distinguish at least five links. The first link is the Son, sent by the Father. The

3

second link is the Holy Spirit, sent by the Father and the Son. These two links are wholly divine, even if, by the incarnation and Pentecost, they form part of human history.

The third link is the church, which immediately leads into the mixed zone where the divine is fused with the human. The church gives an expression of itself in the communities that it in turn sends, and they constitute the fourth link. Each community in turn sends out its representatives, those who are called missionaries, and they are the fifth link.

It will be especially to this last-named element that we shall be directing our attention in what follows. "Missionaries" will mean here persons who, by baptism and the faith, participate in the priesthood of Christ[1] and are trained and ready to live by the gospel in a milieu other than their own, with the aim of proclaiming the kingdom of God and of convoking the church there. Their distinctive charism is that of being animated by relationships with persons of other milieus and other religions or ideologies. This function—or better, vocation—is transcultural. This definition covers all baptized persons— clergy, religious men and women, lay men and women—who have this charism.

With the missionary completing the chain of persons "sent," we come to the third type of person involved in mission: the one to whom mission is directed—in this case, the one who lives in an ambit or culture in which the proclamation of the gospel is not yet a fact.

It can be argued that the milieu or culture, rather than the individual person, was the originally intended recipient of mission, at least of the mission referred to in Matthew's Gospel (Mt. 28:19). Matthew speaks of *ethne*, "peoples," "nations," not "individuals."

Despite the fact that we have long been accustomed to identifying "the people" with the inhabitants of a given nation or national state, the two concepts are not coincidental. Almost all modern states are composed of a *number* of "peoples." In Africa, Asia, and Latin America there are dozens of states, but within their borders there are dozens of thousands of peoples.[2]

Another reason why the concept of "people" must be made more exact is that it will be a basic concept for the identification, more and more detailed, of those to whom mission is directed. A people is not the sum of the individuals who compose it, but the complex made up of the stable relationships that they form among themselves. Hence to distinguish one people from another it is necessary to focus on this "complex of stable relationships," that is, their lifestyle, their way of viewing reality, their way of resolving problems. The social sciences have studied the concept of "stable relationships" in depth, and today they commonly use the term "culture" to describe it. Every people, accordingly, would have its own culture, and every culture would be formed by the "models" that facilitate conduct and interaction. These models recapitulate the particular realizations of a given people, not excluding material realizations (artifacts, products of technology more or less advanced). But the essentials of a culture will always be found in its traditional ideas, derived and chosen from the history of a given people and transmitted by means of symbols.

When therefore Matthew orients the missionary mandate to "the peoples," "the nations," he seems to want to point out a strategy also: to reach individual persons through their culture.

It would be fascinating to compile a missionary atlas of the peoples who have not yet been reached in this way. It would especially interest the present generation of missionaries, who have often been told that the era of geographical mission (when a people stood for a territory, a nation) is giving way to that of cultural mission (where people means especially culture, lifestyle). An attempt in this direction has been made by a Protestant body; it took as its criterion that a people was "not yet reached by evangelization" when less than 20 percent of its members formed part of the community of believers.[1] But this criterion, by itself, may be insufficient, too extrinsic.

For the present purposes, we restrict consideration to the *city as a culture*, because it offers to its residents not only a "common territory" but—and this is much more important—a totality of models that compose a fully particularized lifestyle. This does not at all mean that every city is a people, but that every city as such reveals a culture that is sufficiently its own to deserve to be studied individually as the specific object of mission.

It is not possible in the present work to investigate in detail the culture of particular cities. Nor do we intend to treat of the city in general, as such. Our aim, more circumscribed, is to piece together the constants that are characteristic of the metropolis in the so-called Third World.

Urban

"Urban," the second term to be defined, here covers all the "things" that characterize the fact of the metropolis. But, just as for the term "mission," so too here it is more correct to speak of "process" than of "things." The central interest is in the *process of urbanization*, which can be defined as the phenomenon by which millions of men and women move en masse from rural to metropolitan areas, and—more importantly—which transforms their lifestyle.

The first, more evident, consequence of this displacement is the new, higher proportion of humankind living in cities. In order to subdue the earth (cf. Gen. 1:28), human beings do not now tend to spread out evenly over an inhabitable surface; on the contrary, they tend to concentrate themselves, choosing as their preferred habitat certain nerve centers, whether already established or consciously sought out for some valued resource.

This is a relatively recent phenomenon: before the industrial revolution the overwhelming majority of persons lived in rural areas, resorting to "nerve centers" only for specific requirements. It is also an impersonal phenomenon: it has not been willed expressly by any individual or group. Initiated by developments apparently independent of it, it then proceeds under its own momentum, in most cases escaping subsequent control by human calculation.

It is a process that profoundly affects the lives of the persons who are caught up in it. And this is the second consequence of the mass migration to the cities. What comes into being is a new order of relationships among persons, radically different from what is obtained in rural areas and heavily imposed on newcomers. In this way too it is an impersonal process: "urban" is not something chosen by individuals, but the collective condition of all those who live in the city.

For mission, this new complex of stable relationships as the "culture" of the metropolis is the more disruptive and decisive aspect of all that is urban. It is a complex that is formed, as we shall see, by the regularity that patterns the normal interaction among residents and imposes on each one of them a particular way of reacting to reality and of behaving in daily life. For what concerns mission, "the urban" is first and foremost this conditioning.

There are therefore two elements that typify the modern, urban people and differentiate it from others: the geographical element (surface reduced to a strategic site) and the sociological element (particular system of relationships). These two elements together have long since constituted a sign of the times. It is the sign of urbanism, which must be of interest not only to city-dwellers but to everyone because it has disturbed the centuries-long equilibrium of human residence patterns and has introduced an unheard-of "second" natural law that now extensively regulates life in common. It must therefore be read as a possible indication of the divine plan of salvation for our generation and for successive generations.

God's Plans

The third term that must be defined for this study concerns God's plans for the contemporary city.

For humans, a plan is a rational effort to select the basic objectives of a certain course of action and to mobilize the resources, institutional and material, needed in consequence. The effort takes place on two fronts, that of formulation and that of implementation.

To formulate a plan means to make calculations in terms of priorities, available means, and linkages with the energies at one's disposal, according to the evangelical example of the tower-builder (Lk. 14:28). To implement a plan means to make the effort to transform calculations into actions, work, and results. All that is involved becomes part of a process: the process of planning.

Properly speaking, the plan of God is one of *God's* works, not humankind's. But it assigns a definite sphere for human reflection and activity. Under this aspect it is the sphere assigned to those in mission.

What is this sphere? In order to give an answer, it is helpful to distinguish between two moments or levels of a plan. There is the universal level, the level of a general plan, valid for all times and situations. And there is the particular level, or particular plans, where the general plan is applied to particularized human situations. Consequently there will be as many particular plans as there are human situations, but all of them will be coordinated and confluential with the universal plan.

As regards the universal plan, the task of mission is to communicate it to the world, according to the words of Saint Peter: "And he commanded us to preach to the people, and to testify that he is the one ordained by God to be judge of the living and the dead. To him all the prophets bear witness that everyone who believes in him receives forgiveness of sins through his name" (Acts 10:42–43).

The contents of this communication can be summed up as follows: God has a plan of salvation for humankind and God is realizing it in history. The key point of this plan is that God reveals himself to be a Father who loves the world of humankind so much that he sends his Son, with the mission of saving those human beings. And the Son becomes incarnate, takes a name—Jesus—lives among us and with us, showing us the image of the human being in its plenitude and loving us all the way to death on the cross, and loved by the Father all the way to resurrection, Easter. In this way the Son becomes the sign, the sacrament, of the Father's love for us, a love that pardons and sanctifies. This same love, in the interior life of God, is revealed as a Person—the Holy Spirit—who, sent by the Father and the Son, continues in the church the mission of Christ. The church thus becomes, for its part, the sign and sacrament of Christ: "I in them, and thou in me—that they may become perfectly one, so that the world may know that thou hast sent me and hast loved them even as thou hast loved me" (Jn. 17:23).

Thus the church, in the working out of salvation, becomes the heart of the divine plan because it is made up of those who, having been evangelized, believe, and, believing, evangelize. The sphere assigned to the work of the church, and hence to those in mission, is well defined in the missionary mandate: "Go, therefore, and make disciples of all the nations" (Mt. 28:19). "Go into all the world and preach the gospel to the whole creation" (Mk. 16:15). The gospel, the object of the proclamation, is nothing other than the good news of the salvation brought to humankind by the plan of God.

The sphere for each particularized plan is enlarged by being brought into the tasks that mission is called on to develop. It is clear that it is not the task of mission to formulate the plan: it firmly believes that the plan has already been formulated by God. It can, however, and must discover the plan, committing itself, according to the very lucid words of one of the internal documents from the fourth Synod of Bishops (1974), "to base itself on concrete realities because it is precisely in this context that God is present and reveals himself to us. [Concrete realities] become signs of the times that must be read, scrutinized, and interpreted in order to understand the designs [*lege:* plans] of God for today."[4]

In particular plans—always as something to be discovered—there will be found the confluence of the impulse that comes from God (mission) and the impulse that comes from humankind (in this study, the urban reality). As mission uncovers, step by step, a given particular plan, it responds to its summons, actualizing the plan in those aspects that require human collaboration. The modalities of each particular response will vary according to the elements of each particularized human situation. But the essential lines of such a response can be pointed to by a generalized reality, such as is the urban reality, leaving then to the individual collaborator the search for the immediate modalities in which the discovery and implementation of the particular plan for diverse urban situations—that is, diverse cities—is to be realized.

Before all else, each particular plan will reflect the essential lines of the universal plan. And these lines will become criteria for discerning what is a sign of that plan and what is not. For this discernment to be effective, a profound faith in the hand of God within every human reality is necessary. It is not by accident that the solemn promise "I am with you always, to the close of the age" (Mt. 28:20) is an integral part of the missionary mandate. If the Lord is with us, signs of his active presence cannot fail to be present. It is as Mark wrote: ". . . the Lord worked with them and confirmed the message by the signs that attended it" (Mk. 16:20).

The Emergence of the Metropolis

The city as a characteristic human habitat is a fact that goes far back into history. Some scholars, like Blumenfeld and Mumford, would trace its origins back to the era of the caveman. But it is more commonly dated about 5,500 years ago.

Most scholars are also in agreement that the history of the city can be divided into two overarching epochs. The first, and longer by far, is that which preceded the industrial revolution. The second period, relatively short but very intense, is that which extends from the industrial revolution to our own time—an epoch not yet closed. Some scholars—for example, Weber and Riesmann—stress the enormous differences between the two epochs and doubt that it is realistic to treat of the two in terms of the same history, that is, the same concept of city.

The City of Antiquity

According to Sjoberg, the first cities would date back approximately 5,500 years and would be those in the Mesopotamian region: the famous Ur, Babylon, Seleucia. A millennium later came the cities of the Hwang Ho (Yellow River) valley in China and those of the Indus valley in India. More or less contemporaneous were the cities of ancient Mexico (Teotihuacán).

In Africa and Europe, the first metropolises seem to have been Alexandria and the Greek cities, especially Syracuse.

The oldest cities, of course, hardly numbered more than 10,000 inhabitants, but with respect to previous clusterings—in caves, tents, pile dwellings, built-up villages, or, at the most, large encampments of nomads—they represented a qualitative leap forward and the point of departure for a long, drawn-out, multimillennial technological and organizational development.

To understand why this is so, it is necessary to note from the very beginning that the phenomenon of city is connected with certain major technico-scientific discoveries. The discoveries are in the area of primary, essential human needs. In practically all the regions where major cities arose—the Mesopotamian fluvial zone, the Nile delta, the Hwang Ho and Indus valleys —it was due to the discovery of irrigational technology on a large scale, hand in hand with the cultivation of grain, a product rich in nutritional potential, which can be transported easily and stored for prolonged periods of time. By extension, the modern discovery of new means of transportation means only that essential life provisions become reachable from a vaster territorial arc.

These discoveries have to do with *essentials* of human life: only when a substantial economic base is assured, and a number of persons freed from the daily struggle for their own survival, permitting them to devote themselves to such functions as government and social organization, intellectual research and applied technology, is the door opened to urban life.

But these discoveries by themselves do not bring about the qualitative leap forward. A body of organizational knowledge is also needed. With the discoveries, specialists emerge, and the division of labor and social life becomes more complex. Institutions take on more prominence, and an organizational hierarchy is needed to harmonize and integrate the various specialized activities.

A third condition required for the birth of a city is accessibility. In fact, the first cities were always sited at natural meeting places of diverse cultures, such as the valleys of Asia and the Central American corridor.

Once formed, the cities developed economic, political, cultural, and religious functions. They became mercantile centers, seats of the accumulation and distribution of riches. As such they became centers of power, often military and colonial power (over neighboring territories and other human settlements weaker and less developed). This is particularly evident in the history of ancient Asia Minor and ancient China.[5]

The Modern City

In the mid-nineteenth century another qualitative leap forward in the history of the city took place. Again it depended on technological discoveries, but this time they were not linked with agriculture and social organization, but with the capacity to exploit new sources of energy and to create new means of production. This was the large-scale use of the machine. The phenomenon occurred first in the West, where the capitalist system, developed by the bourgeoisie, acted as catalyst.

The most dramatic aspect of this new phase was precisely the very rapid displacement of populations from rural areas and their concentration in the cities, where the new means of production, namely, factories, were sited, capable of exploiting the new energy sources—carboniferous minerals at first and later petroleum and electricity.

Whereas in the ancient city, population concentration proceeded at a slow rate and the flow from rural to urban areas was relatively nondisruptive and even sometimes reversed, now the cities, under the pressure of mass movements, exploded.[6]

Sustaining and accelerating the urban expansion, the factor of extraordinary demographic growth entered in, resulting from scientific and technical progress in the field of medicine, which we shall examine in chapter 3. Here it will suffice to point out that this progress permitted control over natal, postnatal, and early childhood mortality rates, with an effect of geometric proportions on population growth.

As to the process of urbanization in the Third World, it must be noted immediately that it was not dependent on the industrialization factors that produced it in Europe and North America. It proceeded at its own pace, so to speak, or better, under the influence of more complex factors, which we shall go into later. We shall first touch on the rhythm of development of the "modern" city, making use of numerical data published by the United Nations.[7]

In 1850 there were only 94 cities in the world with a population over 100,000. By 1900 that figure had grown to 291; by 1950 there were 760 such cities, with a combined population of 241 million—that is, approximately 10 percent of the world population.

During the first half of the twentieth century, while the total world population doubled, that of the cities quadrupled.

In 1950 the most urbanized parts of the world were Australia, northwest Europe, North America, northeast Asia, and the south of Latin America. In those areas, about 52 percent of the population living in cities of 100,000 or more inhabitants was to be found. Africa was the least urbanized continent, with only 9 percent of the population living in cities with 20,000 or more inhabitants.

In succeeding decades, however, the USSR and China showed the highest rates of urbanization. In 1959 urban residents in the USSR reached 48 percent of the total population, as contrasted with 32 percent in 1939. The annual growth rate from 1950 to 1959 was 4 percent. In China about 20 million persons migrated from rural to urban areas between 1949 and 1956. It was the largest population displacement in all history. The corresponding annual growth rate would be 6.5 percent. In Europe and North America the rate of urbanization reached its apex toward the end of the nineteenth century. It declined from 1930 to 1960 and, in some countries, declined again from 1941 to 1951 because of warfare and other causes, such as the economic crisis of the 1930s and the growth of suburban areas.

As regards the continents, the Third World population of the metropolises of Asia and Africa grew at a more vigorous rate in the twentieth century than in the nineteenth. The phenomenon then invaded Latin America: after 1900 the rural population began to move en masse toward the various national capitals, reinforcing the impulse of concentration.

The Siting of Metropolises

A decisive factor in the origin and development of almost all Third World metropolises was the historical fact of colonialization on the part of European peoples. Cities such as Madras and Calcutta, Hong Kong and Singapore were born as support bases for imperialist interests; they exercised commercial, administrative, and military functions. These cities, and many others, in Latin America and Africa as well, sprang from the concerns of the European population residing in them and the interests of the overseas metropolitan centers—not from the needs of the local populations. But the "foreign" elements served as a pole of attraction and a model of development. The physiognomy of many cities in the Third World mirrors this origin and also explains certain "schizophrenic" structurings.

Although many of the individual factors that explain urbanization in the Third World if taken one by one coincide with those that govern urban phenomena in the First World, their interrelationship is not the same. The most outstanding difference is that industrialization precedes urbanization in Europe and North America, but follows it in the Third World continents.

A quick survey of the major factors in urbanization will clarify the patterns of interrelationships and the directions that the urban process has taken in the two worlds.

Colonialism, only faintly alluded to so far, has long been a historical factor and, as such, essentially diverse in its impact on each continent. And it would be dangerous to think that its vitality is spent. As we shall see in chapter 4, it generated structures and equilibriums in the present international order that tend to perpetuate the reasons why the city of the Third World remains oriented outward and has not succeeded in providing public services and employment for the rural zones that circumscribe it. With some exceptions, for example, Brazil, it is the historical factor that explains the present articulation of the Third World metropolis. Geography did not change with the departure of the colonialists.

The demographic factor also works differently in the two worlds. We have already noted that populations have been growing at more accelerated rhythms in Asia, Latin America, and Africa. Because the resources of the countryside remain the same, the "excess" population is forced to move toward urban areas, even if their needs cannot be met there. Urban immigration, as a result, is more substantial in the Third World.

The economic factor is closely linked with the function of satisfying the needs of the "excess" population. And it is here that the causes of urban growth in the Third World stand out with greater obviousness. Here the city is not industrialized. At most it manages to provide some minimum of public services. In the First World public services followed productivity; in the Third World they precede it. The reason for this is to be found in the urgency of providing the basic needs of the immigrant population from rural areas —an urgency addressed to the same city that is called on to create new jobs.

The political factor does not seem to have reduced the tension. Preoccupied with the administration of new political subdivisions, it has tended to concentrate itself in the national capital—thereby enhancing its attraction for the "excess" population. The capital becomes, in many cases, the only national population concentration, and usually grows at such a pace as to be far ahead of any urban planning.

The cultural factor, finally, acts upon the ensemble of the interrelationships of the historical, geographical, demographic, economic, and political factors, offering a modicum of meaning to urban life. We shall see later how the metropolises of the Third World are culturally very different from those of the First and Second worlds.

Beyond doubt, the best way to assess the import of urbanization in the Third World is to begin with its terminal points, that is, the Third World cities themselves. In Asia, Latin America, and Africa today there are seventy-two cities with a million or more inhabitants. What are these cities and where are they found on the surface of the three continents?

Asia

Two-thirds of all the Third World metropolises—forty-eight out of seventy-two—are in Asia. All told, some 132 million persons live in these forty-eight cities.[8]

Accurate, up-to-date statistics for mainland China are not available, but the data at our disposal indicate that there are eighteen cities there with a population over 1 million. They are Shanghai (10,820,000), Peking, the capital (7,570,000), Tientsin (6,280,000),Lü-ta (Lushun-Talien, formerly Port Arthur-Dairen; 3,600,000), Canton (3,000,000), Shenyang (formerly Mukden; 3,000,000), Wuhan (2, 226,000), Chunking (2,165,000), Harbin (2,000,000), Changchun (1,800,000), Sian (1,500,000), Nanking (1,455,000),Tsinan (1,200,000), Tsingtao (1,144,000), Chengtu (1,135,000), Taiyuan (1,053,000), Fushun (1,000,000), and Shiukwan (1,000,000).

In India, four of the eight metropolises with populations exceeding 1 million are on a coast and trace their birth or their extraordinary development to Western colonialism: Bombay (5,971,000), Calcutta (3,149,000), Madras (2,469,000), and Ahmadabad (1,586,000). The other four cities in the million-plus category are in the interior: Delhi, the capital (3,288,000), and Kanpur (1,154,000) in the north, Bangalore (1,541,000) in the south, and Hyderabad (Haidarabad; 1,607,000) centrally located. In addition India has nine cities with populations between 500,000 and 1 million: Nagpur (866,000), Poona (856,000), Lucknow (749,000), Howrah (738,000), Jaipur

(615,000), Agra (592,000), Varanasi (584,000), Madura (549,000), and Indore (543,000).

Indonesia, with a total population greater than that of Japan, has three cities in the million-plus category: Jakarta, the capital (5,490,000), Surabaja (1,552,000), and Bandung (1,200,000), all three on the central island of Java. There are three other major cities: Medan (636,000), at the extreme north of the archipelago, Blambang (Palembang; 583,000) on the island of Sumatra, and Semarang (642,000) on Java.

Pakistan has two cities with more than a million inhabitants: Karachi, the capital (3,499,000), and Lahore (2,165,000). There are four other major cities: Lyallpur (822,000), Hyderabad (628,000), Rawalpindi (615,000), and Multan (542,000). Only Karachi is on the coast.

The three other Asian Third World nations with more than one city in the million-plus category are South Korea, with Seoul, its capital (6,889,000), Pusan (2,454,000), and Taegu (Daegu; 1,311,000); Turkey, with Istanbul (2,547,000) and Ankara, its capital (1,701,000); Taiwan (Formosa), with Taipei, its capital (2,089,000), and Kaohsiung (1,020,000).

The other Asian Third World cities with 1 million or more inhabitantas are all capitals of their respective nations: Teheran (4,496,000), the capital of Iran; Bangkok (Krung Thep; 4,130,000), the capital of Thailand; Ho Chi Minh City (Saigon; 3,460,000), the capital of Vietnam; Rangoon (3,187,000), the capital of Burma; Manila-Quezon City (2,444,000), the capital of the Philippines; Baghdad (1,491,000), the capital of Iraq; Dacca (1,320,000), the capital of Bangladesh; Damascus (1,042,000), the capital of Syria.

There are also the two major city-states that are direct descendants of British imperial outposts: Hong Kong (4,407,000) and Singapore (2,278,000).

Other major Asian Third World cities with a population between 500,000 and 1 million are Beirut (800,000), the capital of Lebanon; Aleppo (779,000), the capital of Syria; Kabul (749,000), the capital of Afghanistan; Izmir (Smyrna; 637,000), the capital of Turkey; Colombo (592,000), the capital of Sri Lanka (Ceylon); Kuala Lumpur (557,000), the capital of Malaysia.

Latin America

Sixteen Latin American cities have a population exceeding 1 million. Five of them are in Brazil: São Paulo (5,925,000), Rio de Janeiro (4,252,000), Belo Horizonte (1,107,000), Recife (1,061,000), and Salvador (1,007,000). It is interesting to note that the first three form a *megalapolis* ("conurbation"), occupying 2 percent of the total national territory but containing 25 percent of the total national population. São Paulo alone houses 34 percent of the nation's industry.

Mexico has three cities in the million-plus category: Mexico City, the capital (8,628,000), Guadalajara (1,641,000), and Monterrey (1,091,000). Colombia also has three cities with populations in excess of 1 million: Bogotá, the capital (3,102,000), Medellín (1,195,000), and Cali (1,003,000).

Six other Latin American cities with a population of more than 1 million are the capitals of their respective nations: Lima (3,158,000), Peru; Buenos Aires (2,975,000), Argentina; Santiago (2,662,000), Chile; Havana (1,861,000), Cuba; Montevideo (1,230,000), Uruguay; Caracas (1,035,000), Venezuela.

Some other capital cities do not reach a population of 1 million but are major urban concentrations: Santo Domingo (923,000), the Dominican Republic; Guayaquil (823,000), Ecuador; Guatemala City (701,000), Guatemala; La Paz (655,000), Bolivia; San Salvador (500,000), El Salvador.

Other major cities: Córdoba (903,000), Rosario (821,000), and La Matanza (658,000) in Argentina; Porto Alegre (870,000), Belém (565,000), and Fortaleza (520,000) in Brazil; Barranquilla (719,000) in Colombia; Quito (600,000) in Ecuador; Netzahualcoytl (580,000), Aczapotzalco (545,000), and Leon (Leon de los Aldamas; 526,000) in Mexico; Maracaibo (652,000) in Venezuela.

Africa

There are only seven African cities with a population exceeding 1 million. Three of them are in Egypt: Cairo, the capital (5,084,000), Alexandria (2,312,000), and Giza (1,246,000). The others are Kinshasa (2,008,000), the capital of Zaire; Casablanca (1,808,000), Morocco; Addis Ababa (1,083,000), the capital of Ethiopia; Lagos (1,061,000), the capital of Nigeria.

Africa has nine metropolises with a population between 500,000 and 1 million: Algiers (904,000), the capital of Algeria; Ibadan (847,000), Nigeria; Dakar (790,000), the capital of Senegal; Nairobi (736,000), the capital of Kenya; Accra (717,000), the capital of Ghana; Rabat-Sale (616,000), the capital of Morocco; Tripoli (551,000), the capital of Libya; Tunis (550,000), the capital of Tunisia; Dar es Salaam (517,000), the capital of Tanzania.

What is the Metropolis?

These names and statistics from the urban Third World of today, even if they sensitize one to the dimensions of the problem, run the risk of posing more questions than answers. This happens almost always in the merely quantitative approach to an essentially human situation. Names and figures must be integrated, highlighting what more closely touches concrete persons in the cities. It is precisely this aspect that will be of greater interest to missionaries.

A city is something more than a collection of masses in one physical location. As a "mode of life in common," the city must be considered as a "life mechanism," that is, an artificial ambit, the fruit of human genius and effort, where life is no longer a matter of reacting to nature and adapting oneself to it, as in smaller communes, but of imposing a measure to one's life and that of others—to nature itself. The city is the space that humans have created for humans, molding nature and subduing it to their own interest.

But if every city "creates an ambit," not every ambit respects the conditions necessary for living together in a human way. We must spell out the essential conditions required for living together in a human way, in order then to use them as evaluation criteria for the city, to determine whether the cities are truly fashioned for human beings.

An objective point of departure would seem to be the consideration of the fundamental needs of the human being. True, it is not easy to pinpoint the indispensable needs of the human being. But today the substantive documentation of the United Nations is available on this matter.[9] The entire treatment by this international body, from the very beginning, of fundamental human *rights* is reducible, basically, to a search for a universally valid answer to the question: What are the basic human *needs* of our time?

In the documentation prepared for the world conference on the environment (Stockholm, 1973), a list of "basic needs" was drawn up, which can be taken as a reliable guide. It can serve here as an explication of the objective criterion mentioned above—especially because the list was compiled with the metropolis in mind.

Human Needs

In what way do the natural and artificial ambits of life satisfy or frustrate human needs? This is the most pertinent direct question because it does not focus on the minimal biological base for subsistence but probes for the characteristics of an ambit that would permit an adequate individual and social life. The document mentioned states the following: "We know that persons must eat, must have shelter, must be in good health, and must live in some form of family or clan. Beyond this minimum we enter a zone where there are considerable cultural differences and also a notable ignorance of facts."

To give them a sharper focus, all these needs can be fitted into four categories: (*a*) employment—in response to the need to "be independent," to have a personal role in "shared life"; (*b*) housing—not only in response to the need for protection against the physical environment (cold, rain, sun) but also as a base of privacy; *(c)* public utilities and services—in response to the need for food, medical care, hygiene, education, communication; *(d)* community —in response to the social needs of public order, training, civil, cultural, and religious life.[10]

As is only logical, the four categories are referred to the ambits of "life together" in all parts of the world. But the purpose here is to see how and to what extent the metropolises of Asia, Latin America, and Africa are adapted and prepared to correspond to this schema of needs.

The Response of the City

In terms of the United Nations study, it can be said that the metropolises of the Third World do not measure up to the first three categories of needs: employment is not available, housing is not available, the most elementary of utilities and public services—at least for the masses living in the cities—are not available. And despite the great efforts already made or in process, the situation is not only not reversing itself, it is becoming worse: the cities' response to these needs is less and less what it should be.[11]

As to the fourth category of needs, on the other hand, there is a glimmer of hope: at least in recent years these cities have managed to offer the masses of their inhabitants a strong sense of community life. In this respect they differ from the metropolises of the First World.

Even more interestingly, within the United Nations and other similar bodies, there is a tendency to use this positive aspect to respond more adequately to the voids identified in the other three categories. In other words, the better human community aspect is used as a basis for remedying the faulty response of the city to the needs of employment, housing, and public services.

We should now see more concretely how the situation in the Third World continents measures up to these four categories of basic human needs.

Employment: Unemployment is often the first harsh reality that dissipates the hopes of the immigrant newly arrived in the Third World metropolis. It takes different forms, from the absolute impossibility of "getting by" to the various modalities of underemployment, including irregular, occasional, and uncertain employment. Because the dividing lines between unemployment, underemployment, and irregular employment are very imprecise, research in this field is difficult and the results ambivalent. But some data have been collected.

In a study based on investigations made in preparation for the World Employment Program of the International Labour Office, Professor Paul Bairoch concluded that between 10 and 20 percent of urban work potential in the Third World is unused. From 1950 to 1970 the mass of unemployed urban workers tripled, with an absolute increase of at least 20 million persons. Underemployment is not included in these figures: it escapes statistical control.[12]

The same sources point to the immediate causes of the phenomenon: the increasing population density; the disparity between rural and urban earnings (which makes many—too many—dream about having a place in the city); the increase in rural youth population—once they acquire a minimal education, they leave for the city with the hope of a better life. It is a fact that the cities do not cope with the massive demand for employment; even when new jobs are created, they are never sufficient to absorb the newly arrived immigrants.

According to Bairoch, it would be useless to look for a solution to this serious problem in the acceleration of existing patterns. This would mean to risk transforming the greater part of these cities into vast camps of indigents, in which a new international humanitarian organization would have to take upon itself the distribution of food, quickly, in a multitude of Romes, but Romes without empires![13]

The problem is more acute in Asia. About 200 million Asians are already without work and an estimated one-third of them live in cities,[14] which means that the disparity between their condition and that of the more fortunate residents is unmistakably visible. Characteristic of Asian unemployment is the low adaptability of the unemployed to work that does not correspond to their aspirations and the status they intend to preserve. This lack of adaptability is perhaps explainable in terms of strong social biases and the "impassable barrier" that surrounds diverse castes and categories.

Urban unemployment is less visible in Latin America than in Asia. Many succeed at running their own small business or at least earning their daily bread by themselves without having recourse to an employment office. But the discrepancy between unemployed work potential and available jobs is no less severe. The major difference between the two continents seems to be that the unemployed Latin American work potential vegetates in the sector of private services—that is, in activities of extremely low productivity. In addition the programs drawn up by authorities for vocational training or retraining have a very mild impact, whether because of poor health conditions, or irregular work attitudes and habits, or the low level of instruction.[15]

In Africa, too, the number of immigrants to the cities exceeds the number of jobs available. The excess finds a way to survive in domestic services or handicrafts. Here we encounter the phenomenon of so many women who work as domestics, or retailing merchandise, or similar self-employment. Again, underemployment aggravates the problem. Training, here, accomplishes very little: among the more frustrated and disillusioned are precisely those who have completed their studies with success but cannot find work and are constrained to a parasitic existence.[16]

Housing: That the city is more than the sum of its inhabitants leaps to one's eyes from the second characteristic of the urban world in Asia, Latin America, and Africa: in almost all cases, the number of inhabitants exceeds by far the number of dwelling units. The city does not offer shelter to all those who seek it there.

The problem is serious because it touches on one of the essential needs of the human being. Since the time of the cave-dwellers, in whatever type of society, the human being has always had a dwelling. The phenomenon of homelessness is a phenomenon specific to urban civility.

In 1970 it was calculated that it would be necessary to construct from eight to ten new housing units for each 1,000 inhabitants to provide for future needs, assuming that the useful lifetime of a housing unit would be thirty years.[17] In fact, construction from then to now averages one-half to three dwelling units per 1,000 inhabitants. We are a long way from an adequate response to the needs. And it is precisely in the metropolises that the discrepancy is most acute. The reasons are absence of effective planning, absence of an organized and flexible building industry, absence of a credit system, and absence of qualified construction workers.

Inhabitants who do not manage to find a dwelling tend to provide for themselves in unauthorized settlements. A few years ago this was the case for 30 percent of the population of Dakar, Dar es Salaam, and Lusaka; 35 percent in Calcutta, Karachi, and Manila; 44 percent in Colombo; approximately 50 percent in Recife, Maracaibo, Guayaquil, and Mexico City.[18]

Using statistics supplied by the United Nations, from one-half to one-quarter of the urban population in *Asia* lives in hovels, under inhuman conditions, to the prejudice of their health, productivity, and social well-being. Housing is, beyond a doubt, Asia's most serious social problem. In 1960 it was calculated that 23 million housing units were needed to cope with the real needs of the continent, excluding mainland China and some other, smaller states. Ten years later, the figure, at least for India, had doubled. Still more serious: new units always end in the hands of the affluent. And so we confront such facts as the 600,000 persons who sleep on the sidewalks of Calcutta. In Manila the population grows at an annual rate of 4.5 percent (from 1948 to 1957), while that of the slums and shantytowns grows at a rate of 12 percent (from 1950 to 1967). Today the slum population constitutes one-quarter of the entire city population.

The same situation obtains in practically all Asian metropolises, to the point that, according to the United Nations, the degree of disorder and of urban depression goes beyond the imaginable. The majority of immigrants who arrive every year from rural areas ends in hovels and huts, and it is not rare for unrelated families to occupy a single room, subdivided horizontally or vertically. Under such conditions, rentals of course become exorbitant, and those who are weaker suffer the more from it.

The overpopulation that characterizes the cities of Asia also aggravates the problem of employment because it contributes to the unstable nature of the work potential. The immigrant who finds work is not inclined to send for his family from his hometown: he does not want them to have to sleep on the streets or in a single room shared with others. There is room only for the single person willing to join with a family of relatives or a group of fellow villagers, or to sleep in an alleyway or at the place where he works. He does not find a fixed residence and the unity of his family is not reconstituted— with all the easily imaginable consequences.[19]

That a housing problem also afflicts the cities of *Latin America* is unavoidably obvious to even the hurried visitor, who will be overwhelmed by the sight of the immense layers of huts, *favelas*, that invariably circumscribe the metropolis. The peripheral zones, usually uncultivated land, lend themselves to the building of do-it-yourself houses. The situation is different from that in Asia where virtually every last square foot of land is cultivated right to the very edges of the cities, and, at any rate, is too precious to be turned over to immigrants. Thus, whereas immigrants in Asia concentrate in the older sections of the cities, or in the few parcels of land that cannot be cultivated (the banks of waterways, exposed riverbeds, swampy land, or the city streets), or on boats in rivers, canals, and ports, in Latin America they settle down in shantytowns.

In *Africa* too what housing is available is almost always overcrowded and lacks even a minimum of public services. Slums are on the increase. And there is no escape, especially for the less well-off because everything is left to the mercy of free enterprise. In Kampala, the capital of Uganda, for example, housing is divided into privileged and reserved zones: Bugolobi for civil servants, Kolelo for the wealthier, Nakawa for the less wealthy, Rugaba for Catholics, Namiremba for Protestants, Kibuli for Muslims. The location and quality of housing depend on one's finances and origins. For those who do not have much, little is available.

The overarching problem, on all three continents, seems to be that of the development and rational use of land suitable for housing. It is not only a question of privations and resources. It is also, and perhaps primarily, a problem of the conflict of interests among owners, authorities, and the homeless masses. It may also be a problem of architecture and city planning: it seems that the older apartment buildings and the more compact of the newer ones do not provide the necessary social and communitarian environment. It also happens frequently that in the renovation and modernization of historical city centers, entire communities are uprooted.

Utilities and Public Services: Besides employment and housing, the ambit needed for "living together" has another essential element: the physical and social infrastructure necessary for "survival" under a roof—such things as streets, water, electricity, sewers, retail stores, public transportation, and many other things (such as hospitals, schools, meeting halls, libraries) that come under the overall heading of "public utilities and services." If the prospects for "a roof for everyone" in Asia, Latin America, and Africa are not rosy, those for the infrastructures are no better. It is a fact that governments in the various countries have not given priority to these physical and social needs, preferring to concentrate their resources on industrialization. The idea, however, that a response to these human needs would also favor economic growth has gained some ground.

In *Asia*, civil authorities rarely manage to give their cities satisfactory provision of running water, electricity, sewers, means of transportation, streets, garbage collection, and sociocivic services such as hospitals, schools, and social welfare agencies. The urban population grows too quickly—at a rate well ahead of all expectations, or at least in excess of administrative resources and capacities.

In Jakarta, the capital of Indonesia, the population of 5.5 million is housed in a vast conglomeration of settlement concentrations without sewers; for the most part, drinking water is not available and public transportation is not provided. The pattern in Bangkok and Manila, apart from the central boulevards, does not seem any better. In Taipei the same bus network of the 1970s must meet the demands of a passenger increment amounting to 60 percent in a decade. In Calcutta, a sixty-mile stretch along the Hooghly River, housing 8,200,000 persons, is bereft of sewers for about half of its surface area, with the result that a little rain is all that is needed to flood the small canals that feed into it. The drainage system was built from 1895 to 1905, for a population of 600,000. Today 8 million tons of mud have accumulated in it, reducing its flow capacity by 50 percent. In addition the forty-seven cleaning crews cannot keep even one-third of the 40,000 public toilets clean or collect more than a modicum of refuse. Volunteers are often called on to dig out passageways in the mounds of rubbish. The Hooghly River, which provides nearly all the drinking water, frequently becomes brackish because of tidal backwashes that raise the salinity twelve times above the tolerable level. The pumps often stop, and the brackish water gets into the massive pipes leading to water-supply lines for a distance of more than 600 miles. The family that has drinking water is fortunate.[20]

H. Lubell, of the International Labour Office, has said of Calcutta that it is a labyrinth of crowds, poverty, organized and spontaneous violence, mutilated beggars, "sidewalk residents," and pockmarked, malilluminated streets, all of which manages to leave one with the impression of irresponsible vitality, creativity, and exuberance. In its glory it was the commercial, financial, industrial, political, and cultural center of all India. After two centuries of decline, it still is.[21]

Conditions are no better in *Latin America*. In Brazil 45 percent of urban communities do not have a good water supply, and only 34 percent have installed their own sewer systems. The figure is 29 percent in Chile.[22]

In *Africa* it is the medical services that are most insufficient vis-à-vis the multitudinous needs of the cities. Diseases rage, and they are often the ones connected with the lack of hygienic urban conditions: tuberculosis, typhoid fever, and malaria.[23] Streets and traffic also cause problems for the African cities, especially those that, having become administrative centers, attract new immigrants; they cannot meet the increased demands for needed services.[24]

Community: The human being is a social being. Employment, housing, and public services do not suffice for human fulfillment; there is also a need for society. As Barbara Ward has written:

If the right to shelter is a basic human right, it cannot be fully enjoyed unless there are corresponding rights to community, or rather to those human benefits which can only be provided by a community. Some of them are social—health, literacy, employment, personal security. Some of them are physical—pure water, good drains, clean air, access, and mobility. Some are cultural—freedom of expression and choice, continuity, responsibility, effective influence, beauty, great art, the right to visions and dreams.[25]

The first sociologists studying the metropolises of the West observed that one of the principal traits of their inhabitants was "anomie"—the feeling that they were rootless, isolated, forgotten by everyone. Society was missing. But this does not seem to be verified in Third World cities. Here much can be lacking, and is lacking, but the spirit of society is not lacking. The poor still know how to help the poor.

It is true that on occasion the compacted masses in urban jungles have erupted into acts of collective violence. It has been theorized that such masses constitute an explosive potential capable of bursting into class struggles, racial struggles, and guerrilla warfare on such a scale as to threaten the rest of the world. And in fact there have been some such explosions in recent years. In 1966 there were the Shiv Sena riots in Bombay when Marathas wanted to keep non-Marathas from certain jobs. In 1968 in Kuala Lumpur, the capital of Malaysia, Chinese and Malays clashed, with a heavy loss of human life. In 1971 there was shooting in San Salvador, Peru, when shantytown huts were erected too close to the Pan American Highway and to the wealthier sections of Monterico. But these were exceptions that seemed to confirm the general rule of the presence of a spirit of collaboration stronger than that of confrontation. The general impression is that everyone wants to live together, and therefore in peace, even if each one lives in one's own "community."

In *Asia*, M. Juppenlatz, studying the slums of Manila, observed a high degree of social order, with elaborate hierarchies and strata, which practically eliminated the temptation to revolt. In a mass of 4 million persons, he distinguished five groupings: 10 percent lived along the banks of waterways, earning their livelihood from fishing; another 10 percent earned their livelihood from making and repairing nets for fishermen; 20 percent lived in slum areas, waiting to move into better housing as soon as they could save up what it required. The other two groupings were refugees from the Visayan islands (population 1,208,000) and immigrants from numerous depressed villages who, as soon as they could, would return to where they had come from. In the heart of each of these groupings there was noted the same spirit of solidarity with and co-responsibility for the others.[26]

In *Latin America* too a spirit of collaboration, of concern and respect for what belongs to others among the poor in the city has been noted. In Peru the shantytowns have been studied and the stages of their "progress" singled out: *itinerants* arrive in the city and provide for themselves as well as possible under the circumstances. After a while they become *prospective settlers,* joining with other itinerants to take over some unused plot of land. The third phase is reached when the group manages to keep the police at bay. The final stage is reached when the authorities are forced to accept the situation and even sometimes see to it that running water and other public services are provided.

In Rio de Janeiro the authorities openly solicit the cooperation of the slum-dwellers, in order to improve their life conditions. There is an organization,

CODESCO (*Companhia de Desenvolvimento Comunal;* Community Development Company), which provides building materials to encourage them to build their own houses.

In *African* cities, urban immigrants are often received and settled in by persons from their own ethnic groupings. This reinforces the communitarian spirit and even addresses the question that overwhelms the immigrant: How will I "find myself" in the anonymous city? Close-knit networks of interaction are stabilized on these bases, facilitating the urban integration of the newly arrived.[27]

Not everything is going badly for the cities of the Third World. Urban scholars from the First World often lament that Third World cities are dirty and monotonous. The cities of Asia, Latin America, and Africa can indeed be dirty, but they are anything but monotonous! There is suffering; many feel themselves superfluous because they are unemployed, many feel cut off because they have no place to live, many see themselves deprived of things that others take for granted, such as water, electricity, streets, city cleaning, sewers, and public transportation. But in their suffering they see themselves supported by others who share the same privations. And this support is expressed in the most diverse forms of communality, hospitality, and celebration.

Without this support it would be more difficult to explain why violence and crime are not the *rule* in the Third World. Not that violence and crime are unknown: everything fosters them. Young persons grow up without the warmth of a decent home, among the rotting refuse piles, and the electrical switches and water faucets that do not work. They have the impression of not counting for anything, and of being destined to remain "out of it." In such circumstances it is an easy step to join in with outlaw types or violent groups for exploits of pure vandalism or for banditry and terrorism—to which the cities are prone. The police are unable to control them. Only the attitudes of cooperation by the larger community can contain them.

But when persons are encapsulated in so-called zones of intensive construction, in many-storied apartment buildings, the attitudes of cooperation give way to those of isolation and segregation that spawn vulnerability, insecurity, fear, anonymity, the sense of rejection, revolt. The seedbed for drugs, criminality, and violence was never before so well prepared.

The City as a Sign of the Times

In taking account of the situation of the urban masses, it must be recalled that we are not studying any one city in particular, but cities in general—in other words, a great part of the world's population. This means that we are confronting a situation that cannot but be a sign of the times.

How are we to read it, interpret it? First of all, it must be analyzed in depth. A historical, spatial, and social sketch only reveals symptoms, from which to turn back again to a more complex and deeper reality. We cannot pretend to decipher a sign without deepening our analysis to its very roots. The first stage, therefore, of this study of urban mission will be precisely that of examining symptoms. Only by discovering the "why" of them will we be in a position to ask ourselves: What do they mean in the framework of God's plans for humankind?

There is another immediate reason for going beyond the symptoms. Urban mission cannot be indifferent to the problems and human suffering so much in evidence in the Third World. The waves of refugees to Hong Kong in the 1940s saw a burgeoning of social services on the part of the church, for example, in the form of training centers to combat the plague of unemployment. In Santiago de Chile missionary Sisters, together with their grassroot communities, struggle with all their means to provide housing for the homeless. In Kinshasa there is a Catholic center for human promotion that seeks to provide the citizens with that they need to ameliorate their lot.

But the response to the more immediate and more visible disasters is often a course of action based on symptoms, not underlying causes. The attempt is to assuage a fever, not to get to the source of the fever. Urban mission must try to go deeper, to the very roots, in what it undertakes, while not ignoring the concrete and immediate suffering of the people. It must get to the causes in order to reverse the intrinsic orientations of the cities, to humanize them, and make the presence of the kingdom of God appear there. Today the pursuit of this type of activity has become an imperative for urban mission.

Moreover, as must be evident from the preceding pages, the symptoms have become so massive today that all direct action on them becomes merely symbolic. There are so many needs, even those of the most urgent nature, experienced by the urban population that resources cannot be found to respond to even a minimal percentage of them. This is realized by Mother Teresa, the great missionary of Calcutta, standing in the breach for many years in her adopted city, and, in the person of her Sisters of Charity, in many other cities. She does not continue her work under the delusion of being able to resolve the problems, but rather, in the conviction that her testimony can be a sign of hope for the hopeless.

And here, even at the level of symptoms, there is a clue. The "compassion" that the poor arouse in us helps us find it, in tuning with the heart of Jesus who, attentive to the multitudes, offers himself to them as their shepherd and liberator: " He has anointed me to preach good news to the poor. He has sent me to proclaim release to the captives and recovering of sight to the blind, to set at liberty those who are oppressed, to proclaim the acceptable year of the Lord" (Lk. 4:18-19). The unemployment, the lack of housing and of public services ignite in us solidarity with them, and empathy with those in whom nothing can extinguish the spark of vitality, of optimism, of collaboration that animates them. For us who often find ourselves drained of initiatives and of hope when we think about the gigantic undertaking that urban restoration entails, this is *their* testimony.

Some years ago the diary of a shantytown woman in São Paulo, Brazil, was published. It is a fascinating story of a daily battle with hunger. She managed to eke out a living by salvaging paper and other scrap from refuse heaps. And she never gave up hope:

> *May 15[1955].* This is how I see São Paulo. The governor's palace is the living room. The mayor's office is the dining room. The city is the garden. The *favela* is the place where the rubbish is dumped.
>
> *Dec. 25, Christmas.* José [her son] came back with a stomachache. I know why: he ate a spoiled melon. Today they dumped stuff near the river. I don't know why those idiot merchants throw away the rotten food near the *favela*; the small children see it and eat it. I think the merchants are playing with the people, like Caesar when he tortured the Christians. But the Caesars of today are worse than the Caesar of the past. The Christians were being punished for their faith, but we for our hunger. At that time those who didn't want to die had to stop loving Christ, but we can't stop needing to eat.[28]

This is the kind of sign that prompts us to go on, from the vital reaction that the "prey-symptom" sparks in us all the way to the sin at the origin of the new oppression.

2

A SYSTEM TO BE UNDERSTOOD

As arduous and arid as it may be, the task that must be undertaken in this chapter is essential for urban mission. To go beyond appearances, in order to arrive at a diagnosis of underlying causes, has long been an integral part of mission. It is not only a matter of avoiding the risk that missionaries find themselves the unwitting and unwilling collaborators of the secret influences responsible for the serious disorders in urban life. Nor is it simply a matter of knowing how to treat evils at their roots. Knowledge of the city is an imperative for missionaries if they are to interpret it as a sign of the divine plan for contemporary history, a history decisively conditioned by the urban phenomenon.

The Concept of Social System

As a framework for construction to come later—that is, as an instrument of knowledge—the concept of social system seems most suitable. For urban mission, the important thing is to know how to build bridges in the direction of city inhabitants. "Social system" means, primarily, a system of bridges among the members of a society.

Under this definition a city is not simply its establishments, or its edifices, or its means of communication. It is not contained by its problems and their solutions or by the individual persons who live there. It is much more, as personal experience has probably made clear to many readers. This study therefore will attempt to sum up the *entirety* of the city by considering it as a system of stable relationships by which the residents "compose the city." The conceptual framework for this study will be a model for understanding better this complex of human relationships.

"System" refers to a collection of parts forming a whole. This definition can be applied to the most diverse of realities: an automobile, for example, is a collection of mechanical parts, which, correctly interconnected, compose a system devised to travel from one point to another in space. In the present case, of course, the reality goes beyond the mechanical: the parts and the whole are social realities—at once less visible and less static but, from the missionary viewpoint, much more important and much more vital.

For just this reason, the social system derives its physiognomy less from the nature of its "parts" and more from that of its "whole," that is, the way in which the parts fit together among themselves. In other words, the linkages between the parts are more important than the parts themselves.

Social reality incorporates a paradox that clearly distinguishes it from whatever other reality, mechanical, physical, or biological. Its "parts" are molded by the characteristics of the "whole," and the "whole" is molded by the way in which the parts are related among themselves. Technically, the network becomes the structure. For this reason the individual parts are often called "structures."

The interaction between persons, realized in precise, stable, and recurrent models, generates and perpetuates this order. When persons interact—and this is the heart of what "social" is—they do not do so in an absolutely original way, but according to inherited *models*, in stable *groups*, in line with *values* shared with others, in precise *roles*. This phenomenon gives birth to the social system.

Interaction is something distinct from the persons involved in the social system: it does not depend on them but on the recurrent and modeled behavior not invented by them but transmitted and "given" by them. The persons who interact consider the presence of the other "actors" and draw conclusions from it before deciding on their own course of activity. They find themselves in a system in which their own "actions" are conditioned by those of the others. Then too they share with these others a whole complex of expectations about what will happen, inasmuch as the actions of diverse actors tend to be similar in a situation that is often repeated. This is the source of the regularity in models of interaction.

The Rural Community as a System

Before applying the concept of social system to the complex reality of the city, it will be helpful to sharpen it by applying it to the simpler and better-known reality of the small, rural community, that is, the rural town or village that comes immediately to mind when one thinks of a small, self-contained residential community.

The village or hamlet is, in one sense, the whole, but from the social point of view its "parts" are not the buildings, the streets, the land, or the five hundred or a thousand persons who reside there. The parts that are of interest to this study are the groups, the values, the roles. The persons change (they die), the houses are torn down and rebuilt, streets are changed, new public services are introduced—but the village is still there, thanks precisely to its system of groups, values, roles. It continues because it answers to the basic exigencies of every human community.

This leads back to the theme of *needs*, already touched on in the preceding chapter. But now the focus is on the collective aspect of needs. Every collectivity, in order to perdure, must be able to reproduce itself, train the newborn to its way of life, assure for everyone food, clothing, shelter, order, and security, and transmit a meaning of life that sustains the exertions and reverses of daily existence. To each series of needs will correspond a precise function of the collectivity. The ensemble of these functions constitutes the system.

Concretely, each person forms part of a family. This is the predominant type of group to which are entrusted the functions of procreation and education of new members, and, in general, that of providing for their biological needs. To another type of group is entrusted the function of assuring "law and order": the village council, or informal group of village leaders, or the equivalent. The meaning of life is communicated by the fact that all inherit the same "world outlook," considered as "taken for granted," a datum. This is the aggregate of values accepted by all. Sometimes this aggregate of values is unified in a religious vision and supported by a special institution (in a Christian community, the "church").

Among the "parts" of this system, the most characteristic is that of roles. It will be worthwhile to deepen here the concept of role, as also in order to grasp better the meaning of recurrent interaction and the social system that derives from it. Leaders are not the only ones who have a role to play: within each family there are roles no less vital for the functioning of the rural community.

The idea of "role" is taken from the theater, where an actor recites on stage a predetermined part, interacting with the other actors to simulate determinate situations. The actor must say certain things, do certain things. The other actors know it and expect the others' lines and actions. This is at the very basis of their interaction. If an actor "invents"—says or does something not in the script—trouble results. The system collapses. If it is only a matter of a stage performance, the matter ends there, but in real life a role is a more serious matter.

When, for example, someone gets married, the person must enact (not "act," not recite) the part of husband or wife. That part is not invented by the individual; it is already stabilized, sanctioned, expected, and demanded, and not only by the marriage partner but by the whole social group. They all have a defined, inherited, motivated idea, linked with values and expressed in clothing and laws that no one would call into question about what a husband or wife must do. These expectations serve a twofold function: to make clear to married persons what they must do, and to oblige them to do so. The interaction between husband and wife thus acquires clear directioning, recurrent lines. Jurists would call them the "rights and duties" of husbands and wives. But the role extends to a field of conduct that goes far beyond the rights and duties stipulated by law. It is clear that an obligation on the part of the husband implies a right on the part of the wife, and vice versa. More than that: it implies another spouse—the role of another spouse. Their interaction runs its course and finishes on the projectory of this reciprocity. And this implies a fixed linkage, a two-way bridge between the two persons who take upon themselves the two reciprocal roles.

The impact of the system on the individual becomes more evident. Belonging to a group obliges the individual to accept a certain number of roles, and the values shared in common oblige individuals to adapt their conduct to what is expected of those roles. Thus a major part of the individual's life is "prescribed," in the sense that individuals must correspond to what the others expect of them. The behavior of the individual is oriented in this way to the goals of the system. In passing it can be noted that missionaries, if they are not aware of what is taking place, can end up by accepting the roles defined by the system, and not those defined by the gospel.

The general structuring of the village is relatively simple. The differentiation of groups and values is minimal: the family, or clan, does everything or practically everything. Families procreate, educate, work, buy and sell; they transmit the meaning of life, reaching into the complex of common values. In the area of values, in fact, there are no remarkable differences: they are the same for all, and all obey an aggregate of very stable, unwritten norms handed down from generation to generation.

Roles, on the other hand, are somewhat more differentiated. There are those that are independent of the family group, such as that of "mayor" (village head) or "priest" (religious authority, spiritual head; the one who invokes the "world beyond"). Where society has evolved more, there are also more specialized roles resulting from a division of labor: mechanic, mail carrier, doctor, teacher, merchant.

In its dynamic aspect this structure finds expression in what are called "social processes," which give content to the linkages between groups and roles, singling out their particular force. Thus survival becomes a concerted and attainable goal by reason of demographic and economic processes; social order is assured by political processes; the meaning of life is asserted by cultural processes.

On the basis of this preliminary sketch of the social system, it is now possible to formulate four questions that will gradually introduce us to the more complex system of urban community:

1. What are the group categories that seem to prevail in the city? We speak of "group categories" because there will be no attempt here to list all the groups present in the city—it would be impossible—but only to classify them in their more generic aspects.

2. What are the values that regulate the life of each type of group identified?

3. What are the social roles that are found helpful in the identified groups or that better express the identified values?

4. What is the resultant structuring of the whole formed by these groups, values, and roles? What is the content of the processes that pass through these structures or linkages?

The City in the First World

The distinction between urban and rural community does not have much to say to those who were born and grew up in a city. Nor does it have much to say to those who were born and grew up in the country. But for missionaries, generally educated and trained in the predominantly "rural" traditions of the church, and then immersed in life and work in a metropolis, the distinction exposes a basis of experience that renders it eloquent. Just like all the other traditions developed over the span of two millennia of history, missionary methodology has almost always been bound up with contexts of a rural nature. It can even be said that missionary thinking on the "natural law" is conditioned by a long habituation to rural life, and it would be hard to find verification in the type of urban life experiences of recent decades.

For the missionary the differences are not simply visible, they are problematic. For example, consider the territorial "plan" of a rural village: the houses are on streets, the streets converge on a center, the center serves the community needs. Each house represents a family, and almost always a cultivated area or a small business ("cottage industry").

In the city, everything is different: its very dimensions make a bird's-eye view more difficult. It is not a question of several hundred inhabitants but of hundreds of thousands, which highlights the difference as to the factor of population density. The social element (population) takes the upper hand over the physical element (terrain). The relationship between social and physical is not left to spontaneity, to tradition, to heritage, to the free initiative of individuals or families, but is organized, because a terrain of the same dimensions in an urban setting must serve more families or even more groupings of families.

Urban community has been studied in the West precisely from the point of view of these differences. Hence arose the "theories of contrasts." Tönnies, for example, focuses on the new models of social relationship created in the First World city born of industrialization, and distinguishes between a "community of cohabitation" *(Gesellschaft)* and a "community of participation" *(Gemeinschaft)*.[1] The first is rational, calculated, instrumental, and generates relationships in which the will to live in common is cemented in an impersonal way, by well-defined contracts. The second, traditional and rural, is founded on a spontaneous solidarity, like the accord that exists within a family. Here the personal relationship (person to person) predominates; in the other, the functional relationship (role to role) predominates. Both of these are idealized types of society, not fully verified in concrete communities, but intended to facilitate one's understanding of social reality, throwing its orientations into relief. The city would thus be more in the direction of *Gesellschaft*. This does not mean that it would be less natural than *Gemeinschaft*.

Emile Durkheim, the father of modern sociology, saw the root of contrast in the process of specialization or "division of labor."[2] In the village, solidarity is almost mechanical because each person is capable of doing everything that needs to be done, and hence any one person can take another's place, with the result that nothing is ever lacking to the "whole." In the city, tasks are divided, broken down; to fill all the diverse tasks, specialization is necessary, and a "title" or social recognition. And it is enough, to give an easy example, for city garbage collectors to go on strike to provoke a crisis for the entire life-support system. Solidarity, therefore, is even more necessary, but must be reasoned, thought out, organized. The predominance of the social leads to a predominance of the political.

Redfield argued that the sense of contrast could be reduced to that of a continuum spanning the passage from rural to urban society.[3] But even in this interpretation, the theories of rural-urban contrast (regardless of which aspect is stressed) do not measure up to empirical research. Students of urban reality have often come upon spontaneous relationships of great intimacy and solidarity. The continuum, according to Christaller, is not between rural life and urban life, but between villages—mini-cities with determinate functions—and the metropolis-center.[4] This idea will be expanded in the following chapter.

The "theories of contrasts" had a negative and a positive effect. The negative effect was that some scholars created a "myth of the village," claiming that it was a better and more natural habitat than the city. The positive effect was that it threw light on and yielded more precise ideas on "the urban way of life," that is, on the fact that life in the city is a different way of life. This way of life certainly merits closer attention by urban mission.

With these premises, it is now possible to pose the first question, in reference to the city of the First World: What types of social groups seem to prevail in it? Empirical research has brought to light some answers that must be of interest to urban mission because they allow for the identification of particular groups with which a specific evangelical dialogue must be opened.

The expression "social group" here means persons who, in whatever way, find and feel themselves together, and in consequence have a common identity that permits them to consider themselves united and different from the others—"we" as opposed to "they." Unity is defined by its common finality and also by certain norms of behavior that govern interaction. All this requires at least a certain minimum of contact and communication among the persons who compose a group.

Citizens

"Natural Areas": The concept of "social group" must be broad enough to embrace both large and small groups. It can, therefore, include the discovery of the Chicago researchers, whose findings are summarized in *Human Communities* by R. E. Park: the cities are composed of "natural areas" connected among themselves; that is, a commercial core, residential zones, industrial

zones, and satellite cities (suburbs). Thus, they say, every American city has its slums, its ghettos, its immigrant colonies. Almost every city has sections inhabited by bohemians and vagabonds who find there a freer, more adventuresome, and more solitary life than in any other section. These are the so-called natural areas.[5]

These sectors are called "natural" because they started and grew as a spontaneous response to the phenomenon of the city. And they continue even when city planners consider them no longer desirable; consider the case of city slums, for instance. They are also "natural" in that they are the creation of inhabitants, past and present, each with its own collective "personality" and its own particular functions that serve the city, especially in the socialization of the immigrant.

Without having been planned, the natural areas are connected among themselves by the specific functions that each of them develops within the "whole," functions that converge in the global function of the city. The Chinatown in Chicago, for example, performs the function of receiving Chinese immigrants and smoothing their way into the urban life of America.

The concept of natural areas, developed in the period between the two world wars, retains its valid interpretative insight: it reveals how the city, while remaining a qualitatively diverse entity from the parts that compose it, cannot be explained without those parts and without their history, nature, and mutual relationships.

The consequences on the pastoral plane, as seen by the chaplains and pastors who ministered to the North American immigration of the previous century, led to the formation of ecclesiastical communities out of these natural areas. They were the missionaries of the "national parishes," helping immigrant groups in their integration into the new nation and in their Christian dimension.

Functional Groups: The occidental city is also characterized by groupings based on "specialization." The finalities of most urban groups are very specific, which accounts for their great number and their multiple interaction. Even the family group, which controls practically the whole finality of functions in the rural context, takes up only certain limited finalities in the city: procreation and supplying for the affective needs of its members. For everything else it resorts to other groups, such as the school, the clinic, and the employment office.

Thus it is that the city entails a whole range of groups, distinguishable by their finalities, which can be classified according to the criterion of the needs to which they correspond. Sociologists thus arrive at six basic categories of groups: educational, economic, political, religious, welfare, recreational.[6]

All these groups have in common certain characteristics that clearly distinguish them from rural groups: all of them are "temporary," in the sense that individuals will remain a part of them only until they obtain what they sought in the group. And they are "simultaneous," in the sense that someone can be a member of a number of them at the same time, because no one of them absorbs the totality of the individual member's life. They are also "separate," even physically: someone may reside in a house, work in a distant office, find entertainment in a third locality, and so forth. They are also "formal"—that is, formally constituted with their own norms, hierarchies, structures—and they develop and communicate with one another only indirectly. To be sure, given their strong specialization, all these groups are complementary and hence take their place in a context of reciprocal interdependence.

The experienced missionary will agree with these observations. The city is this way. But there can be reluctance to admit the "normalcy" of this situation. Missionaries may have a rural model of life deep inside them, and it becomes the criterion by which they judge the urban way of life. This substitution of criteria is a luxury that urban mission cannot allow itself if it truly wants to come to terms with the world where it is at work. The behavior of citizens must be judged by criteria that take account of their specificity.

The implications of this position become evident when the second key question is posed: What seem to be the values that regulate the life of the groups just identified?

The Citizen Mentality

The meaning of "social value" should be spelled out. "Value" means something worth devoting oneself to in earnest. If this attitude is shared by a number of persons, there is a *social value*. The "thing" worth devoting oneself to is an abstract and generic principle, which becomes more concrete in "consciousness," is articulated in a series of finalities and objectives, and becomes the stimulus and norm of behavior that involves a number of persons in concert. Social value is a cultural fact par excellence, a measure that permits the same persons to evaluate single or collective actions and situations. In other words, value is also a "point of view," a judgmental criterion. A congeries of values is therefore also called a "mentality."

A value or sum of values often expresses itself by a symbol or symbols. A luxurious car or a university degree are things desired not only for the comfort or expertise they carry with them, but also as a sign of prestige, of a position reached in society. Symbols are very important because they make the values of a group, a society, immediate and perceptible.

The question arises: What is the origin of social values? Why are certain values shared by a number of persons and become "group values"? Are the "things" that are worth an effort chosen as such by individuals who then discover they have something in common, or are they imposed by the groups that individuals belong to? The question is a profound one and would merit a study in depth. Diverse schools of sociology give diverse answers. For this study it is important to highlight here that this line of thought is connected with that of social classes and categories, because every class or category has its own system of values and symbols, which are bound up with economic factors but are not reducible to them.

Karl Marx, starting with history, identified two social classes—the bourgeoisie and the proletariat—as the protagonists of the history of all existent societies, a history that he reduced ultimately to a class struggle for power. And this kind of struggle, according to Marx, takes place in the city, because rural ignorance cannot comprehend it.[7]

Max Weber, more cautious, identified other classes besides the two singled out by Marx. Further, for the individual he distinguishes between class position and social position. The first is rooted in economic factors, such as capital, the means of production, riches, supervisory employment; the second is rooted in the prestige accorded to an individual and expressed by symbols.[8]

If this is so, social position exists first of all in the mind of others, and only later in the mind of the person to whom the position is given. It is the others who assign to the individual a place in the social scale, on the basis of one's origin, one's profession or that of a family member, but especially the titles one has acquired—"titles" in a broad sense standing for "symbols": it could be a diploma, a certain notoriety, a possession, a mansion, a position of power, or the like. When all is said and done, a social position depends on the judgment of "the others." In society the individual has the "specific weight" that the others attribute to the person, to a large measure independent of one's merits or efforts. No one can escape the system.

Social Classes: The term "class" is not used here in the Marxist sense, but in the sense in which it is commonly used in everyday language: a grouping of persons who have the same social position. As has already been pointed out, no such entity exists "out there"; a group of persons bound with each other by real contacts and lines of communication is not a physical reality, as such, but a *mental* reality, one of categorization, inasmuch as all the persons who are at the same social level are "put together." This involves a stratification of the residents of a city into an idealistic pyramid, from the masses, considered as its base, up to the privileged elite.

Such a stratification simply does not exist in the small residential collectivity of a rural character. There, only one or two families will enjoy a position of prestige, almost always inherited; all the others are on more or less the same level. Rural society exhibits very little stratification.[9]

It is the city that brings social stratification into focus, concentrating a population in a reduced space and articulating it into numerous, visible, and consistent strata. In an urban population, the following strata emerge. First there is an elite, somewhat numerous, constituting the "upper class." Then, a "middle class," fairly consistent, which often exercises important roles. And then there is the stratum of the "have-nots." Of course each of these strata can be further subdivided, and sometimes subdivisioning is called for. For example, in Western society, the so-called middle class is clearly divisible into an upper and a lower classification; the proletariat would thus belong to at least two categories: those who have a fairly secure and protected income-related employment, and the "marginals," the unorganized, unprotected subproletariat.

Incidentally, it should also be noted here that the social stratification of the Western city is very different from that of the Third World city, which shows much greater variety. Generalization ignoring this difference would have no basis in reality.

Those who compose a social class are more or less on the same level of education, prestige, and financial means. Financial means, although a conditioning factor as to social position, is neither an exclusive nor a predominant criterion. The social "esteem" of an individual or a family remains a uniquely cultural fact. The following can be determinative class criteria: occupation, belonging to a certain clan or caste, academic degrees or titles, race, membership in religious bodies or particular associations.

It is commonly said that a social class is not organized. This is certainly true, nor could it be otherwise in the case of an abstract reality. Nevertheless it should not be forgotten that political parties and other movements often direct their efforts to specific social strata, in their attempt to get them involved in their pursuits and to represent them. Even if they officially describe themselves differently, certain political parties are clearly "the party of the middle class," or "the party of the upper-middle class," or "the party of the proletariat." Certain opinion movements direct their efforts to specific social strata and are supported by them.

This should put one on guard when attempting to excise the content—the *vital* content—of the concept of social class. It was not by chance that Marx made of it the pivot of his social and political conceptualization. Missionaries will have to sort out the diverse social classes of their populations, as the bearers of diverse values and interests, and therefore as the recipients of a particular mode of language and a particular pastoral course of action.

Besides being of importance to the organizers of political and other movements, the concept of class also has dynamic importance for individuals: generally speaking, everyone attaches great importance to the image that others have of them, of their family. And they act in such a way as to influence the mind of others, acquiring the values that society considers more positive, and exteriorizing the more efficacious symbols. Those who belong to the higher classes exert themselves to maintain the symbols of their position; those of the lower classes exert themselves to acquire the symbols of the higher classes. This is a facet of the process of social mobility, which is a very slow, almost static, process in traditional societies, but very rapid in modern societies.

Thus social position, beginning as a passive connotation, is transformed into a value, and as such motivates the conduct of the individual. Maturing then into "class consciousness," it can become the powerful political and revolutionary driving force that is well known to us.

Social Values: If persons derive their values from the social class they belong to and from the higher social class they aspire to, it is still true that they are taking them—more generically—from the city, which has its own specific culture and hence its own values. Sociologists have identified a whole series of the social values characteristic of the First World city.

The first value is *resourcefulness*, which prompts individuals to make the best use of what is at their disposal. In the economic sphere, this tension promotes technology; in the social sphere, it promotes formal organization. Another value is *secularization*, by which human problems are resolved by human means and are not handed over to a naturalistic fatalism or to prayer for divine intervention.

The value of *efficiency* is shown by the person who makes judgments after the manner of a "doer," an "achiever," rather than that of a "follower." It searches for ways of doing things that will be more efficacious, more sure, more rapid, over and above their intrinsic properties. *Competition* for the attainment of goals replaces the spirit of cooperation of the rural community, and progress toward a higher class becomes a means of personal promotion. *Pluralism*, finally, supports survival in a regimen of competition, granting to all the right to follow their own principles and their own methods, with the proviso that they respect the principles and methods of others—in the final analysis, to respect the ideas of others in order to be able to adhere to one's own ideas.

That these values of Western urban life must have great interest for the missionary is obvious. The gospel is also a complex of values, and it tends to conflict with other complexes. The missionary must be aware of these other values. One danger to be avoided is that of presuming that the conflict of the gospel with the values of the city will follow the lines of the conflict between the gospel and rural values. Another danger for missionaries is that they will fall under the influence of urban values to the detriment of gospel values. There have been cases of missionary initiatives carried on under the banner of resourcefulness, efficiency, and perhaps even competition. Not that resourcefulness and efficiency—and sometimes even competition—cannot offer fertile ground for the seed of the Word, but priority must be given to the gospel values, putting resourcefulness and efficiency in their service and not vice versa.[10]

Once again it is a matter of bringing to light the hidden mechanisms of the urban way of life. It is now time to pose the third key question, which will lead to reflection on the concept of role.

Relationships among City-Dwellers

What types of roles characterize the occidental city? Using the criterion of the collective functions assigned to roles suggests that four principal types emerge:

1. The self-regeneration and survival of the system are provided for by the roles that are taken care of in the family and the "natural area," the *demographic* roles.

2. Another series of roles, *economic*, covers the general function of providing for the material needs of the citizenry in their limitless variations.

3. Another complex, more restricted but not less important, is that of the roles that assure orderly cohabitation: *political* roles.

4. Finally come *cultural* roles, which can be defined as the complex that supports the socialization of city residents and the motivation behind their conduct.

Demographic Roles: The urban family provides for the self-regeneration of the collectivity, as does the rural family. But there are differences. As we have already indicated, the urban family "specializes" in the roles of procreation and the sustenance of the emotional, affective life, delegating to other groups the economic and political roles, and in part the educational, recreational, and social-assistance roles that it exercises in a rural setting.

Even in the demographic sphere, the family has lost some measure of its monopoly, subject as it is to outside controls and influences more or less overt; consider the "slavery" associated with tiny apartments.

It must also be noted that the city does not receive all its citizens from the urban family: immigration also fills that role.

Economic Roles: At the turn of the present century, Max Weber saw economic roles as the ones that most radically identified the Western city. For him the city was, above all else, the marketplace that not only distributed the goods wanted by the collectivity but also put producers and consumers on a plane of parity. Market transaction is an exchange of goods, an exchange that implies a reciprocity and equality between persons; I give you this much because you give me this much. Here is the heart of the social role.

For Max Weber the specificity of this exchange consists in the fact that it is carried out with *reasoned* criteria, which then shape the whole life of the citizen. The fleeting marketplace association becomes the model of urban interaction. The marketplace transaction, in contrast to all the other communities, which always presuppose a personalized fellowship and usually parentage, is radically extraneous to all forms of fellowship.[11] Marketplace exchanges are carried out simultaneously and anonymously in full view of all the other potential buyers and competitive sellers. It promotes impersonal, secondary, relationships and roles.

Political Roles: From its birth, the Western city developed the civic body and within it its characteristic political roles. Thanks to its marketplace-type functioning and the economic forces it generates, escape from the vise of parental ties is possible. The right to urban real estate, freely purchasable from its owner (and thereby the instrument of credit and capital), permits the emancipation of the individual citizen. Individuals thus enter under the jurisdiction of a common right, exclusive to them. And the groups cemented by bonds of parenthood lose their hegemony as constitutive elements of the city.

Often, however, this is arrived at by way of a revolution, as happened in Geneva and Cologne.[12] The important thing to remember is that the social change to urbanism results from displacements of the positions of influence of social classes or social groups—whether the displacements come from interaction or conflict. The positions of influence are then translated into political roles taken up by individual members of the prevailing classes or groups. In some cases the civic body as such takes over the reins of power in the "nation"; in other cases the more affluent bodies do it.

Cultural Roles: Most of the inhabitants of metropolises often have to deal with one another but do not have to know one another. This allows individuals to pass easily and rapidly from one ambit to another, and encourages the fascinating but very dangerous experience of living at the same time in diverse worlds, contiguous and nonetheless rigorously separated. All this tends to confer on urban life a superficial and casual character, to complicate social relationships, and to produce new and divergent types of individuals, according to R. Park.[13] And, we may add, new types of roles.

Park's observation summarized in the preceding paragraph, the fruit of his empirical researches, confirms Weber's intuition that not all citizens belong to the civic body. It is not easy for the immigrant to assume a role and thereby find a place in the urban system. Adaptation and assimilation yield to competition and perhaps conflict for the few roles obtainable.

It seems, however, that the vacuum is compensated for by the various integrating roles that are to be found in the "natural areas." How this takes place is discussed in chapter 5. What is of interest here is that even when active roles cannot be found by immigrants, they become the counterbalance to other roles, as suggested by newspaper want-ad columns for "services offered" and "housing wanted." They are already consumers, "available workforce," the easy victims of pressure tactics. Through the roles associated with each of these "zones" urban culture augments its hold on the immigrants—and makes them citizens.

The theme of cultural roles is of direct interest to urban mission. In sociological language, it too has or offers a cultural role in the city. It is the aim of mission to communicate a "new meaning" to the lifestyle of the collectivity. The theme of cultural roles becomes more concrete and more interesting when we realize that citizens do not receive the "new meaning" by way of the generic communication of values, but primarily by way of the roles that they take upon themselves. It is thanks to those roles that the message becomes "life." It is thanks to them that "the things that are worth an effort" become precise, concrete commitments that link in solidarity the person filling a complementary role with the others.

The attempt to identify the common characteristics of urban roles is not without interest. It was L. Wirth, another representative of the Chicago school, who treated the city primarily as a cultural fact, a special way of life. The creature of growth rather than creativity, the Western city is understood by him as a relatively large, dense, permanent settlement of socially heterogeneous individuals. This type of cohabitation develops impersonal, superficial, transitory, and calculated relationships.[14]

Seen in this light, the main difference between rural and urban roles would reside in the image that individuals express to others. The rural person is happy to be considered understanding and cordial by others; the city person wants to be considered lucid and detached. In large measure, urban roles are what condition the inhabitants of a metropolis to project an image of themselves as objective, reasonable, impersonal, and to consider relationships with others as a means, not an end. Rural roles condition rural persons to be subjective, affectionate, very personal in their social relationships—relationships cherished as an end in themselves.

A ready explanation of this fact is that practically all urban roles are acquired; they are the fruit of personal efforts gained in struggle. Rural roles, on the other hand, are assigned, inherited simply by belonging to a certain family or group.

Structures and Processes of the System

There is an obvious connection between the characteristics of the urban roles and the values proper to the Western city outlined above. Their convergence is not accidental; it comes from the fact that the city is a "whole" composed of parts. This is the logical place to pose the fourth question: How does the whole composed of groups, values, and roles come to be structured and held together?

The purpose here is not to develop a theory about the city, but to identify the channels through which the reciprocal influence of city and citizen passes. These will be the channels best suited to urban pastoral activity.

Perhaps the best way to understand the profile of the whole, or aggregate, or system constituted by the Western city would be to think of it as an extremely divided reality. The very expression "urban community" is practically a misnomer. To the spatial agglomeration there corresponds an extreme social fragmentation. Divided horizontally by the "natural areas," vertically by social stratification, psychologically by memberships in a plurality of groups and by the assumption of innumerable interchangeable roles, urban population is characterized by the emotional isolation of individuals, families, and small groups. By "emotional isolation" we mean that the vast solidarities founded on primary relationships are lacking. But it does not mean that there cannot be other solidarities of a vast radius, founded on interests or functions.

It is precisely in the formation of these new solidarities that certain small but powerful groups expend their energies—the groups that succeed in forming the others into a hierarchy and controlling their destiny. The structural composition of the Western urban system thus contains a few centers that unite innumerable other groups, not by holding them together directly (except to a minor extent) but by conditioning them to some form of control. The same system is explained functionally by the interdependence of all the groups: it suffices to control certain nerve centers of interaction to control the ensemble.

A scale of generic social values shared by all citizens is the "cement" that holds the entire city together. This scale of values justifies and to some extent supports the social stratification and the entire hierarchy of groups and roles, even if not always in all their incidental details. This scale of generic values is then integrated by the particular scale of values that is developed within each larger grouping. But the cement of generic and specific values would count for little were it not "armed" by roles. Roles are indeed the armor of the cement that holds the city together.

This ensemble lives in a tension that is part of its very structure. In one way the city is poised toward conflict between its divided and asymmetrical components; in another way, though, it is attracted to consensus for the maintenance and perfecting of its global unity. Despite everything, the city believes in the city.

The component parts of this "life in tension" are spelled out by the social processes. If its structure highlights the static aspect of the system's armor, its roles highlight its dynamic aspect. Social processes, like roles, are particular and recurrent models of social interaction. For clarity, they can be classified into four types.

The first process, often called *demographic*, provides the "gray matter" of the city: massive population, geographic density. It is a "living" matter, moving and growing in creative dialogue with its physico-biological ambience. (Chapter 3 will highlight what happens when more and more persons are concentrated in less and less space.)

The second and third processes channel the *economic* and *political* impulses of the city. Their "historical alliance" is a characteristic of the occidental city. Barbara Ward pictures this city as a "conveyer belt": millions of persons moving in regularity from rural to urban areas, from agriculture to industry. The new technology reached these sectors at the same time; as it reduced the work potential of the former, it augmented that of the latter. In the name of increased productivity, agriculture had to give way to industry's call for more workers. This was especially the case in the beginning, when a city like Manchester in England advertised for "hands," not "skilled workers," for its factories. The mortality rate was still very high at that time, and European migration was largely to the New World. Families, as they adapted themselves to urban life, gradually became smaller, even before the advances in the field of medicine that changed the mortality rate.

Western urbanization therefore had its start, by a fortuitous historical coincidence, before the demographic explosion. The "conveyor belt" could transfer "manpower" from preindustrial society to the industrial city without too much trouble. But this does not mean that urbanization in the West forms *the* paradigm or sets *the* pattern for all urbanization. It happened in a certain way in the West by a chance convergence and nonconvergence of historical factors. The Asian, Latin American, and African worlds will have their own processes of urbanization; they do not have to adopt the Western model.

Urban mission will be particularly interested in the fourth type of social processes, that which takes place at the *cultural* level. This too, like its corresponding roles, points to a specific lifestyle.

The population that "uses" the city is very concentrated, very mobile, very heterogeneous. It is "encapsulated" in apartments, not in houses spread out over a given terrain. The annual change-of-residence rate is high. Persons from diverse backgrounds, often speaking diverse languages, find themselves thrown together.

The division of labor is complex, but clearly oriented toward industrial products and the service industries. Everyone specializes in a certain competency, and thereby becomes more dependent on the others.

Relationships of an impersonal, fleeting nature predominate. Individuals deal with one another "through a screen," not face to face. Often they are identified by numbers, uniforms, badges, not by names.

All this takes place in close connection with the region that surrounds the city, in a precarious, new city-country equilibrium. The city attracts the rural population because of its markets, its entertainment places, its centers of power, and its lifestyle. And the city, for its part, depends on the countryside not only for food and similar resources, but also for the relaxation and "unwinding" that it makes possible. In the majority of cases, the entire rural area becomes a function of the city, so much so that the Western world, industrial or postindustrial, can be defined on the whole as an urbanized world.

The City in the Third World

The cities of Asia, Latin America, and Africa took their origins differently from those of the West. The most ancient among them—those of China, India, Mesopotamia, and Egypt—were linked more closely with political than with economic processes. Often they were born or developed in consequence of a ruler's decision. A potentate treated citizens in the same way that he treated stones and streets; he would construct a city and then have persons brought in to populate it. Traces of a true civic body or of the consciousness of the rights of citizenship are, accordingly, very few. And because the potentate was often a warrior as well, with an army at his disposition, the city was his fortress, the place where he defended his possessions and the staging area for his conquests of additional possessions, which he brought back in the form of goods and slaves, but also the products of handcrafts and new techniques of artists and creative thinkers. From this point of view, the city was a shrine of the humanities, a place and a factor of cultural growth.

G. Bettin has written:

The Chinese city has the physical appearance of a great fortress, and the direction of its development was from the outer walls to the central marketplace. Economics was not the decisive factor: the only consumers were the well-off, and their economy was fed by taxation. Ownership did not result from business but from expertise in political administration. The key role was not that of citizen-merchant but that of mandarin-functionary (which did, however, have an impact on business, in the form of imposing taxes on merchandise).

For its part, the city of ancient India did not even have a free economy. The privileged castes forced the masses to work for them. The city was the stronghold of the ruler and the "superior" castes. Even later, when corporations came into possession of certain rights, they did not succeed in transforming their victories into effective political power.[15]

Gideon Sjoberg has sketched a functional profile of these ancient cities, some of which, for example, Mecca, have been there for millennia. What functions did they develop? Their population rarely exceeded 100,000. In the absence of stabilized monetary controls, their economic activity was slight. The urban configuration tended to gravitate around a center that was political and very often religious; the ruling body exercised its authority from within that center. A rigid hierarchization precluded passage between that group and the masses living on the periphery, segregated by ethnic criteria. Traditional values, accepted by all as absolute, sanctioned this state of affairs. Religion ruled daily life. It is interesting to note that, unlike the home in the Western city, the physical space of residence served diverse functions. One building houses the clan-family—grandparents, and their offspring, spouses, and children—and the most diverse roles were played there. The socialization of the citizens took place in the home; their roles within the family were the measures that they applied to themselves.[16]

T. G. McGee, in his studies of more recent phenomena, observes that Sjoberg's profile does not fit the cities that developed as a meeting-place of two cultures, the so-called colonial cities. Cities of this type were also found in the ancient world, but the ones of interest to us are those in Latin America from the sixteenth century and those in Africa and Asia from the nineteenth century. McGee writes:

It is the towns which grew up in the period since 1800 in the tropical areas of Africa and Asia which are perhaps the best example of the "colonial city." These towns were broadly of three types: (i) those towns which represent a mixture of the industrial city and the preindustrial city. Frequently, as in Kano [Nigeria], they were administrative centers of the indigenous societies and a colonial administrative structure was grafted on to the already existing preindustrial city. (ii) The towns which were connected with the exploitation of minerals, such as Luanshya [Zambia], which were wholly industrial in nature. (iii) The large port towns which acted as the receiving and exporting centers for the colonial empires.

The last-named were perhaps the most ubiquitous. . . . Such cities were brought into existence to satisfy the needs of commerce . . . yet [they] were characterized by a political and social structure which was no less hierarchical than the preindustrial city. The colonial administrator and businessman was alien from those he administered, and there was virtually no entry from the indigenous ranks into the ranks of the administrators. This, then, was a stratified society similar in pattern to that of the preindustrial city. [In the words of Redfield–Singer:] "The city was a grouping of communities, each of which carried on its pattern of life in a different way. Thus the old patterns of economic organization in the form of guilds persisted side by side with the 'rational' organization of production of goods, with expediential relations between buyer and seller."[17]

Groups

These particularized systemizations remind one of the "natural areas" of the Western city; if there is a major difference, it would be in the fact that they stand out more obviously and they are more homogeneous (think of the fishermen in Hong Kong). The Asian and African city has been called a "juxtaposition of villages."

As regards smaller groups, they are generally less differentiated and less specialized than their Western counterparts. The family still exercises most of its traditional functions, as also that of the acculturation of immigrants. Through its networks linked with parentage it also generates the groups that regulate the production and exchange of goods.

Values

The social stratification of Third World cities is much simpler than that of First World cities. The absence of a consistent middle class is one of the first data an observer notices. In fact, a civic body conscious of itself seems to be missing, and the impression is easily gained that the urban masses do not challenge the fact that the city belongs to the elite of the upper class. In this sense, the expression "lumpenproletariat" is not without foundation.

A scale of social values different from that in the West is in force—nor could it be otherwise, granted the absence of a self-conscious civic body. This absence is attributable largely to the weight of the long colonial domination and to the creation, in many places, of a countervalue mentality difficult to eradicate—the conviction, namely, that only whites can belong to an elite and gain access to economic and political controls.

What confronts us, then, is a complex of values that distinguishes only two social classes: the class at the summit, those who have everything: education, wealth, power; and the class at the bottom, those who have very little. They are two strata that live near each other but have only a minimum of interchange.

Within each stratum are complexes of specific values, largely autonomous to each stratum. And although the upper class replicates, so to speak, the values of its corresponding class in the West, the populous class has its own lifestyle, characterized by a spirit of community that distinguishes it from the city of the First World.

Roles

Social roles of the Asian, Latin American, and African city are more personalized and less "secondary" than those more efficiency oriented in the occidental urban system. Third World urban roles more closely approximate rural roles. Even a division of them made on the basis of functional criteria would be of little use: the boundaries between one role and another are never distinct or rigid.

Structures and Processes

Structures: The Third World urban system is less complicated than that of the First World urban system. Segmentation develops on the plane of the "natural areas," and thus follows the horizontal rather than the vertical lines of social strata. Structural disequilibrium is acute. In the lack of an articulated stratification, a very few have very much, and the very many have little or practically nothing. The same proportionality is repeated in the use and ownership of city property.

To this structural disequilibrium, however, and perhaps contrary to expectations, there is not a corresponding tension greater than that in Western cities. This results from the centuries-old tradition of acceptance of the situation (a tradition that colonialism was happy to maintain, so far as possible, because it served its interests) and from the nonexistence of the values that would detonate the contradictions.

In his study of Calcutta, Professor A. Detragiache of the University of Turin makes these observations:

> It has a two-part society, with profound fissures between the two parts. The dualism, however, does not lead to an explosive conflict. There are two reasons for this: the heavy weight of political control and the extremely low degree of sociopolitical awareness on the part of the marginal or emarginated sector. The territorial reality—that is, the urban configuration—is that constituted by the far-ranging development of an urban fringe characterized by areas of suburbanization of the higher classes fleeing the city center, and by the very extensive formation of slum areas. The central nucleus of the city is divided into two sectors: the business sector and the sector of urban blight, where the lower strata of the population reside. Putting it very simply, these are the most outstanding characteristics of the city in an underdeveloped country, of which there are many in Asia and Latin America.[18]

Social Processes: The *demographic process* is very different from that in occidental cities. In the Third World the city grows at the same time as—not in advance of—the demographic explosion brought on by control of the mortality rate, especially infant mortality. This growth, then, coincides with restrictions of a political order imposed on emigration to other continents. The European emigration to the Americas and Australia has no parallels here. In addition, the fall in the birth rate in Western cities, which accompanied the increase in affluence, is not echoed here. Urban fertility is not lower than rural fertility; in Cairo, for example, it is above 30 percent.[19]

The *economic process* also develops along different lines from the same process in Western cities. In the colonies the only technology put to use was that for mining and agriculture, for exportation. Apart from a few nations that have recently incorporated a true process of industrialization, the Third World cities grew without a transformation of their whole economy that would have been parallel to the growth of the First World cities. The city did not emerge as an industrial center needing more workers *in situ*, promoting productivity and economic expansion. At the most only one economic function was developed, in relationship with a metropolitan colonizer (or, more generally, with Western multinational corporations). And even there, where industrial development began, capital-intensive production methods are in place today, demanding a maximum of capital and a minimum of labor, in contrast with the overabundance of potential workers resulting from the demographic process mentioned above.

The *political process* often gives support to the movement toward a foreign capitalism extraneous to the true interests of the Third World city and its inhabitants. As in the ancient cities studied by Sjoberg and Weber, the political factor tends to prevail over the economic: it is the sovereign—or his equivalent today—who determines the fate of the citizens, altogether apart from any law of economics.

Another difference from the Western city comes to light at this point: while the Western city is never left without close relationships with the region surrounding it and, on the contrary, draws its lifeblood from this interdependence, the Third World city, even after political decolonization, does not succeed in reestablishing authentic relationships with its own geographic region and remains trapped in the net of international capitalism.

The *cultural processes* of Third World cities go back to their remote roots in archaic political regimes and colonial eras. Even when these cities are now in a stage of capitalist or socialist penetration, they have their own lifestyle, which has a heavy rural imprint. For example, it is the head of the clan who mobilizes the others to "act and produce"; the impulse does not come from the interests and initiatives of individuals under the direction of someone in charge. The economic process, in other words, is subordinated not only to the political process but also to traditions and customs. Even when this has some positive consequences, the fact remains, as Barbara Ward has pointed out, that certain cultural processes are obstacles to the assembly mechanism of a painless and beneficial urbanization. It is a fact, for example, that many cities have adopted only the more negative and less functional aspects of the Western urban system, such as wastage of energy and the unmonitored speculation on real estate and other essential goods.

The City as a Sign of the Times

All the divergences noted thus far, when taken together, make it clear that urbanization in the Third World differs from urbanization in the First World. And even from this preliminary and theoretical sketch of the urban system and the factors that shape it in the Third World, we already have a fairly clear idea of what must be the roots of the painful and harmful symptoms of unemployment, inadequate housing, and the lack of public utilities and services.

They are roots of a political and economic nature that derive their nourishment from the type of demographic process in effect. They are roots that seem to be sustained by the cultural process, but can also be called into question by it. Once we deepen our knowledge of the demographic, economic, and political processes (see chaps. 3 and 4), we will be in a better position to grasp the ambivalence of the cultural processes of the cities in the Third World (see chap. 5).

The urban system is an unmistakable sign of our times. Its diffusiveness and its implications for the relationships among human beings are only too evident.

Among the various "parts" of the urban system, its values will be of special interest in this study in the attempt to see the city as a sign of God's plans. Its values are what sustain the cultural process, where urban mission must penetrate the city. They weld together the multiple pieces and give meaning to the "whole" that the city constitutes. These values will be a major help in understanding the strategic bearing of the city-sign in itself. The reader will be able also to see through their apparent abstractness, uncovering them in the concreteness of the urban behavior patterns in which they express and manifest themselves.

Pope Paul VI, in *Octogesima Adveniens* (1972), summoned Christians everywhere to investigate in greater depth the meaning of the city and of the migration to the city:

> So there is every reason to ask this question: Granted all he has accomplished, is not man turning the fruits of his efforts against himself? In rightly converting the resources of nature to his own use, has he not become the slave of the objects he has made? . . .
>
> The rise of densely populated cities, which is clearly a stage in the development of human society and is now irreversible, poses problems for man that do not admit of an easy solution. How can he set limits on the growth of cities, provide for their proper organization, and inspire citizens with a concern for the welfare of all? In the disordered growth of the present, new proletarians are born. They settle in the heart of the city, from which the wealthy sometimes withdraw. They take up their abode in city outskirts, and their squalid misery is a silent protest

launched against the overindulgence in luxuries to be found in the cities themselves; for in the latter, goods are wantonly consumed and often wasted. The city does not foster fraternal encounters or mutual aid. It favors divisions and even neglect. It stirs up new forms of exploitation and domination whereby some people turn the needs of others to their own use and reap reprehensible profits. Many miseries lie hidden behind the façades of houses, unknown even to the closest neighbors. Other forms of misery are in full view, in cases where human dignity has been cast aside: delinquency, crime, psychotropic drugs, eroticism. . . .

Christians, aware of this new task that they must shoulder, should not lose heart in the vastness of the city which lacks any trace of individuality. Let them be mindful of the prophet Jonah who spent much time wandering through the great city of Nineveh to proclaim the joyful news of God's mercy; the sole support of his frailty was the word of almighty God. To be sure, the city is often depicted in the Bible as a place of sinfulness and arrogance, where man prides himself on being able to build his life without God, or even to stand against Him as a potent adversary. But there is also the holy city of Jerusalem, the place where God is encountered, the promise of a city that will descend from heaven.[20]

May we not see urban mission as the sign of Jonah (Mt. 12:39) in the bowels of the earth? From within the dark beast of urban processes will there not come the proclamation of the salvation of Him who rose from the shadows of death? But it will be necessary to enter into "the whale" of the demographic, economic, political, and cultural processes in order to assimilate them, bury ourselves in them, and from within them point to the face of the new city, the city of the kingdom that is coming.

3

MORE PERSONS IN LESS SPACE

In its complex and rich articulation, the urban system could seem to be autonomous. It is, however, anything but autonomous: the city is part and parcel of the very recent and very rapid expansion of the world population—one of the most significant signs of our time. What does the Lord intend by permitting such a growth in the family of his children in this century? Urban mission must search for an answer, investigating the most important currents of the interdependence of city and demographic explosion.

More Persons: The Demographic Processes

The implications of this new phenomenon become evident as soon as we consider some statistics. The world population reached 1.5 billion at the beginning of the twentieth century—a figure never attained before. But by 1961 it had reached 3 billion! Today it has gone beyond 4 billion and the predictions are that it will reach 6 billion by the year 2000.[1]

It took humankind thousands of years to reach a population of 500 million; experts calculate that it occurred in A.D. 1650. Today it takes only ten years to add 500 million or more. And the growth rate shows no signs of leveling off; on the contrary, the .83 percent rate in the year 1900 has been doubled—1.7 percent—today. If by the year 1900 it took eighty-four years to double the world population, today forty-one years suffice. And so it is that we find ourselves face to face with dizzying figures: 1 billion persons in 1841; 6 billion by the year 2000.

On the occasion of the Congress on World Evangelization in Lausanne (July 1974), an electronic "population clock" was installed in the central meeting hall. The idea was to impress the participants by clocking, second by second, the world population increase from the beginning to the end of the congress. By the time the ten-day meeting closed, the clock recorded a population increase of 1.5 million persons.

Today the world population grows at the rate of 180,000 persons per day, which means 125 every minute, or 2 every second. And these figures will increase tomorrow. This phenomenon must be taken seriously if the evangelization of the world in general, and of the city in particular, is to be taken seriously. The astronomer H. Sidentopf highlighted its significance by transposing the history of 5 billion years into the proportionate time spans of one year.[2] In his terms of reference, the sun came into being in January; the earth was formed in February; the continents took shape in April; vegetation appeared in November; the reptilian age came to an end by December 25. At 11 P.M. on December 31, Peking man appeared; at 11:30 Neanderthal man. In the last thirty seconds, from 11:59:30 until midnight, the whole course of human history took place. In the last second of the last minute, the population of humankind tripled (ten seconds would be the equivalent of 1,560 years). The weight of the bodies of all the human beings from the last ten seconds would equal the weight of the entire globe.

We cannot close our eyes to this vertiginous process if we are to take seriously the mandate to "evangelize the whole world." We must read in it a sign of the times and therefore interpret it well, probing into its hidden origins. Since 1960 there has been a more acute consciousness of the seriousness of its consequences.

The origins and consequences of this phenomenon involve an unheard-of complexity. They constitute an interlacing of ethical, religious, cultural, political, and economic factors. At their base, however, is the fact of the overcoming of obstacles that used to brake the spiral of ever growing population—namely, disease, malnutrition, and warfare. But above all it was scientific medicine, reducing the mortality rate, especially the infant mortality rate, and keeping it within previously unimaginable limits, that led to the population explosion.

Increased Population Growth in the Third World

A second new fact emerges precisely at this point. Whereas in the West control of the mortality rate followed the initial period of prosperity that accompanied industrialization, in the Third World continents of Asia, Latin America, and Africa it came unaccompanied—that is, without the preceding or concomitant transformation of behavior patterns. Thus, while a lower birth rate, thanks to social changes, accompanied the introduction of new medical advances in the West, fertility remained high in the Third World continents. The rest of the world is expected to augment its combined population by 500 million persons before the close of the present century, but the three Third World continents are expected to augment their population by 2,500 million. The total population of the Third World will then constitute three-fourths of humankind.[3]

The "Excess" Population Migrates to the Cities

It is perfectly clear that the expanding world population does not multiply uniformly over the world, at a consistent rhythm, in the populated areas where new growth occurs. There is a noticeable preference for urban rather than rural sites. Migration to the metropolis is a third new fact of crucial importance.

Statistics bear out this assertion: while the total world population doubled during the first half of the present century, that of the cities with a population of more than 100,000 quadrupled.

Asia: Asia is still a predominantly rural continent. But with 480 million persons in 1970 living in concentrations officially considered urban, its urban side is quantitatively impressive. That urban population figure exceeded the *total* population figure for Africa and Latin America as of that date. The urbanization rate, however, was 21 percent (the percentage of the population residing in cities), which was lower than that for Africa and Latin America. And the movement toward the cities exhibits major disequilibriums: it is almost exclusively toward the principal cities, especially the national capitals; they have been growing at an annual rate of 5 to 10 percent, while the other cities have been growing at an annual rate of 2 percent. Bangkok, for example, with 2.7 million inhabitants in 1968, was thirty-two times larger than the second largest Thai city, Chiangmai, with only 34,000 inhabitants.[4]

Latin America: The overwhelming majority of the 300 million Latin Americans live within a coastal zone no more than 185 miles wide. With the exception of Ecuador, Brazil, and Colombia, each country has only one metropolis—its capital. Approximately 15 percent of the Latin American population live in some twenty capitals. A third of all Argentineans live in Buenos Aires; approximately one-half of all Uruguayans live in Montevideo.

The national capitals "make" the nations: they have become the decision-making centers, setting the tone for the national economic and social life. The three most advanced countries—Uruguay, Argentina, and Chile—are classified as 81, 68, and 61 percent urban, respectively, whereas the continental average is closer to 50 percent. The outstanding characteristic in this distribution pattern is the absence of intermediate population concentrations between the metropolises and the small village or hamlet or simply the *hacienda* of the rural area. In Mexico, for example, 50 percent of population concentrations have less than 2,000 inhabitants, and 100,000 of them count less than 400 inhabitants.

Meanwhile the migration from rural to urban areas continues. From 1950 to 1960 Lima grew at an annual rate of 6 percent; Caracas, 7 percent. As mentioned earlier, three Brazilian metropolises—Belo Horizonte, São Paulo, and Rio de Janeiro—house 25 percent of the national population on 2 percent of the national territory.[5]

Africa: Africa is the least urbanized continent, and the least populous. Only 15 percent of the total population live in communities of more than 20,000 inhabitants. But delusion must be avoided. The continent's urbanization rate is the highest in the world, hovering at 5 percent per year. Africa has at least thirty-two cities with a population of 100,000 or more; together they number 30 million persons.

There are enormous differences from one country to another. Niger, where only 1.5 percent of the population live in cities, shows the highest urbanization rate in all Africa—12.5 percent for the period from 1965 to 1970—but only because it started practically at zero. In Upper Volta the total population grew at an annual rate of 1.7 percent, while the urbanization rate reached 10.8 percent. The corresponding rates in Malawi for the same period were 2.7 percent and 10.4 percent. At this rate the population of African cities will double within fifteen years.[6]

We can conclude this short sketch by pointing out one disconcerting fact: in the list of the world's cities that show the highest growth rate, the first thirteen are in the Third World: Bandung, Lagos, Karachi, Bogotá, Baghdad, Bangkok, Teheran, Seoul, Lima, São Paulo, Mexico City, Bombay, and Jakarta.

Will the Third World city itself explode in trying to cope with the population explosion? It is necessary to see at closer range how the city "manages" its growing population. This will be essential for reading this phenomenon as a sign of God's plans in conjunction with the population factor.

These planetary facts—in themselves and as signs indicative of the deeper reality of faith—have extraordinary import. If, as we believe, God takes the individual human person seriously, the spectacular growth of the number of persons whom he "knows by name" must tell something of great importance. Beyond doubt, a new and crucial phase in the history of humankind is upon us. Mission is called to be on the alert. The Lord is perhaps coming in a new way, unsuspected until now, even if implicit in his incarnation.

We must therefore search for the meaning of this sign, analyzing its innermost structure in the light of the faith. It is clear, for example, that the city is at the center of it. In the proven inadequacy of rural areas to cope with the demographic explosion, urban areas have been given the problem. And so the city forms part of God's plans for a more populous humankind.

It is precisely the so-called new nations that are confronted with this problem more urgently. And, with the exception of the Latin American peoples, this means the less evangelized peoples of the world. Mission must interest itself in their cities.

This sign obliges one to follow the same road as did the first Christians. They were small minorities within a composite world that had an enormous potential for change because of its cities. It is the road taken by Saint Paul who went "from city to city" until finally he arrived at Rome. This sign obliges one therefore to probe for its "message" in the clue provided by the "spaces" that mission must direct its attention to, including "spaces" it cannot enter under present circumstances.

Less Space: The Geographic Processes

Basic needs (treated in chap. 1) motivate persons to respond to them in concert, leading to the creation of cities. The consequences that derive from this, sketched in a hypothetical and theoretical fashion in chapter 2, at least in their spatial dimension, will be made more precise here on the basis of a geographic analysis.

This approach will make it possible to unveil some of the mystery that the metropolis often presents to those who ready themselves to read it as a sign. This investigation of the spatial structure of the metropolis will take into account the fact that many things in it obey very exact laws. The usefulness of the analysis to missionaries will depend upon adherence to methodological exigencies, in whatever attempt to interpret the signs of God's plans, to scrutinize well the phenomena before passing on to an interpretation. Furthermore, the geographic analysis should have concrete results because it deals with the dimension of "space," an easily measurable and controllable datum.

This approach raises two questions that in a certain sense reformulate the fundamental problem of the investigation of the *why* and the *how* of "superpopulation" in a few "supersites": Why have these cities—and not some others—become metropolises? How is the space within them articulated?

The first question requires an investigation into the de facto relationships between city and country. We shall do this through the strategic concept of the *accessibility* of the concrete responses worked out to the basic needs of the human person. The second question provides an opportunity to measure the hypothesis of the "natural areas" (treated in chap. 2) against the reality of the contemporary city.

City and Country

The city is for the country what the *Campo* is for Siena: its central "place." This is the opinion of the geographer Christaller, after he found that, among the various human residence concentrations spread over the surface of a given region, there is always one that supplies a complex of services to the others.[7] This one would be the "central place." The complex of services would include an exchange-of-merchandise system, a transportation network, a communications system, a form of government and defense, and other services, depending on local circumstances.

When he analyzed the effects of the distances among the various population concentrations, Christaller always arrived at the same conclusion: city and country are interdependent, with a hierarchy among the functions taken on by each concentration and competition among them for the same "space" of influence. He found too that a part of the rural population always remained untouched by, emarginated from, the networks of services and functions. These are observations that many missionaries have made for themselves, going about their work in a particular locality.

With the help of this model, geographers have gone ahead to identify three processes at work interrelating city and country on the basis of the three data: trade, transportation, and administration.

The first process pertains to the economic order. It consists in the pressure put on the services provided by the "central place" to cover a maximum radius, directly related to the maximum distance that clients or customers of the service are prepared to travel in order to have the service, as also on the quality and other conditions of the service offered.

The second process also pertains to the economic order. It consists in the tension on the "central place" to occupy an optimal site in a given region— that is, on the artery that accommodates the traffic between the larger population concentrations. The difference from the first process is that here it is not a question of space (implicit in the concept of the radius enclosed within the circumference of a circle) but of distance (implicit in the concept of artery, which is equivalent to a line). Was this perhaps the intuition shared by Peter and Paul in their decision to direct their mission toward the cities, and finally toward the "central place" occupied by Rome? What is certain is that mission cannot neglect the arteries that interconnect population centers and their nerve-points.

The third process pertains to the political order. It is sustained by the tension toward complementarity exhibited by the various population centers, for reasons of defense and administrative control. The central issue here is the logic of subsidiarity, perceived by the early Christians when they organized themselves into patriarchates and, from the cities, directed their missionary activity toward the surrounding countryside.

These processes, with the diverse emphases that emerge from particular historical circumstances, converge in a complex founded on the function of each population center as a center of services for the other centers. The expression "central place" can be understood as the top of a hierarchy of functional sites.

Hierarchized complementarity does not preclude interdependence between city and country. In this light, instead of separating urban and rural mission, one should accept and reinforce the ties that exist between them. The more the stress on the importance of urban mission, the more the contribution to rural mission interdependent with the city: what mission accomplishes in the city rebounds to the surrounding rural areas.

The internal dynamic of the rural-urban dialectic can be illustrated by the model of the "isolated state" proposed by J. H. Von Thunen after his research on the distances of suppliers from merchants, the prices offered for their products, and the rents they must pay for their land.[8] The "isolated state" in his hypothesis is situated in the middle of a fertile plain where there is no river or other navigable waterway. A desert surrounds the plain, cutting it off from the rest of the world. The isolated state is the only large human settlement, and hence the only city.

In the terms of this model, the city must provide the countryside with all manufactured products and must receive from it all its food supplies. Growers take to this exchange with refined rationality. They are constrained to use the only means of transportation available. The relationship between the distance (from which food products must be transported) and the prices offered for them is direct: the greater the distance, the lower the net profit, because transportation costs consume part of the gross profit.

But there is a third factor acting by way of compensation, and it too is bound up with distance: the farther the land is situated from the city, the lower is its value, and hence the lower is the rent that the grower pays for it.

Growers adapt themselves to these three factors, and they diversify their production. This remains conditioned by the demand of the urban market, the techniques of production, and the calculations of the growers. In fact, there are other factors at play that Von Thunen, for purposes of analytical clarity and simplicity, leaves aside, but that would easily be identifiable in concrete situations.

The model is rather flexible and has also been found useful for feasibility studies on the siting of industrial installations in given zones, in conjunction with other considerations such as the cost of raw materials, labor, and certain services. Like agriculture, industry too is always looking for optimal locations as regards productivity and consumption. The key concept, therefore, is the geographical one of accessibility. Its concrete measure, at least in the West, is the cost or value of a particular site: the more accessible it is to other particular sites, the greater its value.

This theme is familiar to missionaries, who have always been expert at evaluating and improving the accessibility of their work centers. In Africa, for example, the fact that missionaries have superior means of transportation—motorcycles, and the like—has improved their accessiblity and therefore their work.

The Space within the City

It was not then by chance but in accordance with the laws of accessibility that the metropolises listed in chapter 1 developed exactly where they did. Pursuing this theme, we can see that there are further explanations for the chaos that seems to weigh upon the *interior* of the surface areas at these geographically strategic points.

The fluid and anonymous masses within these cities are also housed according to spatial considerations, which were long ago well identified. This is something that missionaries must make it their concern to understand: they want to sow the seed of the gospel in the most appropriate furrows of urban territory.

Accessibility reaches its highest levels at the geographic center, where governmental networks often converge as well. It is therefore only logical that competition for space among the various groups of this population concentration would be still more intense precisely here.

Statistical analysis of the use of the various spaces within certain cities reveals the existence of distinct zones, with three types of relationships among them.

The Concentric Model: In this model, the value of space diminishes as the distance from the center increases. The center is reserved to business interests, and is surrounded by an initial belt of light industry, according to the schema worked out by E. W. Burgess: around the center there is a transitional zone, invaded more and more by commerce and industry.

A third belt is inhabited by industrial workers, displaced from areas of urban decay but wanting to live near their work. Beyond this zone is a residential area: the apartment buildings and homes of the well-off. Farther still, beyond the confines of the city, are the satellite communes.[9]

The overall structure is clear: to each circle or belt around the center is reserved a particular function that characterizes it as a "natural area."

The Sectorial Model: In this model, the internal structure is determined by the particular layout of the streets that radiate from the center in an irregular pattern. The diversity of accessibility governed by these radials creates zones of diverse quality, at least in terms of real estate value. It usually generates an urban spatial structure in which—as in the concentric model—there are diverse zones with precise functions. These zones, however, are not patterned in belts but in juxtaposed segments separated from one another by radial arteries.

The Nuclear Model: In this model, the city manifests a polycentric—rather than a unicentric—structure. Each composite center develops a specific function. Thus we find a business center, an administrative center, various residential centers, industrial centers. Here we are somewhat removed from the concept of "natural areas" proposed in chapter 2.

Spatial Segregation

Common to all three models is the phenomenon of spatial segregation, not only of economic functions, such as commerce and industry, but of social categories also, such as the poor, blockaded in their slum areas, and the affluent, housed in residential sections.

Economic functions are segregated for purposes of specialization. Specialization and its consequent divisions of labor are normal in the industrial economic order, whether it be capitalist or socialist. But when social categories segregate themselves spatially, they do so under the impulse of other factors, generally cultural.

We must stress the importance of economic factors brought out by the analysis of urban space. When all is said and done, the value of space is defined most concretely by its price. Competition among those interested in buying it tends to assign a particular space to the competitors who at that moment see greater usefulness in it and are prepared to pay more. Obviously this applies only to political systems that allow free trade—political systems that, furthermore, are still in effect in many Third World cities. The economic process, then, converges in that space and emarginates whole categories of residents from zones rendered inaccessible to them because they are beyond their financial means.

The Specificity of the Third World City

The spatial concepts developed above on the siting and internal configuration of the metropolis apply especially to the cities of the industrialized nations, but are also valid in many respects for the whole world. It will be advantageous, however, to highlight the specificity of the geographic processes in Asia, Latin America, and Africa. As early as 1957, a special commission of the United Nations reported that the rapidly developing cities in the less developed parts of the world were creating diverse areas or districts badly integrated among themselves: a modern commercial, administrative, and residential center (for upper-middle-class social strata); an old city quarter with narrow streets and overcrowded residential buildings; a zone of huts or shacks, inside or outside the confines of the city, lacking urban characteristics (with the exception, of course, of population density and urban types of employment).

But the model does have variations, as the United Nations commission reported. In some cases, especially in Asia and northern Africa, the modern city is totally separated from the old city, which retains its traditional handcraft and commercial (bazaar) industries and social organization; it is often subdivided into quarters distinctly characterized by ethnic or religious criteria. Among the ancient cities, some, such as Damascus, have grown considerably and with very few modern elements. In other cases, fairly common in Latin America, the modern city has interwoven itself with the old city, and the expansion of the new often sweeps aside the old, reducing it to a zone of buildings on the verge of collapse. In practically all of Africa south of the Sahara, and in many industrial centers for mining and oil drilling in other regions, it is clear that there never was an old city.[10]

The same report makes the observation that the zone of huts and shacks is generally to be found on the periphery of the cities. In some instances they have taken the form of integral villages, maintaining the traditional social values and controls, analogous to the rural village. More often, however, the zone is a shantytown that spreads out in all directions without even a modicum of formal administration or organization. Such shantytowns can spring up outside the geographic area under urban administration; no authority feels itself responsible for providing city services or applying construction regulations. But even when shantytowns go up within city limits, city officials neglect their needs, especially if—and it is frequently or even ordinarily the case—the residents have no legal rights to the land where they have built their shacks.

The pattern of urban growth in Asia, Latin America, and Africa is also complicated by the siting of industrial plants on the periphery of cities. Workers can come from nearby shantytowns or be housed in satellite communes constructed by employers or the state.

At present the great majority of the poor resides in the older sections of a city, or in self-regulative villages, or in shantytowns on the periphery. There has been very little private residential construction; rentals or sales are possible only to workers who are better paid. Public construction and "aided self-help" have done very little for low-income families, even though they and their problems are becoming ever more important.

The reasons why land within a city or on its outer borders comes to be taken over by migrants are diverse. Peripheral slums grow up on land that for one reason or another is not being used: often it is considered unsuitable or undesirable for long-range construction purposes. The newcomer to the city can simply put up a hut, or pay a small rent to the owner of the land, or, in the case of better-organized groups of workers, obtain from the government permission to occupy it. Land taken over by shantytowns may be swampy, as in Bangkok, or mountainside, as in Rio de Janeiro, or lowland subject to flooding, as in Baghdad, or simply land used for garbage disposal. Undeveloped land of this kind is also often found near the center of a city. In other cases the land is too arid for agriculture and outside the zones provided with irrigation canals or piped water. Some shantytowns are on land that was bought by real estate speculators looking to the future growth of the city; present occupants risk eviction without advance notice.

We cannot therefore say that the city in Asia, Latin America, or Africa corresponds to the details of the models elaborated by Burgess, much less to those by Von Thunen and Christaller. Santiago de Chile, for example, appears to have about 1,000 *barrios* for 3 million inhabitants, and some forty of them control the whole city.

The City as a Sign of the Times

It must be of interest to urban mission to notice how spatial or geographic accessibility shades into social or life accessibility. Physical accessibility "segregates" certain urban spaces for certain functions. But that is not the whole story. Over and above geographic distances—often bridgeable by new communications systems—there are social distances, more subtle and less controllable.

Certain residential zones remain physically accessible to all, but socially accessible only to those who can pay the high rents or buy homes there. The spatial configuration of the city, at bottom, makes its social configuration emerge. The physical becomes social. And this physical aspect better reveals the sign of the city (see chap. 4).

Meanwhile, these considerations on the demographic and geographic processes that animate the Third World cities themselves carry implications constitutive of the city as a sign. Viewed in this light, one fact comes immediately to attention. Before the end of the present century, there will rain down on us another world. The doubling of the world population within one generation says, beyond any doubt, that something extraordinary is happening to the human family. The sign, from this vantage point, speaks very clearly: "Be attentive; the heavy cloud of this approaching world will not leave you as you were before!" The alert urban missionary will immediately draw the conclusion: if mission is considered to be directed to all persons, "all nations," it is of crucial significance that the urban population of today will be twice as large tomorrow.

How will mission succeed in reaching such numbers if even today, after two millennia, it has not found the way to "go to all nations," to gather them into one flock? The demographic doubling seems to be a further impetus toward dispersion of the human family.

But there is another side to this sign: the impulse toward urban concentration seems to be a counterbalance to the impulse toward dispersion. Will not the new city be a sign of the divine plan to unite humankind? If so, will it not be the specific function of urban mission, inserted in faith into this plan, to prepare us for this imminent "assembly" convoked by God? These are thought-provoking questions that we shall try to resolve in chapter 7. But even at this point, they reveal the heart of mission: every person is sacred, unique, worthy of the concern of one's entire life, the subject and object of a plan of divine salvation, a plan that seems to invite all concerned persons to reach out to the multitudes across the structures of the city.

By way of conclusion, a deeper reading of the sign of the city, clarifying the values that sustain the demographic and geographic processes, is possible by a reflection—already suggested in chapter 2—on its groups. Among them the most typical, whether by reason of their statistical massiveness or their diffusion, seem to be those formed by or for new city immigrants. They have a pronounced visibility when their relatives and acquaintances are already city residents, as also when they take up residence in the city areas reserved to slum-dwellers. The roles that develop seem to be characterized by the informality of the intensive, person-to-person contacts aimed at incorporating newly arrived migrants into the life of the metropolis. From this, therefore, emerges the presence of values such as those of survival and of assurance of food and shelter, a sense of belonging, mutual assistance and responsibility within a family or clan, a pioneering spirit and creative flexibility, social affirmation by way of communication, knowledge, and the new lifestyle.

These are values that, by their very range, indicate that the city-sign tends to absorb the whole person, from the struggle for daily sustenance to the vision of a better world. They do this across the recurrent social datum of recourse—recourse, that is, to other persons, in a communitarian spirit, in seeming contradiction to the individualistic spirit of competition that has colored the history of the Western city.

It is precisely this community value that seems of the highest importance in helping to interpret the sign of the city. It reveals an impulse convergent with another impulse centrally present in the history of salvation—that of communion.

4

ORDERLY RESPONSE TO NEEDS

Concentrating more persons in less space, the city reveals its true heart: it is not just a quantitative reality but also, and above all else, a qualitative reality. Ever more dizzying numbers and ever more reduced space converge in it to form a unique system of human interaction, which must be studied as an urban sociality. We can begin with its most visible and statistically controllable expressions. Economic processes introduce us to this qualitative reality, demonstrating that the consumption of material goods essential to life generates unique patterns of interaction and social relatedness. Then consideration of the political aspects of urban life will carry this study to what many consider the fundamental problem of the city: order.

Urban Economic Processes: A Response to Needs

The Western city takes its origin from processes that are uniquely economic, producing and distributing for its residents and others essential material goods such as food, clothing, and housing, on the basis of a process of exchange (see chap. 2). As a privileged place, the city expresses itself through its zone of influence thanks to its organized trade system and monetary control. Trade takes place according to the equilibrium of supply and demand for goods, and it can do so because the equilibrium is objectively controllable by a monetary "pact," or, more precisely, prices.

It is interesting to note that trade and prices do not regulate only the relationships between producers and consumers of goods, but also those between producers and the four basic resources, namely, the entrepreneurial spirit, workers, capital, and land, that their enterprises require. On the other hand, these same relationships generate new roles in the complicated division of labor in which the productive process articulates itself.

As all this affects human interaction, it alters that interaction profoundly. It is of interest to mission, then, because it reveals another dimension of the city as a sign of the times. To understand it well missionaries seek to know how to interpret what the Lord is saying in his own way: the mystery of his incarnation continues today and passes through these urban economic channels.

Economic Functions of the City

It is a striking fact that while the Western city develops a stimulative function in the creation of new employment, the city of the Third World does just the opposite. This is a serious matter because employment is the individual's base for access to essential goods. Only employed persons can buy what they need.

Why is unemployment a hallmark of the Third World city? The reason is to be found in the fact that the Third World city was not historically linked with industrialization but followed a totally distinct course of development. Agriculture and mining (primary sector), in order better to exploit land and ore deposits, disperse workers over an ever broader surface. Industry (secondary sector) does just the reverse. In order to eliminate excessive transportation and communication, it prefers to concentrate workers on a restricted surface—that is, an urban site. Whereas the primary sector exploits land, the secondary sector exploits sites.[1] As the geographic processes delineated in chapter 3 show, the city is essentially a site, and from this it derives, in the West, its orientation toward industrialization. Industries search it out (or create it) because it is an accessible site, where transportation and communication are favored.

On such a site a great demand for industrial products can be developed, a demand that is much more flexible and "maneuverable" than in traditional rural society. In a capitalist regimen, furthermore, where everything rotates around trade and everything "has its price" and is measured in terms of money, the city intensifies the relationship of stimulation between the demand of the consumer and the supply of the producer. The city, in short, concentrates and accelerates economic processes, both national and international.

When industries experience a shortage of workers, a shifting from rural to urban occupation takes place. Thus in the West a "locational" revolution accompanies the industrial revolution. Sites are not mobile, but workers are. The city becomes a vast reservoir of employable workers; the majority of residents in the Western city subsists from employment in industial enterprises. At a later stage this majority declines, yielding its place to the tertiary sector that produces services instead of material goods.

In the Third World, however, where the process of industrialization has only just begun, the secondary sector is passed over and urbanization leads immediately to the tertiary sector. This fact emphasizes the absolute necessity of reading well these signs of the times as they emerge. Just when the Western city was imposing relationships of an industrial stamp on the lifestyle of the city, the church emphasized the renewal of pastoral ministry in a rural vein, according to the model of the rural parish inherited from the Council of Trent. In the West today, having learned from the mistake of ignoring the workers' world, the church insists on so-called industrial mission but it could be leaving aside the other stage characterized by relationships of the tertiary sector which tend to be more interpersonal and less efficiency-oriented.

In the Third World, urbanization arrives *without* industrialization. The rural masses that move to the cities do so for other reasons. Here trade does not stimulate production, and employment opportunties are not abundant. Immigrants do not even represent a demand for consumer products, which could stimulate industry, because they do not have the money to purchase goods and services.

This leap from the primary to the tertiary phase has long been recognized by missionaries:

> When our community of five Franciscan Missionaries of Mary arrived in Intiyaco [Argentina], the foreign corporation that had been operating in the area for years had already departed. The consequences were deeply felt. All the settlements of the district owed their very existence to that corporation—paternalistic and well organized—which had had but one purpose: to extract all the wood products of that rich forest land. It had operated there for some fifty years and had provided employment for a great number of workers, who had put down roots there.
>
> But the day came when the forest had nothing more to give; the corporation withdrew, leaving the workers to their own fate. For those among them who had not been even minimally prepared for self-development, there was nothing else but unemployment. The younger and more dynamic workers moved away. The land itself was very fertile, and would have sustained agriculture and livestock, but it was covered by the remains and aftergrowth of a forest despoiled of its glory. . . . We cleared the land of those remains, and thus helped them move toward cultivation and reduced unemployment.[2]

In this way, the Third World city does not stimulate industrialization, and consequently does not stimulate national economic development. On the contrary, there are those who say that, attracting the rural population, the city cultivates within itself a parasitic concentration that inhibits the normal development of its own resources. Still it does contribute to the economic development of other nations—the already developed Western nations. This is the disconcerting discovery made by more than one researcher.[3]

In fact it has been ascertained that the Third World city in this situation constitutes an essential link in the network of international trade—the mechanism or, more simply, the economic process that regulates the exchange of goods and services among states in the capitalist world. It is a fact that international trade is organized in this way and that the Third World city in it plays a role of linkage and clearance in the relationship between the West and its own national state.

Third World cities are sites for the exploitation of the Third World in favor of the West: this is the paradox of urban economic processes at the international level. It is clear that what we have here is not a symmetrical pattern of complementarity. World trade is not free or "unrestrictive" trade; it is controlled by the Western states in such a way that the exchange of industrial products from the West and raw materials from the Third World continents is not conducted on a basis of parity, as would be the case in free trade. This asymmetry drives home the point that the Western nations are rich only because the unindustrialized nations are caught up in a world trade that keeps them poor.

The capitalist formula of production is not in effect only within the confines of the West. For centuries, and especially from the industrial revolution onward, it has penetrated the traditional rural world of Asia, Africa, and Latin America, transforming it into a world "on the way to" development. The condition of *under*development, which today characterizes more than half of humankind, resulted from the impact of capitalism on this world and can be understood only by understanding its real relationships with it, which are worked out in a process of international symbiosis. The economies of the Third World nations are exploited to the advantage of the West, which speculates on their material resources. They are thus locked into the primary sector. The West buys raw materials from them and transforms those raw materials, using and strengthening its own secondary sector; it then sells finished products back to the Third World. The problem is that in international trade (for the most part and at least until very recently) prices are not the result of the "hands-off" interplay of supply and demand, but are largely controlled by the West.

In this framework, the cities of Asia, Latin America, and Africa take on a very clear-cut function: they become "export-import cities"—cities that export raw materials and import products made elsewhere.

Their economic function is very different from that of the cities of the West. They did not emerge and do not continue in operation to stimulate the national economy, but to serve the international economy. They do not promote internal trade and the productivity of their own industries; they promote international trade and internal consumption.

The Third World city, in short, does not contribute to the secondary sector of its own nation—as the occidental city does—but to that of Europe and North America. Instead of producing, it serves. And not its own people, but a distant one.

This should be a warning to contemporary urban mission. If missionaries penetrate the confines of a Third World city, it is not to develop ties of dependency on their own homeland or on the church, but to help contribute to the correct functioning of the city, called to serve its own "inland" and the countryside around it. Missionaries do not come as representatives of an unknown foreign kingdom, but, in the footsteps of their Master, they come as ambassa-

dors of a Kingdom that is already present in that city. This is the true
Kingdom, assigned the task of responding to the deepest exigencies of the
populations—urban and rural—that depend in any way on that city.

Economic Consequences for the City

Penetration of the cities of the Third World by processes driven by international trade tend not only to inhibit industrialization at the national and regional level, but also to affect the economic processes within the city itself,
blockading it within the tertiary sector.

Meanwhile immigrants continue to stream into the cities, and they find a
way to survive. Inasmuch as productivity-type enterprises have no openings
for workers, they turn to the tertiary sector. And they create an economic
model very different from that of the Western city: a blend of the traditional
and capitalist formulas. It will be worthwhile to study it at closer range in
order to have a more detailed understanding of the economic processes of the
"tertiarized" city of the Third World.

Tertiary Occupations: The tertiary sector, defined as the complex of activities that produce "nonmaterial things," includes such occupations as hair-
dresser, truck driver, retailer, and commercial and administrative personnel.
In the West the growth of this sector is interpreted as a sign of progress because improved productivity by agricultural and industrial technology means
that "fewer workers can do more" and consequently more persons can dedicate themselves to offering their services to others, and more persons can seek
the services of others. But in the cities of the underdeveloped world the advent of the tertiary sector is not a sign of economic progress. There are two
schools of thought as to why this is so. Some say it is a sign of the failure—the
inadequacy—of Western capitalist models applied to Third World nations.
Other say that it is only a matter of a temporary disequilibrium resulting from
precipitous economic progress.

In effect the tertiary sector appears to take upon itself an essential function
in the city, absorbing jobless workers at a minimum investment. An example
from Indonesia may help to illustrate its functioning, and bring out also the
specific economic processes at work.

Majokuto is the fictitious name given to a city on the island of Java studied
by C. Geertz.[4] He concentrated on the two major occupational blocks of the
workers population: the commercial and manufacturing enterprises, based
on impersonal relationships, organized into specialized occupations in a
complex of labor-division and interdependence among the various strata of
expertise, in the Western pattern; and the bazaar, the independent activity of
small retailers, based on ad hoc personal relationships, in small but very
numerous transactions, in a very intense interaction.

The first area entails a process of capital augmentation to the detriment of
employed workers (a capital-intensive enterprise); the second entails the reverse process (a labor-intensive enterprise). The two of them penetrate each

other, reinforcing themselves in turn. How? The bazaar has its fulcrum in the central marketplace, the *pasar*. More than simply a physical space, it is the ambit where all the transactions of small business, as well as urban and rural production, take place. It is essential, therefore, to take into account the flow of goods and services exchanged, the mechanisms governing this flow, and the traditional cultural import of the bazaar.

The goods in question are easy to transport, and the flow patterns that they exhibit are circular, not linear. The image comes to mind of a long row of men passing bricks to one another, over a great distance, slowly building a wall. The regulative mechanism at work demands that credit be possible, that risks be "divided up and shared," and that prices be fluid, in such a way that everyone can realize a small gain. The social import of the bazaar is relatively light: interpersonal relationships are understood to end there, at the market-place.

The family is still the base of the social system in Mojokuto, and the family head feels responsible for seeing to it that the family's offspring work their way into the *pasar*. But parental or family ties do not have a decisive weight on the transactions that take place there. In general this "system" favors the introduction of new participants. A process of self-enlargement means that more persons are involved, the market is more active.

The problem of urban unemployment is mitigated by this system. The virtuosity of *pasar* veterans, the tenacity of their traditions extending to the smallest of technical details in their craft, the internal workings of market exchanges, and the very fluidity of the overall flow pattern are all resorted to in the search for "occupations" or "jobs" when the need arises.

The *pasar* is the heart of Mojokuto; it remains closely linked with the sphere of large-scale industry and with the surrounding countryside.

Two observations of a general nature seem warranted here. On the one hand, a tertiary sector of this type should not be judged by Western standards, or be considered a failure of economic development, or even be taken as a measure of the level of economic development. On the other hand, the fact that it has so many component elements may conceal the germs of decomposition by large-scale industry—the "advance troops" of Western capitalist strategy.

It happens, in fact, that small retailers move from the *pasar* to the Western-type department store (the *kulot*, the *toko* store). This signals the beginning of the erosion of the *pasar* and of the entire network of interdependence between the urban marketplace and rural suppliers. In its "pure" state, the marketplace depends on them for food products, and they depend on it for handcrafted products, services, and occasional employment.

The same phenomenon can be seen in Latin America. Its capitals have not experienced a transformation from an agrarian to an industrial economy: the transformation was one that went immediately to the tertiary phase. And it is not in a tertiary sector centralized in a *pasar*, but in the overcrowded offices of bureaucratic organisms and in the streets where the desperate masses try to sell or do anything at all. The most dramatic example of their resourcefulness is seen in the subdivision of labor among *favela*-dwellers who salvage things to sell from garbage dumps.

In Africa there are the "parking boys" of Accra, Nairobi, and all the other cities that have more vehicles than parking spaces. Motorists drive around the busy sections of the city and suddenly a boy appears, wildly gesticulating, to direct their attention to an empty parking space. The boy will be very young, shabbily dressed, his arms and legs muddied, his fragile body tormented by hunger.

Many of them sleep on the streets or in caves, under trees, or in kiosks. They use sheets of plastic and cardboard to protect themselves from the cold. They smoke cigarette butts thrown away by others and they inhale gasoline fumes to forget—at least for a few seconds—the bleakness of their life. They band together in groups of three or four, or even ten to fifteen. One of them will be the leader, with the responsibility of protection and the fair distribution of food and money. In one year in Nairobi, 1976, their numbers increased by 26 percent. They begin at the age of ten to fourteen.

Father A. Grol, with a group of volunteers, has worked among them. He realized that they were not an "outlaw fringe" cast out by an urbanized society. They did not know the word "trust" or "love"; their experience had taught them to defend and protect themselves, and not to put trust in anyone else. Father Grol began his work by giving them clothing. As their confidence in him grew, he put them into schools, vouching for them. They now have a committee for each group of twenty boys, which sees to it that they always have work to do.[5]

Reduced Productivity: In the cities of Latin America, the economic and political processes are characterized by the massive penetration of the capitalist system, which reaches them via their respective governments. To a large extent this has been the source of the economic growth realized in recent years.

Economic processes in the tertiary sector, by reason of their linkage with large-scale industry, are affected by the overall unification imposed by capitalist production methods. It has an effect on the types of occupation carried on in the tertiary sector.

Since the beginning of colonial history, capitalism has made its presence felt, especially in foreign but also in domestic commerce, progressively penetrating large-scale industry, agriculture, the service industries, finances. Nor does it operate in a vacuum: the older forms of industrial production, agriculture, and services that it has affected must be taken into account. At the beginning of the twentieth century, half the work force in Buenos Aires was composed of salaried persons in private companies. In Salvador (Brazil) in 1970 the figure was 40 percent. Companies of this type work hand in hand with domestic production and self-employed (handcraft) workers who also sell what they produce. The two last-named modes of production are on the verge of being subordinated to the capitalist system.

Large enterprises, for example, prefer to contract for services from independent agencies rather than take on their own employees. They thereby escape social security taxes. This has happened in Monterrey (Mexico), to name but one city.

São Paulo offers another type of example. In a recent study it was ascertained that between 1958 and 1970 the cost of living had gone up drastically but wages remained the same. Workers were able to survive because family members made for themselves things they had previously bought (often the very house they lived in). This indicates that the capitalist invasion does not destroy all less productive models of industry.

Objectives and Resources: There remains the basic problem: the growth rate of more productive jobs is too low to offset the population growth rate.

Attempts have been made to solve the problem by the application of labor-intensive rather than capital-intensive technology. Industrialization could be directed more to the home-construction industry than to the automobile industry. More could be invested in industry that depends less on governmental intervention. Above all, the blind acceptance of models of economic growth successful in the West could be discontinued. On the contrary, something could be learned from their failings.

At stake here are options that are becoming more and more crucial in the Third World. The question of choices, decisions, brings us into the political sphere. Priorities have to be set and who will do this? According to E. Jelin, when national production priorities are formulated by multinational corporations in collaboration with local executives and high government functionaries who represent the interests of those whose goal is profit for themselves, the results are oriented toward capital-intensive technology. To arrive at priorities oriented toward social justice one cannot rely on the goodwill of these persons. A change of priorities demands much more than simply a change of production programming: it demands a thorough going realignment of the equilibriums of power.[6]

This observation can serve as a bridge between the economic and the political spheres in this study. The nexus is evident: if the philosophy of international capitalist trade continues in effect, the city of the Third World will continue to serve the interests of other peoples—those represented by the multinational corporations—and not those of its own people. But it is easier to *say* that this philosophy must be abandoned than to *do* something about it. The major powers—they can be called the First World and the Second World, or simply the capitalist bloc and the socialist bloc—reject this approach. And the Third World cannot content itself with condemning its own exploitation by colonialism or imperialism, ancient or modern; it must organize itself for joint action—such as that which has had considerable success for the oil-exporting nations.

Ordered Response: Urban Political Processes

The conflict between rich nations and poor nations reminds one of the fundamental dichotomy in every discussion of the struggle of humankind with nature. It appears to be an irresolvable conflict, at least so long as the relationships among nations are governed by the interests of the superpowers and by the logic of their "zones of influence"—namely, the present international order. It is a political conflict expressed in terms of condemnation of the present international order, but with its roots in the economic components sketched above.

The World Population Conference held in Bucharest in 1974 made a valid point when it proclaimed that only a new world economic order can resolve the problems of underdevelopment, echoing a United Nations document that condemned the "disorder" in the patterns of international trade. It rejected the idea that development could come about simply by a mechanical increase in productivity.[7]

But other factors are also at play: if integral development could take place with a different configuration of economic relationships, order would be involved—and this belongs to the political realm. It will not be experts in economic processes who will resolve the problems of underdevelopment. At the very most they can only touch up some of the fixtures of the present order. Capitalism is already rethinking its own structures on the basis of a new territorial division of labor, on the planetary scale. A world order capable of liberating the Third World from its poverty can come into being only if the governance of its resources is withheld from the philosophy of the projections being made by the multinational corporations.

As regards urban poverty, the urgent needs were well pointed out by the United Nations conference held in Vancouver (Canada) in 1976, which stated, *inter alia*, that the world does not lack the technology or the physical resources needed to create and regenerate authentic communities. The fact that so many governments in the world met in Vancouver to search for ways to mobilize ideas and resources for creating more human communities does honor to their sense of responsibility and their clearsightedness. To achieve this, the conference emphasized that priority must be given to making sure that communities no longer be considered of "secondary" importance or result from decisions taken on other problems. Their vitality and growth should not depend on economic expansion or the development of other factors; living conditions should be considered a barometer of world development.

Such an ordering of priorities, declared the conference, makes the following demands of governments: better control over the use of land; reserving for the community some part of the proceeds from land sales not resulting from improvements made by sellers; the supervision of all national territory within the framework of community planning; giving a priority to intermediate cities and rural communities to create systems that will sustain agriculture and relieve pressure on the larger cities; the formation of more balanced communities, so as to eliminate social segregations (among social groups, occupations, service industries, residential areas); the introduction of programs for conservation and recycling of usable materials; the development of more economical sources of energy (solar power, etc.); the participation of all in national decision-making processes; the reorganization of national, regional, and local governments, in order to respond better to the urgent needs of human communities; the reorientation of academic and research institutes to see to it that problems having to do with living conditions be given the attention and documentation they need; the commitment of the international community to give the highest priority to the area of living standards in their capital-assistance projects; a commitment to initiate a program of cooperation for the development and amelioration of living standards.[8]

For the underdeveloped nations the Vancouver conference recommended that all self-help incentives be offered to immigrants, including land and the provision of essential public services. It stressed the importance of a smooth transition from phase to phase in the implementation of development programs.

A formidable task, beautifully stated! The means and ideas are not lacking. The only thing lacking is the political will to recognize the problems and work toward solutions. Why is this such a problem? On the one hand, many governments in Third World countries are indeed searching for national development—but on condition that it will not provoke changes in the internal social order. And the multinational corporations, on the other hand, which exert influence over the American government, will not agree to an autonomous evolution of the economy of Third World nations because the international division of labor put in place by them requires that the center-to-periphery structure retain its present interrelationships of production and exploitation. The socialist bloc too finds itself compromised, its own interests conditioned by the capitalist stategy that orients it more toward the creation of its own zones of influence than toward human solidarity.

Léon Tabah, a UN official dealing with demographic studies, was not wrong when he said that "the goals proposed by the UN plan for world population were sacrificed, by and large, to such declarations as: 'A new international economic order must be created!'—as if what those words meant were a matter of common knowledge."[9] Even if everyone knew what those words imply, no government seemed ready to pledge itself to implement them. A "new" order would threaten the "old" equilibrium still in effect which favored those who already have a sizable share of power in their hands.

The concept of order implies the concept of power. Reflection on these two concepts will help to lay a foundation for an analysis of the international political processes that have an impact on the life of the city.

The social order, which includes the economic order, coincides with a complex of models that regulate interaction; those models have the support of a vast consensus or at any rate the support of general acceptance. When such a consensus is formulated, explicated, and in some way imposed, it becomes a political fact. Here, then, the term "order" will be used to describe a formulated and imposed consensus, abstracting from the degree of acceptance on the part of those on whom it is imposed.

To formalize and impose an order requires power. Power is the capacity possessed by an individual or a group of individuals of imposing their will on others who are involved with them in the same social system. Its ultimate base seems to be the effective possibility, on the part of the individual or group in question, to use force if met with resistance.

The military functions of the cities of antiquity (mentioned in chap. 2) involved this same thing: the urban group, which defended the surrounding countryside against third parties, imposed its will on it in return, and this was how it possessed the power to maintain a stabilized order. In more recent times, this power has extended to a network of administrative functions, becoming at once less visible but more diffuse.

At this point the effective distribution of power among social groups takes on a special interest for urban mission. At one time missionaries attempted to initiate a dialogue with local leaders, who had a high degree of visibility in rural systems. But now they must become aware of who really has power in urban zones.

If, in the past, they ran the risk of being identified with a "foreign" power, that of a colonial government, they must now be careful not to align themselves with usurpers well hidden in the very intricate threading of urban life. How is this to be discerned? We shall first see what the situation is from the international point of view, to understand better the political processes that underpin the order that permeates the Third World city.

There is question here of the process of *dependence*, well dissected and analyzed by specialists on Latin America. This continent, in fact, has experienced three moments of "dependence," with profound consequences on its spatial systematization and, therefore, its urbanization.

International Dependence

At the international level, some states occupy a position of power with respect to others, imposing on them a situation or relationship of dependence. Analyzing Latin America from this viewpoint, we see that the first moment of dependence was that of a colonial domination that carried out direct exploitation of its resources. The political sovereignty of the colonial power succeeded in making of this territorial possession a key point in its own expansions. The colonial cities were planned for three purposes: (1) to solidify the political governance and economic administration of the conquered territories; (2) to populate, to some degree, those same territories, consolidating the imperial expansion; (3) to promote commerce with the metropolitan center, and perhaps also with neighboring countries.

This commercial function was particularly successful in the Portuguese cities on the Brazilian coast. By a political decision, they were few and far between. They were linked directly with Lisbon, for imports and exports, without any linkage with other Brazilian centers. Even today more than 80 percent of the Brazilian population lives in the Atlantic coastal zone.[10]

With the coming of worldwide capitalist trade that accompanied the political independence of the Latin American states, we perceive a second moment of dependence, a moment bound up with the exploitation of natural resources that led to the fixing of the national borders that we know today. The continent was divided, historically, into agrarian and mining "enclaves." Enclaves mined raw materials and formed the "company towns" of Venezuela and Bolivia. Agriculture raised products for exportation, and Argentina and Uruguay quickly took to urbanization around their great export, commercial, and administrative centers. Plantations, on the other hand, did not lead directly to the creation of cities: although they required great numbers of workers, they were spread over a vaster surface.

The third moment of dependence, that of postwar imperialist domination, is characterized by foreign investment in Latin America coupled with control over imports and exports, and aligned with the profit-making strategy of the great multinational corporations operating on the world market.

Control over the production of exports was dictated by international money sources; the multinational corporations modernized and developed national industry, basing it on new methods of mass production with a minimal work force.

The strategy of the multinationals was of a world scope and escaped, of course, the logic of local economic and political exigencies. The government of the United States, in particular, offered guarantees for the overall format, providing technical and economic assistance, as well as military and political surveillance. In the 1970s the impact of the new industrialization widened the distance between city and countryside, exacerbating the exodus of the masses from rural areas. And while the agrarian social structure was going to ruin, the urban system was not building up a nucleus of production sufficient to cope with the rural exodus.

Unable to defy or dislodge this alignment of powers, the dependent countries contest its "legitimacy," a concept that is very useful for understanding political processes. Legitimacy is that minimum of acceptance that renders the use of power practicable. If it is true that power rests ultimately on the implicit threat of the use of physical force, it is not less true that its use demands a minimum of justification. Political power can impose its decisions not simply because it has armaments but because everyone knows it has armaments, and at least a certain number of citizens accepts as normal its intervention in foreseeable circumstances. Legitimacy is precisely this minimum of acceptance of power. It is only logical that the wielders of power try to enlarge a minimal base; they do so by communicating reasons to justify their position. They are not blind to the fact that legitimacy does not reside in them, but in the minds of the others who do not have power (or do not have the means to acquire it).

With this in mind, it is easier to understand what happens at the international level: the attempt to diminish the base of legitimacy claimed by the dominant nations. Lacking the means to construct a base for their own power—at least for the time being—the countries of the Third World make use of what they do have: the negative "power" of reducing the base of legitimacy needed by others.

Legitimacy

Against this background, and with the same conceptual instruments, one is better able to understand what is happening in the city. The problems can be put in simple terms: resources—beginning with the land available—are very limited, but the urban population is growing rapidly. In what "order" will these resources be distributed? And who will have control over this "order"? Answers will hinge on the question of legitimacy: What would the legitimate order be? Who will have legitimate control over it?

The first question can be answered in terms of social values. In treating of basic resources, appeal is made, for example, to the right of private ownership of land. The person who has land makes a claim on this value of private ownership, which becomes an element of order to the extent that others accept it. But this line of reasoning can be contested by recourse to a higher value, that of the human person and the right to the spatial dimensions worthy of the human person. The two values clash. When the right of private ownership "invades" an urban site, making of it an object of speculation, a marketable object, may this not be to the detriment of many human lives?[11] In such a case, order can indeed continue to be legitimated in the name of the right to private ownership—but no longer in the name of the common good of the general public. And the base of legitimacy is thereby greatly reduced.

The answer to the question of who legitimately regulates order would look to the representatives of the majority of the citizens, in a democratic regimen. In practice, however, the matter is much more complicated, at least in the Third World, where official representatives, like their colonial predecessors, often do not pursue the real needs of the population (which would coincide with the common good) but the particularized needs of a certain portion of the population (one or another privileged minority).

In terms of urban mission, we can begin with a practical datum. For city immigrants, who normally constitute the great majority of the citizenry, the second question simply does not arise. Those who have power are already identified with the city, and it does not enter the mind of the immigrant that they could be called into question. They are *there*, like the streets and the houses. And their legitimacy is equally stabilized, forming part of the very nature of things. It is taken for granted.

There remains, however, the question of legitimate order. The answer to this question is more problematic. To the extent that an awareness emerges in immigrants—as in so many other residents—that their hardships are rooted in the existing order, they raise the question of its legitimacy.

The decision-making process, therefore, cannot ignore the fact that the city does not belong only to the 20 percent who are well-off. The political process will find a correct solution only when it knows how to provide for the 80 percent a proportionate share in the available resources. The path of a community of *favela*-dwellers toward a residential area furnished with water and sewers, schools and hospitals, and all of it linked with full and diversified employment, would not be so difficult. The immigrant who begins with the construction of a house for himself, and goes on to help with that of a neighbor, would probably be inclined to start up a small construction business *if* public officials would assure him of his right of ownership of his own house, would control the excesses of land speculation, would see to the provision of public utilities and services, and especially if they would treat him as an associate in the building up of the social life of the metropolis.

The necessary technological know-how has long been available: for on-site job training, conscientization programs bearing on the real needs of the community, small outpatient clinics staffed by paramedics, installations for recycling waste materials into methane or fertilizers, and many other similar aids.

But political decisions are needed to establish a just division of investments in public services, in alignment with a model of employment offerings that the city could and should provide.

The City in Order

At this juncture, we can set this study on the tracks of urban political processes, contrasting two situations. The first is that of a city where the problem of the legitimacy of the existing power is largely resolved in favor of the status quo, and the second is that of a city where this problem is posed in open and acute terms.

It must be admitted that, unfortunately, the first situation—"the city in order"—is commonly verified in Asia, Latin America, and Africa. Here, where are found in extreme forms the conditions that Western sociology has identified as the ones that have historically led to urban revolution, radical cataclysms are not in evidence. This has led many scholars to revise their theories on violent social change. And it is part of the reason for the agreement today that Third World urbanization is different from Western urbanization.

From Western social science we can, however, borrow the two concepts of legislation and administration to identify better the political processes at play in an urban situation where legitimacy is not questioned. These two concepts sum up the two ways in which every political regime goes about the problem of distributing power and resources among the various cells of the population. In treating of the control of the city's destiny, what is of chief importance here is the legislation that fixes the criteria for the assignment of space and urban services among the various "contenders," because, as noted in chapter 3, it is precisely accessibility to urban space and services that gives a city its specific physiognomy.

It is normal for a city government to decide which areas and which services will be developed, and for which social group. This is city planning, which, among other things, includes zoning restrictions and the provision of schools, clinics, social services and utilities: streets, public transportation, electricity, water, sewers, and refuse collection.

Also included are the collection and allocation of funds, from taxes and various forms of investment, for the diverse areas of the city and the diverse categories of needs. An attempt is made to establish criteria once and for all—that is, to legislate.

But who actually legislates? Here is the crux of the question. Despite the best intentions and the loftiest declarations, it is, in general, the privileged who influence legislation, reinforcing or at least defending their own privileges. It is not always true that "the one in charge makes the law"; often it is the one who can influence the "official" lawmaker. The true wielders of power in a city are not always the members of the city council, or the equivalent, but also those who can exercise influence over the council. The persons who more commonly do so are financial leaders and those who speculate on land and the social needs of the citizenry.

It seems, however, that for the city, and especially the Third World city, the effective distribution of power is controlled more by administration than by legislation. In this case the executive has gained the upper hand over the legislative. In the analysis of a city, therefore, the administrative processes must be taken very seriously. In Asia, as an example, urban legislation has its place, as a document of the United Nations makes clear,[12] but the effective realization of its workings is something else: notwithstanding adequate legislation and planning, the everyday administration of the city does not have the capacity or the will to confront the needs of the masses, or it is too compartmentalized, with one subdivision blocking another, or it is too stretched out to handle the waves of applicants, or too weak to face up to owners and the vested interests that seek to exploit the situation, or it simply does not have the means to carry out the execution of laws and plans.

For the rest, experience has shown missionaries that understanding a given law well and knowing how to establish good relationships with an administrator is what gives the best results. However, our chief interest here is the process that puts into the hands of administrators the power that they actually have.

It is essential for urban missionaries to understand clearly the functioning of these political, largely depersonalized, processes. Only so can they understand the inner meshings of the urban mechanism. But it is no less essential for them to understand clearly the personal role of the individuals and groups operating within the framework of such laws. Their analysis, in fact, would not be complete if it took in only the impersonal processes. Missionaries must know how to penetrate to those who promote or obstruct them, or simply "let them run on." In short, their analysis must reach to those who really govern a given city. Too often people stop with the impersonal processes, condemning their consequences in terms of manipulation, exploitation, and the oppression of whole categories of persons. But it is essential to go further, to identify the handful of individuals or groups that play a key role in these political processes, maintaining or promoting them, sometimes unwittingly.

It is this element of nescience—on both sides—that often creates and exacerbates the disparity between the objectives of legislation and the harsh everyday reality. In the search for causes, it will be useful to keep in mind that access to power is often obscure in large organizations, and it can happen that some practically unknown person who occupies a strategic position in an urban bureaucracy (or, for that matter, in an industrial, commercial, labor union, governmental, or military bureaucracy) has more power than the person at the pinnacle of the official political pyramid. It is also helpful to keep in mind that power in a city grows quietly, and therefore information on it and its outreach is not easily come upon. It must be looked for.

Here it will suffice to point out two types of interest groups that, by exerting influence on the legislative and administrative processes, manipulate to their own objectives the destinies of entire cities.[13]

The first group is that of the great landowners, building-industry entrepreneurs, and speculators. Because of their de facto alliances with those in control of urban legislation and administration, they often manage to define the nature and time of physical changes within the city, changes that are more evident in the center of the city and on its periphery.

Where socialist governments are well established, this group no longer has power, but with other governments, including military and dictatorial, even if covert, they are there and they have power.

The persons who compose this group are not necessarily in contact or communication with one another. This is an interest group, and it differs from others by its invisibility and subtlety. Common interests are all that form it into a "group." But it is not for this reason any the less influential in imposing decisions on the city.

To this first group we can add those who belong to the business world. Their field of activity is that of "citizen centers." What counts for them is accessibility; they tend therefore to concentrate their forces to assure for themselves the geographic locations best suited to promoting commercial trade and industrial development. It can be a ruthless undertaking that often compromises the common good of the city, polluting the atmposhere or emarginating entire categories of craft workers once housed in the city center.

The second group is composed of those who are ensconced in the residential zones of the city. These are the families and groups that already have a generous portion of the city's services and resources, and they intend to keep what they have, against no matter whom! They insist on "being left alone," cementing their segregation from other groups, especially from immigrants, who, they fear, may disturb their way of life. When they get what they want, it is often to the detriment of others, and this causes divisions and conflicts.

Both these groups draw public administration to their side, thus compromising its mediative function between the various groups comprising the citi-

zenry. Instead of contributing to the common good, and promoting an equitable distribution of what the city has to offer, the public administration
becomes its major source of blockage, lending itself to the game of the
strong. And so the rich become richer, and the poor poorer. The everyday
functioning of the city often reveals a fusion of interests of these groups and
public administrators. The separation of competencies, generally practiced
by the latter, obstructs the unificative and organic spirit of the best of plans.
Time is lost in seeing a plan through to completion, and owners busy themselves with investments in very expensive clinics, luxury apartment buildings,
and the like, to the disadvantage of the less well-off. The political dimension
becomes very clear when fusions of interests bog down city planning.

According to John Kenneth Galbraith, the key to order in the distribution
of urban power remains that of land control. He contrasts socialist and capitalist approaches, saying that perhaps the most urgent need is to admit that
the modern city is—by its very nature—a socialist enterprise, and to see more
clearly the essentially social character of the whole city. The social dimension
of modern urban life is very costly, and the idea that these social costs represent only a modest fraction of the total costs has long since been proved false.
Public expenses must take precedence over private expenses, for it is impossible to have clean houses when the streets are filthy.

Capitalism, Galbraith continues, is woefully incompetent in providing the
goods and services that cities need most. But it is perfectly competent in providing the things that cause problems for the city. Nowhere on earth has it
ever been efficient in the construction of housing. Nor has it ever created
efficient sanitary or transportation systems. These failings of capitalism
have come to be accepted, at least partially, in Western Europe, Japan, and—
understandably—the socialist countries. But they are still considered to be
adventitious, not intrinsic, features of it.[14]

Galbraith's words are a challenge to the legitimacy of capitalism as a mode
of urban organization. How is it to be reworked into an efficient system?
Probably by groups that would work out a diverse body of legislation more
sensitive to the common good.

What is needed is a wider participation of citizens in political groupings
that would educate the populace to take responsibility for decisions affecting
the whole city. In this perspective, a future moment could be imagined when
the city administration—and the legislation it would be acting on—would no
longer take action in line with the partialized interests of a few powerful
groups, but in line with the effective capacity of a maximum of urban groups
to express their real needs. This would be a passage from protest to the formulation of common priorities. And the great majority, from being an object
manipulated by the political processes, would become the subject that gives
them their content. From being a creature of the city, it would become its
creator. As a goal to be pursued, this is enticing because it would give hope to
the most disadvantaged urban groupings, mobilizing them toward valid objectives, even if, in the de facto framework of the interests of a number of

other groupings, theirs would not be the only objectives.

It is inviting too because it opens to us the more fundamental problematic of the formation of truly human communities within the city. No community could ever be exclusively political, except at the price of becoming a monster like those based exclusively on financial interests.

Is this utopian? It could be. But the options are limited: leaving the situation as it is, or urban revolution.

The City in Disorder

When legislative and administrative processes become so extraneous to the realities lived by an urban population that they lose every semblance of legitimacy, the spiral of revolution—whether violent or nonviolent—begins to uncoil.

It is better realized today that violence is not a characteristic of revolutionaries only, but also of the regimes they oppose. If violence means the use of physical force to obligate others to one's own will, then revolutionary violence is not so different from that used by regimes lacking even a modicum of legitimacy. Or perhaps it is only a question of modalities: revolutionary violence to bloody death all at once, or violence to death blood-drop by blood-drop in the drama of injustice from day to day. With legitimacy absent, violence is latent in the threat of physical force that backs up political power.

Violence can be avoided when the force behind the existing power can be controlled and oriented toward the transformation of that very power. In this case the "ruled" become aware of their force and they set it in opposition to that of the "rulers"—*in the name of legitimacy.* If the warning is perceived by the latter, bloodshed is avoided and nonviolent revolution results. Even in this case the use of physical force is "effective" by way of being preventive.

Besides the question of violence or nonviolence, the question of revolution itself remains open: In a city in disorder, where segregation imprisons the masses and inequality renders them even more impotent, what are the perspectives for reversing the situation?

In practice, what are the possibilities for revolution in the cities of the underdeveloped world? As sketched above, the indications are clear. In many of these cities the "ideal" conditions for revolution are verified—conditions that are the consequences of the colossal failure of the economic and political models of capitalism. There is, however, another current of thought here. As a matter of fact, despite the presence for decades of the conditions thought to be "ideal" for revolution, it has not come about.

Other contributory factors are to be observed. There persist in underdeveloped nations, as in the Indonesian example of "Majokuto" presented earlier in this chapter, the traditional rural models, with their extensive capacity to absorb the brunt of a vast work force. Politically, therefore, this type of work, even if less productive than its Western counterpart, reinforces the status quo. Persons who think they have work, even if they really do not, tend to concur that they have everything to lose and nothing to gain by muddying the waters and changing things. Once again we can see how the cultural order cuts across political processes, holding a solution in abeyance.[15]

In all these situations, however, it is acknowledged that revolutionary processes are present, even if they do not always arrive at the goal of political change. And so there remains another question: Who are the engineers of urban revolutionary processes, whether violent or nonviolent?

As pointed out before, once the impersonal processes have been identified, the missionary must look for the face of the persons who animate them. Their identification profiles immediately reveal one clear characteristic: they are persons who have deeply experienced, existentially and conceptually, the disorder of the city, and have done so at the level of the political processes that subjugate, oppress, and exploit the masses of their compatriots. Logically, they are different from the masses, and they risk being taken for deranged and abnormal. But for them, abnormality is normal: they have broken with a "normal" state of affairs that seemed to them unjust. It may be that they are deluded, but it does not have to be presumed.[16]

Persons who occupy key positions in explosive political processes are "polestars," very important for the future of the city because they succeed in articulating its real travail. Before judging them, this future must be taken into account. If the future is to be the same as the present, then revolutionaries must be stopped; but if the future is to be different, they must be taken seriously.

It is not imperative to take the unusual and the abnormal as signs of something negative to brace oneself for and defend oneself against in every instance. Instead, they should be taken as possible signs of political processes that could change a state of affairs justly condemned.

Another characteristic of the animators of revolutionary processes is their scarcity. There are very few of them and it is almost impossible to find them, because they have to go against the stream. The radical disorder is that disorder is accepted or at any rate passively endured by the overwhelming majority of the citizens. Who will awaken the masses? Who will have the courage or the motivation to try to do it? Missionaries, themselves a distinct minority, should not have difficulty in appreciating this characteristic.

There is a certain similarity (not the most exiguous) between the prophetic role of the missionary, namely, summoning others to conversion and renewal, and that of revolutionaries, namely, calling for revision and reconstruction. At any rate it should not be presumed that there is an absolute incompatibility between mission and revolution.

To be sure, in the city in disorder there will be unusual and strange figures who have nothing better to do than preach collapse and novelty, but there should be no problem in distinguishing them from true innovators. The discernment criterion will be in their basic *objectives*, which must be carefully distinguished from *means* to achieve them. The missionary might, of course, have to reject the latter while accepting the former. Judgment will be easier when the concrete urban situation in which the missionary lives is studied. In any event, missionaries will have no excuse for exempting themselves from searching for the values embedded in revolutionary movements.

The City as a Sign of the Times

If demographic and geographic processes seem to converge in the promotion of communion among human beings, facilitating its actualization in their urban setting, the economic and political processes seem to run in the opposite direction, toward dispersion. The hypothesis of chapter 2 is verified: the city is an ambivalent sign.

How should the sign of these urban economic and political processes be read? What special orientation of God's plans do they bear?

A preliminary attempt at answering these questions would consist in identifying the values that govern the urban economic and political processes. This can be done by recalling the common roles that they project. Among them the most typical are found in corporations and industrial concerns, and in centers of government and public administration. As such, they are formal types of groups. The economic process, in contrast, thanks to its tertiary sector, generates groups of an informal type.

While formal groups call for precise and very efficient roles, informal groups generate less specific and more affective roles. As a consequence, the values that emerge from the two of them are on two lines: there are those such as competence, success, competition, profit, ownership, work, tradition, control, power—the formal line; and there are friendship, security, appreciation by others, cooperation, honesty, flexibility, fairness, justice—the informal line. Putting the two lines together to form a scale, it seems that justice comes out as the uppermost value, even though it is interpreted in diverse ways, depending on who invokes it.

Justice thus will be the guide to a correct reading of the city-sign. Is not justice the characteristic feature of the messianic era, the goal and aim of salvation history?

For the moment, then, a preliminary reading makes us aware of a primary appeal to urban mission: the God of salvation cannot *not* invite missionaries, when they make themselves aware of these processes, to share the suffering of his children subject to exploitation and oppression, to go to those suffering. The sign itself becomes a spur to "go to the cities."

5

THE MEANING OF URBAN LIFE

With an absolute minimum of financial and political means, the masses of the Third World have built their cities. This miracle—that is, the capacity of human persons to develop relations with their environment and their fellow humans in such a way that they can live, and even live *well*, in the most hostile of situations—is the cultural process. The capacity for it resides in the human spirit. Exterior elements—worktools, utensils, food, clothing, housing—do not per se establish the quality of life. The overall perception that individuals have of their own situation transforms them when they are put into this "spiritual" context—a subtle but very powerful kind of relationship with the physical and biological environment, the urban terrain, the social reality.

It is certainly of interest to missionaries to understand better how this cultural process helps the disadvantaged to "survive." And this knowledge will also reveal to them the inner meaning of urban life.

The object of cultural analysis was earlier identified with the lifestyle of a social system (see chap. 2). It will thus be the urban cultural processes that will reveal what is at the roots of the social system characteristic of the city. In producing urban culture, it crowns the urban system, assuring its continuation and at the same time setting the stage for its further development. And once again there is a kind of circular causality: the system creates the citizen and the citizen creates the system. From this flows the lifeblood that vivifies the collectivity. Here is the life that explains the city, the same life that the missionary wants to enrich by grafting salvation onto it, bringing it into the process of incarnation, which is the very heart of the history of salvation.

A closer look at this urban culture will therefore be the aim of this chapter. Beginning with the lifestyle of the "natural areas" and of the social classes most characteristic of the cities of Asia, Latin America, and Africa, we shall treat of the plurality of distinct cultures within the same city, and then proceed to the overall urban culture, in which these subcultures converge and interact.

The culture proper to slum-dwellers and that proper to shantytown-dwellers are of course familiar to missionaries. More elusive is the culture of diverse social classes. We shall first examine these two aspects, and thereby gain the knowledge necessary to understand a phenomenon of the highest importance to urban mission: the religious dimensions of the city.

Types of Culture in the "Natural Areas"

Under the impulse of the waves of immigration, urban space changes its physiognomy, especially in what is called, in European languages, the "historical center" of the city and on the city's outskirts (see chap. 3). Slums build up in the historical center; shantytowns arise on the city's periphery. Slums and shantytowns constitute, in sociological terminology, authentic "natural areas," with the clearly distinct characteristics of the other "natural areas" of the city.

City Slums

There are slum areas in all the larger cities. They are "collections" of overcrowded, unsanitary, decrepit housing units in a sorry state of disrepair. Tenants in these buildings are generally craftspeople, small-business entrepreneurs, and manual laborers. How is it that workers in these occupational categories, who normally have the means to afford better housing, find themselves in these substandard conditions?

A specific economic process points to the answer. The historical center of the city, because it is the most accessible part of the whole city, becomes the favorite target of commercial and administrative enterprises on a grand scale. They purchase the land and oblige the residents, including small businesses, to move toward the periphery of the city. Many working persons follow the small businesses; they move away from the city center. The few who remain lose their jobs. Craftspeople and small-business people, for their part, lose their clientele and therewith their income. Constrained by their financial bind, they sublet their own residences to immigrants or persons with even lower incomes. It is only logical that the quality of housing conditions— mediocre to begin with—pays for all this. Owners refuse to do anything about maintenance or renovation. To them it makes better sense to let a building deteriorate, squeezing what rental income they can get from it in the meantime, in the expectation that it will collapse one day, and the lot will be bought by some big company for a higher price than the building would bring.

Tenants are the principal victims in this process. Oppressed by the dearth of space, healthy environment, and employment, they are subjected to extreme pressures, including that of temptation to violence. The area becomes "unsafe," which in turn further depreciates it as a residential zone. An even larger mass of impoverished persons is attracted to the area. But they see themselves deprived of the advantages of city life, relegated to a social prison, a ghetto.[1]

At this stage a strong sense of identity develops among them. The cultural process begins at this point. Feeling deprived and even threatened by the metropolis, a solidarity begins to form among them. They become "we" as opposed to "the others." The sense of unity keeps its strength because it is anchored in something very visible: the area where they live. Communication and interaction become intimate and direct. They all know each other. They form a cluster of subgroupings for mutual defense and support. This culture, evident in every slum subdivision, will express the goals, the norms, and the lifestyle of its adherents, and transmit them to new arrivals. This culture will produce the climate of security and familiarity that makes life possible, and even meaningful, in this situation. Security derives from a knowledge of the extent of the situation—a knowledge that does not reach beyond the slum into "the city." It in fact becomes increasingly more elusive and hostile. The culture of each cultural zone performs a function of mediation, enabling its residents to control the "anxiety" that the city causes.

The internal organization of a cultural area is informal but well articulated. And it becomes very strong: everyone's needs are known to everyone else, and self-discipline functions well because all are in agreement that a certain order must be maintained in the relationships among residents.

Certain internal "moral" norms are also developed in this process, and a specific moral order, involving everyone, takes shape. It offers no alternative: if someone disrespects that order, that person becomes a victim of the confrontation and conflict that it provokes. The only escape for persons who will not accept that order is therefore withdrawal: they must move out. Homogeneity is thus reinforced and a kind of loyalty that consists in "keeping quiet about internal doings" [*omertà,* the famous "law of silence" associated with the Mafia—ED.]. This is the negative side of the culture developed in the slums, but it also offers a wealth of positiveness. Where the metropolis cannot offer a moral order capable of controlling the problems and behavior of individuals, and leaves them to the mercy of eradication and anonymity, in a situation of conflict due to the total lack of norms of conduct, the particularized culture offers them a precise order of norms, fulfilling a primordial exigency of life shared with others.

Hence judging the behavior of slum-dwellers by the criteria of public morality is a mistake. "Public morality" is a morality that would theoretically apply to the whole city, but it cannot even be perceived by those who feel themselves excluded by the city. The contradiction between the "beautiful promise" of the city and the ugly reality of urban life leads to the choice of the values of one's own "natural area." Without that choice there would be an absolute vacuum of values, an absence of norms valid for living with others and for developing a coherent lifestyle.

There remains a considerable problem: How can emarginated individuals find persons they can trust in the city, in the slums? In other words, how can solidarity be recognized? There seems to be an objective criterion: association with a dwelling place. Women and small children spend most of their time in the house. Men are the only ones who "circulate." Identification of the individual—something that is impossible in the other "natural areas" of the city—becomes easy: he is "the one who lives in this house," or she is "the one who lives in that house."

This identification is essential for security purposes.When a stranger moves into a slum and he has a "house" to move into, to give him recognition, he is quickly identified and received as someone in solidarity with the social environment. But if he does not have or find a "house," he is not just anonymous, he is "an enemy," and he has no alternative but to withdraw. Security resides in the fact that the individual knows what others (peer acquaintances) will do; insecurity comes from not knowing what others (strangers) will do. And association with a residence, in addition, lends strength to the spirit of social collaboration. Residents are motivated to develop their common ambience.[2]

The lifestyle of the slums thus will be characterized by a clear and, within itself, consistent scale of social values, which makes up for the discrepancy on the psychological plane between the promise of urban well-being and the day-to-day reality. The solution consists in accepting one's situation of marginality vis-à-vis the metropolis, and doing in it what one must do.

These values of autonomy, however, are worked out in a collective way: for mutual security one cooperates with the others who live and have defined roles in the same neighborhood. The dwelling place and the family concretize these roles, identifying the members of the collectivity with particular dwelling places and distinguishing them from other city residents who "do not live here."

Shantytowners

Shantytown residents are differentiated from slum residents in that they do not have houses in the strict sense of the term. They "take over" a given terrain, in contrast to slum-dwellers who "defend" their terrain against the assaults of speculation. Shantytowners are in a worse situation inasmuch as they can be evicted at any moment by public officials.

The lifestyle that emerges from the shantytowns, however, is not much different from that of slum areas. The problem of security, for example, is repeated, but with an added element: shantytowners must defend themselves from evictions. The threat of police intervention becomes a driving force for consolidation: as soon as a tract of land is occupied, other persons are called in because the bigger the settlement, the smaller the risk of eviction. And together with the values of "dwelling place" and "collectivity," other values take hold, possibly in a more radical way than that observed in slum areas.

Awareness that they must do everything by themselves and "make do" for themselves often has the effect of freeing shantytowners from the grip of margination. As soon as they succeed in self-organization, they change their own life conditions. In Lima, Peru, for example, entire families that have lived in the city for ten years or so are motivated to occupy land not yet given a commercial value, and they have built brick-and-cement houses for themselves. The group was so strong that no authority dared to interfere.[3]

Let it be mentioned in passing that the phenomenon of shantytowns is mainly concentrated in cities in the tropical zones of the Third World. For shantytowners too the value of "family" is primary, more decisive than that of collective solidarity in molding interaction and transmitting the meaning of life.

For Latin America it seems that the hub of this value resides in the mother-children relationship, the role of father playing a secondary role because of its occasional uncertainty and its permanent instability. In this respect the culture of the shantytowns is different from that of the slums: it is the mother who must see to it that her children are given what they need.[4] For their part, the children are often the ones who "circulate" beyond the shantytown environs, to get what is needed from other zones of the city.

As in the case of city slums, it would be illogical to apply criteria extraneous to the situation in assessing the fragility of the family. What is valid for others is not always valid for shantytowners. There are other internal criteria that bring out the high level of their solidarity and interaction. Children must become independent at an early age in order to permit the extreme mobility of their mother, obliged to spend the greater part of the day away from the home. And the nuclear family is part of a close network of relatives and associates that makes possible a whole gamut of reciprocal help. One example among the many that could be cited is Kibuli "village."

Kibuli, "An Urban Village": Kibuli, a "natural area" of some five square miles next to an industrial zone on the periphery of Kampala, the capital of Uganda, was studied by R. M. Solzbacher in 1970[5]. Forty-nine percent of the residents interviewed were living in Kibuli because, before moving there, they knew one or more families already there. This served as a "cultural cushion" for those who, at least initially, felt the need for that kind of support. Others were in Kibuli because they found there a greater freedom, especially from territorial restrictions. Many of them referred to Kibuli as a village secluded from the city, where they could work and "be themselves" with the advantage of a close network of friends.

Although some eighty ethnic groups (from at least eleven different geographical districts) were represented there, the collectivity did not evidence social tensions or conflicts. The anonymity and criminality of Kampala were unknown there. There was even a basis of social organization: the majority, those who shared the same financial and social conditions, had formed a political unity, with a leader. Neighborhood loyalties were reinforced by those of the men who worked in Kampala and by those of family relationship: 54 percent of the families had relatives living in Kibuli. They had a joke to the effect that one of the advantages of urban migration was the opportunity to see relatives more often. Other loyalties formed around diverse religious affiliations, even though Kibuli was mostly Muslim. But formal organizations were lacking, with the exception of ethnic unions and some religious groups.

When they were asked about their own community, the Kibuli residents complained about the condition of their dwellings, sanitation systems, and the streets, comparing them with better conditions in other parts of Kampala. But they thought Kibuli superior to Kisenyi, where the crime rate was high. They considered themselves a social collectivity of poor but honest working persons, coming from diverse ethnic backgrounds but living in peace together. And they considered their residence in Kibuli something temporary. But in city life, the provisional has a way of becoming permanent.

Overcrowding and uncleanliness provoke diverse reactions. The most common reaction in Kibuli seemed to be apathy. A widespread passive attitude did not help the situation: no one took it into their head to collect refuse, and it was thought useless to try to keep a house clean. Many Kibuli residents in fact lamented that they were constrained to live in unhygienic conditions that they would not have tolerated in their home villages, but they thought themselves incapable of resolving such a problem, and shunted the responsibility to the Kampala administration. It thus became a symbol of the "place" where responsibility for their unfilled needs belonged. The suspicions and fears of other city residents arose from the same source.

The greatest anxiety came from the possibility of eviction, if Kibuli were ever demolished by the authorities. If it happened, the only thing they could do would be to return to the villages they had come from. Not having the money to rent an apartment, even an inexpensive one, they had no choice. A good number of them being too old to work, but meanwhile being helped by neighbors, they could face starvation. Panic often broke out because, their level of education being what it was, they depended on "gossip" to keep themselves informed of what was going on. Radio broadcasts were listened to in the framework of the same suspicions and fears. Every governmental statement on urban development became a threat. Strangers seen walking around were thought to be spies of the police or the city administration. The questions they asked were thought to be traps that would lead to their being sent back to their home villages.

But there was also a positive side: every time that the city did something for them—street lights or garbage collection or street repairs—a spark of hope was ignited. It was a sign that Kibuli would not be demolished. On the contrary, in their own words, "Kibuli is becoming a village of the city!"

All in all, Kibuli was a community performing an indispensable function in adapting immigrants to the urban way of life. But its physical conditions gave a dubious identity to the persons who lived there: the image that they had of themselves and the image that, in their opinion, the city had of them was anything but enviable.

Meanwhile, the demolition of Kibuli would not solve anything. On the contrary, it would destroy a reality more important than anything physical: the security afforded by an understood and controlled situation, the integration that promotes self-control in the behavior of residents, the network of

familial and neighborhood relationships that makes life together possible
—and meaningful.

From Illegitimacy to Recognition: At the United Nations conference on
"informal" settlements held in Bogotá in 1970 there was general agreement
that, contrary to what had been thought before, shantytowns were not only
not harmful to the interests upheld by law, but were possibly the correct
solution for urban development in the Third World—a solution tailored to
the exigencies of the poor.[6]

As a result, two years later the president of Colombia gave legal status to
all the illegal residential settlements in that country and launched a new plan
in which shantytowns would no longer be considered "outside the law" or
marginal. They were to become "new towns," "young neighborhoods." This
is the road that has since been taken by the urban planning in effect in the
Third World. It was confirmed by the United Nations conference on human
settlements held in Vancouver in 1976.

Besides the characteristic "natural areas" such as slums and shantytowns,
there are other types, each with its own cultural identity. Missionaries who
work there should take the pains to study them in depth in order to grasp the
lifestyle of each such settlement. Here it is possible only to treat of the "natural areas" that exhibit similar, if not identical, characteristics in a number of
cities in the Third World.

The Culture of Social Strata

Before proceeding to a treatment of the cultural traits of the Third World
city as such—that is, to a *general* discussion—it is necessary to review the
division into strata made on the basis of social criteria. What are the cultural
characteristics of the two strata that typify, with their extreme disparateness,
the cities of the Third World, namely, the masses and the elites?

The masses coincide with the poor, the immigrants, the great majority of
the residents of the "natural areas" considered above. Among the elites are
the wealthy, the powerful, and those who live in the more attractive sections
of the city. It is preferable to speak here of strata rather than classes because
the urban masses of the Third World, confined in their "natural areas,"
seldom come to a true class awareness. More often they constitute and remain
a lumpenproletariat. And the elites too, although they defend their interests
and privileges, do so each without a solidarity or esprit de corps.

The Culture of Poverty

In terms of its statistical consistency and its constant expansion, the stratum constituted by the immigrant and impoverished masses of the cities of
the Third World is truly impressive. In many cases it already exceeds one-
third of the urban population, and before the end of the coming decade it will

compose half in many instances, according to H. Dunkerley, of the International Bank for Reconstruction and Development.[7]

The living conditions of this stratum are in general very low: running water, for example, is provided for only a quarter of the total urban population. The remainder, which includes the poorer stratum, has no such luxury. Sewerage is even worse. Street conditions and public transportation are below an acceptable level.

The fact that these material factors are always taken by the poor in an immaterial context, thanks to the culture that gives meaning to their lives, says much to the missionary. How do the urban masses see their living conditions? The best way to find out may be to refer to the concept of "the culture of poverty" developed by Oscar Lewis at the conclusion of his research in Mexican and Puerto Rican cities.

Urban immigrants live a culture different from that which dominates these cities. In reacting to their condition of margination imposed by the urban system, they become convinced of the impossibility of success, at least as measured by the logic of the metropolis. Rather than fight against the causes of their status, they find themselves constrained to fight against despair. The result of this struggle is the culture of the stratum of the poor, a culture that is perpetuated and reinforced from generation to generation by reason of the early introduction of their children into adult life. Youngsters, following in the footsteps of their parents, cannot gain access to the opportunities offered by the city—schooling, employment, a position in the city administration—in such a way as to derive profit from the advantages that urban social intercourse could offer. According to Lewis, this lack of participation on the part of the poor, perpetuated by their weak organization among themselves and their strong fatalism, characterizes their culture by immobilizing it.[8]

It has also been suggested that the values, attitudes, and behavior of the poor are a reaction to their immediate privations. If these were eliminated, their culture would change. Even if this hypothesis were verified, Lewis's concept of a culture of poverty would still be useful as an explanation of the persistence of the class constituted by the urban poor.

What is of greater interest for this study, however, is the distinction between reaction "to the situation" and reaction "to the values" of the city. Whereas reaction to the situation changes when the situation changes—in other words, it is very elastic—reaction to values is less so. Values are not anchored to concrete situations; they are spread out everywhere. They are "in the air" that everyone breathes.[9]

In Latin America the problem of poverty has almost always been studied in terms of marginality. But what in fact happens? When the city adds to its small industrial base, it turns into a mirage for the rural masses. These industries, putting advanced technology to use, are capital-intensive, not labor-intensive. The immigrants who move into the shantytowns are ignored by the economic and political powers; they are held apart from the "center." In this sense they are emarginated. Two social systems emerge, contiguous but not interpenetrating: the urban system, in the strict sense, and "the system of the poor."

In addition, for the other citizens, the poor become "passengers without a ticket" in the sense that they make use of public services but do not contribute to their upkeep. In fact they act as a brake to the smooth functioning and development of the city.

On the other hand, according to E. Jelin, the percentage of the poor is so high that it no longer makes sense to apply the concept of marginality to them. The urban system should instead be reformed in such a way that they could be fitted into its ongoing functionality, for these human beings constitute positive resources and they could be productive. If only they were to be helped to produce more efficiently the things that they themselves need, everything would be better; but if they are obliged to produce the things that fill the needs only of a particular minority, rather than those of the majority of the population, ignoring the imperatives of social justice, the future will see a crisis.[10]

The Culture of the Elite

It has been observed that in Asia, Latin America, and Africa urbanization has often been accompanied, at least in its initial phases, by a reinforcement of the frontiers between social classes. The gulf between the original, "leadership" population (landowners, professionals, city officials, intellectuals) and the new population (immigrants, laborers) widens. Differences are more visible than they are in Western cities because there is not a consistent middle class. Cultural barriers are even more formidable: the new population is always more traditional.

The lifestyle of the well-off is characterized by a vivid concern for their own interests. Based on the city, they have often been educated in the West or along Western lines, and they know how to close ranks against the "threats" of competitors, taking political power into their own hands. They know, further, how to close ranks against all the others: rarely do they marry outside their own circles, and they keep to themselves as to schools, residential areas, and social outreach. To this aim they tend to display, rather than camouflage, their affluent lifestyle.

The ruling class in the Third World does not always have effective economic wealth as a base. Often it turns to its own advantage the fact of occupying government positions. And so it coincides with the high-placed functionaries, the salaried bureaucrats of high rank, who are in much the same position as foreign colonial personnel in the past.

In some African states, such as Nigeria and Ghana, a small-scale bourgeoisie has taken shape, composed of the owners of large commercial enterprises, plantations, banks, and industries. According to Frantz Fanon, this bourgeoisie is not, however, autonomous: it is too weak to resist the pressures of foreign business interests, and thus becomes directly or indirectly an agent of foreign capitalism.[11]

The Culture of the Metropolis

Specific cultures, associated with "natural areas" or with social strata are evidence of a process of segmentation. There are many such cultures, and they are often in conflict with one another. But the city does not collapse: over and above all the particular cultures is a general culture in which the others converge. This general culture does not have its roots in a territorial base or a particular social stratification, but in the very texture of the urban system. This system is formed by the networks of linkages existing among residents, that is, by the "interdependencies" of the city.

The most interesting research in this field has been done in African cities.[12] This is a matter of some significance because the changes undergone by immigrants there have brought to the surface the resistance of older, ethnic social networks, parallel to the innovative impulses that come from the opportunities offered by the city.

Elizabeth Bott was the first to draw attention to the cultural import of these networks.[13] In her opinion, their formation is due to three factors: the density of relationships, their duration, and the number of persons involved.

Social Networks

Bott distinguishes three types of relationship, which she calls, respectively, categorial, structural, and personal. From each of them derives a social network or meshing in which the individual finds a place.

The *categorial* relationship is superficial, although it may serve a restricted, instrumental purpose. It characterizes casual encounters, such as those that occur in "marketplace transactions," as mentioned in the preceding chapter. City residents tend to establish contact with immigrants in this mode, and they end by creating a series of stereotypes for themselves. Immigrants come to be divided into categories that generally correspond to their respective ethnic groups and places of origin. Immigrants tend to accept the role given to them in this exchange, remaining culturally oriented to the village where their most important relationships are rooted. In this case, social position does not enter into the judgment made about one's behavior. Ethnic and religious preconceptions influence that judgment.

In *structural* relationships, by contrast, the behavior of individuals is evaluated on the basis of their social position; behavior is judged to be appropriate or not in the light of the expectations that one's social position creates. This explains, for example, why the Ibo in Nigeria, when they encounter hostility from other city residents, tend to join special associations founded for their protection. Membership in these associations confers on them a new social status, which is far more than "protection." At the same time it imposes restrictions on them, modifying their external behavior. For instance, they do not ask questions of an employer: their work expectations, and hence their new role as citizens, are "beyond discussion" inasmuch as they are indissolubly connected with the condition of being citizens—something that they very much want.

Finally, when behavior is judged solely on the basis of the direct relationships that bind immigrants, there is the *personal* relationship. Immigrants to Kampala, Uganda, for example, encapsulate themselves in a tight network of friendships and blood relationships, which extend also to the rural areas of their provenance, as noted earlier in this chapter.

Every individual is "inserted" into diverse networks of relationships. Urban culture can be conceived as the framework in which these vital and close networks let themselves be organized. The definition of urban culture as "the social construction of reality" has something to it. In effect it gives immigrants a sense of the virtual infinity of relationships that city life can demand, and it collates them into a unified "spiritual" vision.

This is its appeal to the missionary: the feature of general urban culture that sets it apart from a particular culture or the culture of rural life is its capacity to admit various mini-frameworks within the general framework. This is a characteristic too of pluralism. It is crucial for missionaries to accept this new condition: from a single, uniform vision of evangelical life there must be movement today to a "catholic" vision, in which diversity is taken to be normal. What is essential is to create the conditions for a differentiated realization of the Christian life according to the reference groups and the networks of relationships to which the individual is committed.

In a village, culture is monolithic and uniform. Every type of relationship and behavior is judged by the same standards. In a city the prospects are diverse, according to the reference groups of those involved. Immigrants, newly arrived in the city, find themselves disoriented and they intensify relationships of a personal nature. When they feel surer of themselves, they go on to experiment with relationships of a categorial nature. If all goes well, they finally take up relationships of a structural nature.

Along the way, their mentality changes. The original framework, supplied by the culture of the village, fades into the background. They have acquired a more open mentality, the reaction—favorable or unfavorable—to the diverse cultural frameworks that the city reveals to them. Merely the realization that there are diverse ways of thinking and of reacting to everyday realities can itself be a cultural shock. Absolutes melt away. Their original culture does not of course disappear totally, but it remains as *one* reference among others, "competing" with the influence that new relationships offer.

With their change of mentality, in the urban context of interaction, there comes also for immigrants a change of "social personality," in the sense that they feel compelled to measure themselves against a given model or typology of "the average citizen." The general urban culture develops a view of what the citizen ought to be, and this view is communicated to all residents, of whatever group or social stratum, even if it is embodied in diverse ways.

It will be up to the missionary to point out the position that faith will occupy in this new framework of references.

Urban culture is a way of organizing the resident's relationships with the city and in the city, gathering them into a unique framework that gives them a certain organic orientation, direction, and meaning. Culture becomes the meaning of life. This need for "unity" and "meaning" is a kind of instinct that is inborn in our individuality. But this does not mean that each individual must seek it out for himself or herself. A large part of the work of "putting things into a framework" is transmitted by common experience (in this case, the common urban experience). What the individual must do is to interiorize this common experience and then adapt so as to put order into the thousands of particular experiences of every hour of the day.

Parallels with the Christian task of bringing the reality of life into the vision of faith are immediately evident to the missionary. The subject of faith brings us to a consideration of the so-called symbolic universes, which are a particular dimension of culture. For practical purposes, we have defined culture as lifestyle, treating it as the complex of the conduct, models, ideas, beliefs, customs, usages, and objects that typify the life of a community. But now we must add that all this is connected with a specific vision that permits the conceptualization and categorization of reality on the broadest scale. It is the symbolic universe composed of constellations of meanings: a framework in which one's experiences are fitted in order to give them their ultimate meaning.

Symbolic Universes

Social values (see chap. 2) are not totally dissociated from one another: they form "constellations" among themselves. Certain values draw others into their sphere of influence, somewhat in the manner of stars that shine more brilliantly and act as "suns" around which other heavenly bodies revolve. And these constellations of social values are not independent from one another: they are ordered and harmonized in a coherent universe—the *symbolic universe* in the light of which individuals view their own experiences.

Instead of "constellations" one could speak of "scales of values," and instead of "symbolic universe" one could use the expression "global hierarchy of symbols." The important point is that every culture offers *its own* scale of values, *its own* global hierarchy of symbols.

In a rural setting the symbolic universe (or global hierarchy of values) is monolithic and stable, and is transmitted from generation to generation with little or no change. Not so in an urban setting. The first cultural impact of the city on the immigrant is the discovery that the hierarchy of values is not the same for everyone: each social group has its own version. There is only a certain base model of these group variations that remains fixed: the so-called urban culture—a nucleus of values and social patterns that are so generalized as to be reference points for all residents.

By way of illustration, take social communications. The radio makes known to a rural population that there are diverse scales of values. There are, for instance, the programs broadcast by the government and those broadcast by a revolutionary movement. But in the rural village the ideas communicated by these diverse sources are foreign to and abstract from everyday life. As soon as the villager moves to a city, however, these ideas become concrete and immediate because the villager-immigrant discovers that some persons listen *only* to the revolutionary station. The anchoring of the reference framework of the other radio station—the only one that was "legal" in the rural village—begins to slacken, to the point where the immigrant realizes that, at bottom, both of them are partially right. There are therefore two ways of viewing things, and both of them have their own legitimacy. Apart from their diversity, there is a single universe of symbols that the two stations accept.

Here we want to dwell on one aspect of the symbolic universe shared by the inhabitants of a metropolis: the complex of symbols that help to give meaning to that which transcends empirical experience, or better, to that which appears to be transcendent within empirical experience: in other words, religious experience, a fundamental fact of human culture. Religion has been defined by sociologists as the human response to the ultimate questions of life: death, evil, suffering, the "why" of things, the beginning and the end—a response that builds a bridge between empirical and supra-empirical realities.

If symbolic universes are models of socially objectivized meanings that are referred from one or another part of the world of day-to-day reality to a world intuited as transcending this day-to-day life, as Thomas Luckmann suggests,[14] then religion is the symbolic universe that includes the others, giving them a definitive and absolute meaning.

The term "objectivized" is used here in reference to the process whereby the results of subjective experiences become a common heritage. From this common patrimony individuals "subjectivize," that is, assume and interiorize diverse elements: they make their own what serves them to answer the essential questions mentioned above.

Symbolic universes have also been called the "umbrellas" of particular meanings, constructed and objectivized by diverse social groups to collate and interpret their own individual and collective, humdrum and historic experiences. They are "umbrellas" in the sense that the individual, together with others, finds shelter under them from the "shower" of the particular and unrelated stimuli and facts of everyday life. They are also a "roof" under which the mass of everyday stimuli and facts can be gathered and dealt with, emotionally and conceptually.

Cultural Processes and Religion

Peter Berger has proposed a schema that could be useful to missionaries for identifying and making use of the cultural factors of the city, searching among them for "bridges" for the gospel.[15] Human individuals create society, says Berger, by exteriorizing the social order imaged by them; society generates cultures by objectivizing this image; individuals in consequence accept society and culture by arriving at an identification between *nomos* (image, concept, model) and *cosmos* (universe, understood not only as the sum of realities external to the human individual, but as the harmonization of meanings, as a symbolic universe).

Religion is indeed the attempt to form a cosmos. Its organized expression is the religious institution, which generally includes such elements as worship, creeds, religious conduct, and—for Christians—a sense of church. Acceptance of the religious institution by the individual comes from what is called "religiosity." The distinction between religious institution and religiosity is paramount for understanding what happens in the urban context, and especially for verifying the claim that in the West urbanization, by its very nature, brings about the decline of religion.

It is undeniable that religious doctrine, practice, and organization lose ground in an urban climate characterized by a diversity of religious groups. It is a climate that inclines persons to notice the differences among the various expressions of religion; the final result is to give the religious option the appearance of being something personal and private. It is also a climate that favors (recall the definition of the city as "the social space constructed by humankind") the perception of a world corresponding to human manipulation and, as such, lacking a sacral character.

The process of secularization takes place in the city; in fact urbanization and secularization go hand in hand as parallel processes, even with a certain degree of interdependence. But this does not mean that urban culture rules out the existence of a nonempirical zone; it simply means that religion is no longer viewed as the solution to human problems, but as something that is beneath and above the problems that face humanity. In other words, the function of religion is seen in its capacity to get persons involved with their immediate problems, but preventing them from exhausting their resources in that effort and awakening them to an awareness that there is something genuinely human that goes beyond them.

Secularization characterizes the passage from a rural-sacral society to an urban-secular society. The latter is based on the presupposition that it is possible to regulate the world and the history of humankind by human intelligence. It therefore favors individuals who are adept at taking initiatives and using reason. External reality does not have to be endured passively; it can be changed.

It is a mistake to think that secularization eliminates religion. It can lead to the emergence of a more personal form of religion, more liberated from the external supports of a given social system. To think that religion/tradition and secularization/modernization are absolutely coterminous pairings is a mistake. To understand better the process of secularization it is not necessary to view religion exclusively in its institutional form and, in the case of Christianity, as the institutional church. What is necessary is to view it, rather, as religiosity or the source of values that integrate and legitimate the various components of daily life.

In this sense secularization impinges on certain religious values only when it questions their de facto involvement in a given issue and suspects that the survival of such values is the more or less dysfunctional residuum of an outdated social order. It asks, for example, why the church maintains an "order" and practices that have such a deeply rural bent to them; why it attracts especially the elderly; why it gravitates toward traditionalist groupings. In other words, secularization searches for the reasons why the church-institution no longer satisfies all religious needs, which is a far cry from denying that such needs exist.

Secularization seems therefore to be part of a particular historical process that makes a spectacular invasion of the city but does not take the form of an assault on the primary function of religion. This distinction is very helpful if one keeps in mind that, in the final analysis, secularization "purifies" certain elements given to religion by the religious institution. Religion perdures, it could be said, by renewing its contents.

The concept of religion, then, should not be reduced to that of church, especially if it is agreed that religion should exercise a role of moral authority in society. It would thus discharge its function of furnishing a cosmos—symbolic universe—to city-dwellers.

Some sociologists have arrived at conclusions in this regard that may seem surprising: the existence of a specialized institution (church) would no longer be necessary to assure the existence of religion itself. The reason for this goes back to research into the fact that religion, as soon as it takes shape as a specialized institution, separates itself from society at large. Distances are created, as happened for the Christian faith after Constantine. Various explanations have been proposed: the doctrinal ensemble elaborated by the church is more complex than is really necessary; certain formalized and imposed moral norms are too remote from daily life; the label "religion" comes to be attached to certain specific deeds or types of activity, as when it is said that "religion is for your free time."

The tendency of the religious institution to "dig a grave for itself" is particularly accented in the city, where it becomes a segment in the very dense and complicated network of urban compartmentalization. In other words, as soon as the religious institution makes itself something special and takes a distance from society at large, it becomes an urban compartment accessible only to initiates. How are the others to find fulfillment of their religious needs—needs that in fact, as we have seen, do remain?

Individuals may try to make a collection of disparate religious elements, "pieces" dissociated from an institutional order and institutional membership, to construct their own religious framework or universe. It will be a precarious and fragile framework of reference, but it will at least serve to give a meaning to daily life in the confusion and flood of the stimuli and values of urban existence. The phenomenon of "invisible religion" or "religion without a church" has been the object of study and discussion—a consequence of the secularization that invades society and every member of it. This kind of religion will have a function of the highest importance in assuring social cohesion among residents of the metropolis even if, paradoxically, it will not support—as did the religious institution—the existing social order.

In this context the problem of religion could even be formulated in terms of the relations between the individual and social order. This brings us back to the very first cities in history when religion played a role essential to society, furnishing it with values that made life possible for its members. Human beings cannot live on bread alone. It is not enough to provide for their biological needs. Motivation and "spirit" are also necessary. So long as society searches for symbols and is sustained by them, religion is an irreplaceable element in it. Society and religion search for and support each other. Religion does not concern itself exclusively with the invisible.[16]

It would be well to add here that the cities of the Third World—unlike those in the West—have not been administered such a massive dose of secularization. Those in Latin America are permeated by a popular religiosity with Christian tinting. The cities of Africa reflect the influence of traditional religions—Islamic and Christian—although the distinction between religion and religious institution has begun to make its presence felt. The cities of Asia have their own religious coloring (excluding perhaps Japan and Hong Kong); even Saigon and Hanoi allow Christian religious institutions to maintain a visible presence.

The City as a Sign of the Times

This reflection on urban cultural processes leaves three impressions that can also be viewed as signs for urban mission.

The first is a sense of astonishment at the human spirit that, notwithstanding the difficulties of certain urban situations, manages not only to survive but to give meaning to its own life. Christian mission, addressing the whole person, should not be overly impressed by slogans such as "human beings cannot think about God if they do not have enough to eat."

The second impression regards the unifying impulse that seems so fundamental in combating even the strongest divisive processes proper to the city. Residents find a certain unity of life within the "natural areas" of the city and perhaps also within the framework of their own social stratum. Not only that: besides the unity of life at a lesser level, there is also the unity of the general urban culture, founded on values that stand on their own against adverse experiences. Urban mission, called to unite the dispersed children of God, is not discouraged by the multiple barriers of urban pluralism. Inasmuch as it is itself a sign of unity, it should be the first to perceive and favor the unifying impulse present in cultural processes, including urban cultural processes. They are always expressions of the human spirit.

The third impression touches more directly on missionary methodology. The point has been made with emphasis, and with reason, that transmission of the gospel demands "translation," not only in local tongues but in the whole cultural universe of the evangelized group. There must be a "passage-way" to them. It is therefore advisable that in transcultural mission (as we have defined mission in the strict sense) cultural leaps be kept to a minimum. It would be better, for example, for a group to be evangelized by missionaries from a culturally close, rather than culturally distant, group. Generally speaking, a culture resists penetration by another culture.

It is true that this kind of resistance is appreciably reduced in the city. Immigrant city dwellers are faced with a plurality of cultures and are led to relativize the culture of their origin. They therefore become more open to other proposals, not excluding those of Christian mission. But it must immediately be pointed out that if proposals coming from beyond one's own cultural context are seen as compensating for the dissolution of a reference framework or as making up for uprootedness by membership in a strongly charactered and structured religious group, it does not instill confidence in their profundity and authenticity. They are fragile and fleeting "enticements" bound up with a psycho-social situation, not with the intrinsic content of Christian proposals. Christian proposals—that is, the message of the faith—must integrate the values of the culture of origin with those of the urban culture, not substitute for them.

Impressions gained from urban culture thus become directions. But here we can go beyond the reading of the sign of the Third World city and extract the values that animate the groups that are more representative or more characteristic of them. They are the groups that form spontaneously in the slums and shantytowns. These are the groups that succeed in shaping the great impulses of the city into models and roles characteristic of the intensity of interpersonal relationships and the weight of exchanges and reciprocal services. We can even outline a nucleus of these values, which can find expression in endless modalities: survival, security, the warmth that comes from membership and friendship, cooperation, community, family, loyalty, employment, ownership, creativity, flexibility, order. It is not simply a reproduction or continuation of their previous rural culture, but a truly new framework that integrates elements of their original cultural world and new elements proper to the city. Some of these values we have already encountered in our treatment of other processes (demographic, economic, political), and this was inevitable, granted that these processes are sustained by the cultural process.

It seems too that we can detect a basic gravitation toward three of these fundamental values: cooperation, community, and the intense articulation of exchanges. Cooperation, community, exchange: these are values that bring us very close to the "communion" that is an essential element of the concept of the People of God, the church—a concept whose rightful place is in the very core of the divine plan for the salvation of the world.

We shall return to this point after an analysis of the formal response to the challenge of the city, which will complement the informal reponse sketched in the present chapter.

6

URBAN PLANNING

If urban cultural processes are the spontaneous response of the human spirit to conditions met with in the metropolis, planning is an attempt at a reasoned and deliberated response. In this sense it is also an expression of an important component of urban culture: secularization.

This chapter seeks to take the bearings of the counterprocesses worked out by urban planning—in the spirit of secularization, to be sure—to regain control over demographic, geographic, economic, political, and cultural processes, with the intention, naturally, of canceling their negative effects.

In the past, missionaries often found themselves in a pioneer situation, and sometimes still do today. In some rural areas of the world, missionaries have to begin from scratch and do everything themselves. There simply is no one else who will take any interest in certain human groups, except perhaps to exploit them. The situation in a city is very different. There it is not necessary to presume that one is alone, or to succumb to the temptation of elaborating "one's own" solution to the problems. True, missionaries in an urban setting do sometimes have the impression that they must start from zero, but this comes from not knowing what others have done in a similar situation, or from a lack of information and awareness of the science of urban planning, which searches for a general and organic solution to problems. The effort to learn about and welcome the findings of urban planning will help all people interested in missions to arrive at a consciousness of solidarity, showing what others are doing and what can be done by those wanting to enter into the positive currents at work in the reconstruction and restoration of the city. In addition, city planning cannot but contain some indications or signs of God's active presence in the city.

The Concept of Urban Planning

In the discussion of political processes, we noted that the harmonious growth of the city is blocked by the knot that represents control over its surface terrain. Urban planning seeks to untie this knot. It does so because of the well-known fact of common experience that individuals, if allowed to

95

pursue their own interests, their own inclinations and preferences, will never act in such a way as to achieve the maximum common good of the city. No one of them, singly, is capable of making the decisions that, all in all, would attain the highest possible degree of collective well-being.

This is obvious. But a consequence derives from it that is accepted favorably by practically no one: the necessity of restricting the activity of the individual. This is the central concept in the urban planning process.

The problem confronted by urban planners is now more specific: To what extent and by what means can the liberty of the individual be restricted, in the name of the collectivity?

An initial response to this question is this: it is necessary to control, by appropriate legislation (and its timely implementation), the use that private interests can make of urban land. The liberty of the individual can and must be limited. This would allow for the "minimum" necessary to make urban planning possible.

But, at least for the cities of the Third World, it seems that this "minimum" will not suffice. Two schools of thought have emerged among those involved in urban planning. One group—represented by architects, engineers, and other "technicians" of city planning—aims at a rational use of land and the utilization of various techniques for the optimal deployment of physical space. The other group—represented by social researchers, who work with the concepts of "social space" and "social distance"—aims at the improvement of urban interaction. The first group emphasizes the availability of urban land; the second group emphasizes the availability of a long series of public services and utilities.

Aware of how the physical generates in the social, and vice versa (see chaps. 3 and 4), it seems evident that individual human freedom will be restricted in both views. More precisely: freedom is social; it must be exercised within the community and not in conflict with the essential needs of the city.

The two emphases among those involved in urban planning—the one stressing physical space, and the other stressing social space—are therefore complementary and they call for interdisciplinary support among all participants. Here we touch on another focal point of city planning. It does not spring only from disciplines such as geography, economics, demography, sociology, and psychology, but also from those more oriented to human action, such as political science, urban studies, public administration, and the arts of government, public education, and the use of the means of communication. Experts in all these arts and sciences that deal with "the public" must collaborate in a joint process. The action that city planning is aimed at is the best catalyst for arriving at a synthesis among the diverse competencies in their approach to concrete problems and projects. It is not a matter of obtaining isolated though erudite solutions from diverse disciplines, but of obtaining, through a convergent use of their various concepts and techniques, a better understanding of the problems. An operative decision can be taken only on an ample, articulated base.[1]

These decisions will regard such themes as the more equitable distribution of well-being among the various urban groups, the tapping of public and private resources, the use of public power, and especially the designation of the points of intervention most likely to lead to correction of the harmful results of the urban processes in effect.

In doing this, city planners find themselves faced with a choice: either they limit themselves to an objective analysis, accepting the fact that political figures will be the ones to make the final decisions, or they involve themselves in influencing those decisions. As it is, many of them take the second option. A purely theoretical scheme for the city seems to them useless. What value would it have other than academic?

Before taking action, another question must be answered: Whence derives the mandate of city reformers? The question cannot be answered in general terms by saying that it comes from the groupings that compose the city population, for we know that their interests are often in conflict. The answer given more commonly today—with some caution but also with ever increasing insistence—is that the city planner-reformer acts in the name and as an expression of a consensus that emerges from a participatory process. Caution is urged by the danger of setting up a dictatorship of expertise in place of a dictatorship of private interests. The process of participation must be genuine. If the various urban groupings are invited and encouraged to take part in the planning from start to finish, there will be grounds for expectations of convergences among diverse interests, and these convergences can serve as the mandate to city planners.

The Contents of Urban Planning

At the International Level

Planning at the international level, to stabilize order in Third World cities, will pertain to national governments in concurrence among themselves. One problem here is that each of them is very jealous of its own prerogatives. But governments could compare their experiences of success and failure in order to help in developing new, scientific approaches and formulating international norms, thereby assisting one another in the elaboration of planning programs for their own cities.

In this direction, the United Nations through its Human Settlements Centre and Foundation (also called HABITAT), has already done much. Its purpose is to promote an international, interdisciplinary, humanistic approach to the great problems of cities and smaller human settlements. The central HABITAT team, counting twenty-five members from eighteen nations, is composed of urbanists, engineers, journalists, architects, research specialists, a lawyer, a documentalist. Its very composition reflects the spread of the situations, competencies, and problems within its purview.

It is a matter of interest that the HABITAT team asks for help, at the level of the communication of experiences and ideas, from missionaries and church groups. This was done especially in preparation for the United Nations conference on human settlements held in Vancouver in 1976. This conference succeeded in focusing world public attention in general, and that of political authorities in particular, on the problems of the cities. The exchange of ideas, plans, and methods already tested in the various sectors of the urban problem—housing, transportation, refuse disposal, environmental pollution, administrative models—set in motion a deeper and broader analysis of the problems.

But what is especially sought, and what HABITAT continues to seek, is a transition from the sphere of work reserved to technical experts, government officials, and scholars to the open, public sphere. Efforts are being made to interest the general public in what HABITAT is doing, and thus to educate the public to a more perceptive appreciation of its part in the transformation of the city. *Participation* is what it wants to promote.

Only on the basis of a great awareness and broad-based participation will the process of urban planning find a place in the political processes treated in chapter 4: only when urban administrators sense that the base of their legitimation is tottering can a diverse use of power for a better-ordered, more human city begin.

At the international level, therefore, the specific contribution that can be made to urban planning will consist in sustaining the values that are at its base. For government officials and technical experts to work on the kind of planning that is needed, they must be convinced of the seriousness, urgency, and complexity of the urban challenge. They must above all be convinced that the momentous internal processes of the city cannot be "played" with, by favoring the interests of a minority (well-off) to the detriment of the masses (not well-off). This merely adds to the accumulation of explosive tinder already present. Only an educative process of international impact will lead the privileged to abandon their defensive isolation. This is precisely the kind of activity that international organizations such as HABITAT promote.

At the National Level

Although it is indispensable, education to a deeper awareness of urban problems is not enough by itself. Taking action to correct the irrationalities of certain processes is also needed. And here international structures cannot accomplish much. The power of taking action is concentrated in the hands of the government of each nation. Even the United Nations, founded on the principle of the absolute autonomy of each member state, cannot undertake urban planning in the full sense of the term: it cannot oblige any nation to renounce its autonomy, not even in the name of the international common good.

Efforts being made at present are principally in the line of decentralization. The most significant political results are concentrated in this zone of urban planning. The goal of decentralization is that of defusing the demographic explosion that was swelling the cities and thus crippling their ability to provide adequate employment, housing, and public services. Attempts are being made to stop or at least control the process of urban immigration. It is being done in conjunction with the economic strengthening of other geographic points of national territory.

Urban planning thus takes on the form of a geographic process. Development plans for Third World nations head in this direction when they launch and implement highway projects, the development of natural and tourist resources, new strategically located housing centers, and the like.[2] But once again it is a process that goes up in political smoke because it entails the reinforcement of local authorities. Nevertheless this type of objective is laudable and was in fact singled out for praise in the preliminary working document of the United Nations conference on the human environment (Stockholm 1973). Barbara Ward and René Dubos wrote:

> One of the most important proposals is that of creating opposite poles of regional development to ease the tension on urban centers and divert part of the migratory flood that has been moving inexorably toward them. Of course the projection of new centers of regional development must take into account—as was done in the planning for Malaysia—existing resources, communication networks, other urban centers, and so forth. But localized plans, which have shown greater variety and have been favored by a higher degree of implementation, can reinforce the potential offered by national economies at the beginning of the 1970s for a more efficient decentralization of industrial development, and consequently for that of urban development as well.[3]

An example can illustrate what is taking place in this sphere. Many Asian governments, following an integrated strategy, are trying to build up their less developed regions because, as has been known for years, it is migration away from them that causes problems for the cities. A planning center was opened in northeast Thailand with the task of assisting and giving advice to the fifteen provinces in its jurisdiction in formulating their own development plans. It contributed also to the formation and utilization of channels of communication among those in charge.[4]

A diverse strategy has been embodied in the Philippines where urban planning begins in rural areas.[5] According to information supplied by the United Nations, the Philippine plan for stemming the flood from rural areas—threatening to submerge the cities—is based on the idea of encouraging the rural population to stay where it is. To this end, production of rice and other basic foods would have to be augmented, and the overall level of life would have to be raised: electricity, entertainment, and other "facilities" of city life need to be provided.

Migration to Manila (for the advantages that country-dwellers dream they will find there) would also be discouraged by an intelligent program of education via the mass media. Other possibilities, such as the relocation of shantytowners to smaller cities or even their home villages, are too fraught with problems.

But what still remains at the planning stage, or is being implemented in a very patchy way in the Philippines and other Asian countries, seems already to be reality in mainland China. In a lecture to a conference on the urban explosion, held in Oxford in 1974, N. Maxwell, of the Institute of Commonwealth Studies, claimed that, at least from this point of view, China has solved this problem: Shanghai's population is no longer on the increase; on the contrary, it is "losing" 100,000 residents yearly. The slums, the unemployment, filthiness, vice, crime, inhuman working conditions of twenty-five years ago have all given place to public housing, full employment, cleanliness, order, cooperation and participation by all in neighborhood committees. Urban planning, long since in an advanced state of implementation, proceeded on four frontiers.

The first stage called for help and encouragement to be given to rural inhabitants, Maxwell said. Land formerly held by great landowners was divided up for them, and they were shown what could be done with better organization. The poorer were encouraged to join forces together, in small "squadrons" (six to eight families) of mutual assistance, and they began to familiarize themselves with cooperative methods. Not all these "squadrons" succeeded in getting a better hold on life, but the success they experienced was enough to give birth to hope. When initial experiments succeeded, the next step was "elementary cooperatives" (eighteen to twenty families): land was worked in common, under unified direction. These cooperatives were the equivalent of village units.

At a later phase, toward 1955, the land was put to the use of all, and the entire harvest was distributed according to the work done by each person— no longer according to capital investment, as in the past. Advanced cooperatives took shape. Around 1958 these cooperatives began to be federated into much larger organizations called "collectives" ("peoples' communes") and were adopted by the state as basic administrative units. The names were changed: the simple village cooperative became a "production squadron"; the advanced cooperative became a "production brigade"; the federations of cooperatives became "peoples' communes." The communes interconnect and harmonize the various productive forces. At the brigade level a clinic or mechanical workshop would be constructed; the same brigade would manage its own school and the processing of agricultural products. At specified times work would be organized for irrigation projects or road building.

At the commune level, Maxwell continued, instead of a clinic there would be a hospital; instead of a workshop, a factory; instead of a primary school, a secondary school. Within the framework of its own financial autonomy, the commune would be responsible for its own public health services, its own educational programs, even its own self-defense. When agricultural areas were organizationally ready for it, mechanization of agriculture followed, and then the second front was opened: the cities and controlled urbanization.

In Chinese urban planning, as described by Maxwell, there was no provision for new cities. Even when it was decided to tap the Tuching oil deposits, officials opted for a series of medium-sized towns, at fixed distances from each other and each of them self-sufficient as to food supply, that is, provided for from the countryside surrounding each town.

There remained the problem of the big cities already in existence. After the chaos of the civil war, disorder reigned supreme. Rehabilitation proceeded at a number of levels, from the physical removal of thousands of tons of rubble out of Peking and Shanghai, to the health and social education of the masses.

Signs of success could be seen by 1960, even though levels of urban development remained below those in the West. True decentralization could then begin. Major industries located on the coastline were moved to the interior, beyond the rural areas that had fed urban immigration in the past: concentrations on the coast were dissolved and the stage was set for reversing the direction of the flow of future migration.

The guiding principle was centralized planning, localized control. The industrial production unit was not simply the factory; it was the factory *and* a center of medical, educational, housing, and other services for workers' families. The principles of self-sufficiency and self-responsibility were called into play. Redimensioning of existent cities was also expedited by other factors—for example, the sending of young college graduates to rural areas where they served as "barefoot doctors."

At the basis of all this, Maxwell concluded, there is a political will and a political projection: the Chinese phenomenon is a classic example of the predominance of the political process over economic and social processes.[6]

The Chinese experience allows us to draw some conclusions of general interest for urban planning at the national level:

1. The building up of rural areas, creating new jobs and new public services, means the restoration of the city to its original function: a "mechanism for life together."

2. A logical geographic distribution of poles of development brings with it the creation of new human settlements, which—precisely because they are new—can be planned from beginning to end.

3. It is still possible to reverse the illogic of having ends serve means by reversing the policy of siting a labor force where the interests of an industry dictate, in favor of siting a labor force where the interests of community development dictate.

4. Conservation of resources is not only possible but can be linked with the social goal of providing employment for all.

The Chinese experience, fruits of a convergence of original historical factors—as urbanization in the West has been—and the Maoist revolution, cannot in all likelihood be repeated. But there is no denying that it represented a noteworthy effort in responding to the urban challenge.

Third World countries have something to learn here, especially as regards how China seems to have resolved the problem of urban unemployment. Substantive employment programming at the national level—even though it is not the solution to all problems—can make a considerable contribution to ameliorating the condition of the poorest categories of workers, better distribution of national income, and especially favoring the real participation of all in the governance of society. The nonworker has no weight in society. The worker begins to have some weight, and consequently begins to have some minimal influence on social services, public utilities, and consumer goods.

In Latin America, for instance, the failure of economic development has often been the result of the centralization or—but it comes down to the same thing—the maldistribution of economic processes, of power, of technological and social modernization among the various parts of the nation. Everything is concentrated in the capital. Both the public sector and private enterprise prefer to invest in the great metropolises. Industries are sited near exchange centers—that is, where the have-not groups are already concentrated—as also the universities, the major hospitals, the nerve centers of the mass media, and so forth. As a consequence, more employment opportunities emerge here, which become a further stimulant to immigration from rural areas and all other parts of the nation.

A seemingly irreversible vicious circle is in motion. Evidence on all sides points to the need to stop that motion. The difference here between China and Latin America is that in China theory was quickly implemented by political involvement, but in Latin America everything seems to stop at the level of education to values. True political initiative is rarely even mentioned.

At the Local Level

Urban planning at the national level exerts its influence through geographic and demographic processes, but at the local level, that is, within the cities themselves, it operates through economic and political processes. The task of urban planners is to distribute the scarce resources among the various segments of the population, assigning benefits and costs equitably.

But this "assigning" inevitably involves conflict with specific interests and privileges. The question of "power" arises. For whom is the planning being done? In whose name? What right does it have to impose specific objectives, control mechanisms, and sanctions?

The theme of power is generally overlooked by the social sciences, with the exception of sociology and management science. But it is a theme that cannot be sidestepped if realistic planning is to be undertaken: incompatible objectives generate clashes. In due course a choice must be made. It is naive to think that effective planning could be purely administrative. Even if it were to begin only with the adoption of systematic methods and more productive techniques, sooner or later there would be conflict with specific interests, and therefore with power groups. Urban planning is unavoidably in the political sphere, and it involves political decisions. These decisions, for their part, will be based on the priority given to one or another set of values.

The question of the values that motivate urban planning is a fundamental question and must be treated explicitly. It is widely accepted today that urban planning must be done with an eye on its "consumers" who will incorporate their needs in it by their participation in the planning. Planners, therefore, will have to let themselves be guided (and they are doing so) by the wishes of a people "on the way to being planned."[7]

Unfortunately, awareness of this necessity is being translated into reality at a very slow rate, at least as regards the cities of the Third World. For example, many Asian cities* have a regulatory plan, but often it has to do only with scenic projects to beautify the capital, regulating its physical appearance. This is a positive and even necessary concern, but it certainly is not the highest need or the deepest aspiration of the people. The people, the great urban masses, are not at the center of the interests of such plans. The most ambitious of such plans, that of New Delhi, which has been worked on for more than thirty years, does not do justice to the surging impulses of the social and economic processes springing from the rapid and unforeseen expansion of the city.[8]

Then too, city plans are generally of an indicative rather than an imperative nature. Legislation that would make them obligatory has not been enacted. Even when a city government enters into urban planning with good intentions, its implementation becomes problematic because of the great number of incompetent local agencies and authorities interfering with one another and often contradicting one another. In the city of Calcutta in 1959 there were no less than seventy official agencies charged with the regulatory plan and its various segments. One can easily imagine the bureaucratic conflict and confusion!

Another obstacle is that of the weakness of local governments. Often they do not have even a minimal strategy for the assignment of space and even less legislative clout to make a strategy respected.

If regulatory plans have remained on paper in Third World cities, it is because planners have not taken account of the political processes that still dominate their economic order. Or when they have done so, they have adopted the model of Western cities, thus allowing urbanization to take its own course instead of controlling it and directing it to the needs of the people.

The question remains: Do planners succeed in identifying the real objectives of their work and mobilizing the available resources to achieve them? In fact, the very essence of urban planning can be expressed in the formulation of objectives, the choice of priorities among them, and the successive mobilization of human, institutional, and material resources to achieve them.

*Teheran, Karachi, Delhi, Bombay, Calcutta, Colombo, Rangoon, Bangkok, Singapore, Jakarta, Saigon, Manila, Taipei, Seoul, Tokyo, Osaka, Nagoya.

For the cities of the Third World there should be no problem about formulating objectives: there are many obvious lacunae to fill. The needs of the majority are cries that reach the ears of even those who are most unwilling to hear them. And still practically nothing has been done: only in recent years has there been movements toward a correct formulation of urban objectives.

The myth of Western development and its urban models has blinkered Third World urban planners. Many of them have studied in the West and they still think that what they should be aiming for are the levels and standards of employment, housing, and public services in effect in the West. But these levels and standards are beyond the resources of Third World cities and do not even correspond to the expectations and lifestyle of their own people.

There are some, however, who are beginning to perceive the "secret" message of the millions of urban immigrants, and they are making others think about development of Third World cities in terms of models proper to them, related to cultural, economic, and political patterns of their own social reality.

As regards housing, C. Correa, an urban planner in Bombay, has said that to satisfy the enormous demand for housing in India, it would be necessary to begin with 12 million housing units, at a cost of $6,000 billion—without thinking about streets, sewage, neighborhood stores, schools and other necessities. Rents would be double what would-be renters could pay. Correa suggests another approach: the abandonment of the Western housing standards implicit in his calculations, with concentration instead on the use of clay as a building material: houses made of clay bricks, with a wooden roof. The people would be happy to live in such houses. They would cost from one-third to one-thirtieth less. True, they would last only fifteen years or so, but even that could have some advantages.[9]

As soon as objectives are defined in local, non-Western terms, the discrepancy between goals and resources is reduced as if by magic. To reformulate goals in a perspective adjusted to the real expectations of those concerned means to makes programming more realistic.

It seems that this approach is gaining ground in the Third World, especially in the critical matter of the "natural areas" of shantytowners and slum-dwellers. We shall look quickly at how this approach has been, or could be, worked out in terms of the four major aspects of urbanization detailed in chapter 1.

Employment: To multiply jobs greater weight has to be given to the informal tertiary sector, to the home-construction industry, and to labor-intensive industries of low technological content.

Industrialization geared to automobile production could be deemphasized. The home-construction industry should be intensified, progressing from private to public housing as the return on investment increases, in an equitable proportion between private housing (for the better-off), municipal housing (for qualified workers), and "do-it-yourself" housing for the poor. This would be an economically valid and socially appropriate decision. It was put into effect in Singapore, with the interesting consequence that it was possible to plan not only housing but the whole ensemble of an urban community, with its public services, factories, commercial buildings, schools, and clinics, assuring relatively easy accessibility and respect for the environment.

It might seem uneconomical to invest in the sector of private housing. But it is not. Those who build or improve their own homes make a contribution to the whole city, and do so at minimal cost by not importing materials from abroad and by using the services of acquaintances and local workers. Often some of them go on to start their own small home-construction business. The investment is returned—very soon—when a room is rented to a friend to set up a tailoring or plumbing business. And all this takes place without having to worry about the standards of efficiency obtaining in Western countries.

Housing: To see more houses built, public officials must provide "communal facilities" that families cannot provide for themselves, and then let them do what they have shown they know how to do, that is, build their own homes. From public sources should come general plans, streets, water, a sewer system, schools, clinics, provision for neighborhood stores, public transportation, and especially legal and secure ownership of a home once it is constructed. Of course not everything can revolve around housing. Generally speaking, all projects have to be aligned with the productive economic processes in the true sense: agriculture, mining, industry, handcrafts. But facilitating ownership of private homes, which helps to break the stranglehold of speculation on land and serialized construction, is advantageous for all the economic and social processes. A homeowner is more respected by those in charge of public services and their maintenance, seeks a deeper self-integration into the life of the city, upholds public order more, and works better. And for all this, high-cost housing, reflecting Western models and methods, is not necessary. Modest do-it-yourself homes work out very well, even better from a psychological point of view, provided they are enhanced by security of possession and a certain stability of value.

Public Services: The Chinese example mentioned above contains suggestions for putting in place the services needed in Third World cities, where much can be done by personnel with less training than would be needed in the West.

Some services merit special attention. Schools are an example; basic changes in the educational system are needed. Secondary schools, where intermediate-level strata are trained—the future "squadron leaders" of society and commerce—cost *ten times less* than a university, and they yield more. But governments do not invest in them even a tenth part of what they put into the facilities and functioning of a university system. It is a miscalculation. Intermediate schools should be emphasized by having more money invested in them and by giving them more prestige and public recognition (for example, by empowering them to grant titles that would be recognized). Graduation from an intermediate school should be thought of as an "achievement in its own right," a "point of arrival," not merely as something required for admission to a university. And their educational programs should be more functional with respect to the real needs of urban communities.

Here too prospective changes must be aligned with economic indicators: fewer capital-intensive enterprises which require a higher technological content and more sophisticated specializations, and more labor-intensive enterprises. And they should be aligned with another problem area: the need to lighten overweight bureaucratic apparatuses, generally created in cities in an inept if not positively dangerous response to the need to create more jobs; fewer doctorates and more diplomas in technical fields; fewer bureaucrats and more really effective social workers. This should be the goal of educational planning.

Community: Employment, housing, public services—all unified in settlements permeated by the spirit of community. This objective, which would be unrealistic in practically all Western cities, is possible in the Third World. Barbara Ward writes:

> The various opportunities to group urban activities in districts with their own jobs and services, to exclude all but the occasional car, to develop bus lanes or interurban rapid transit railways, to install basic services—power, water, sewage collection, with a keen eye for conservation and new techniques—become all the more practicable when one remembers that half the new communities will be on new land, not cramped and confined within the existing metropolis. Provided land speculation is strictly stamped out, tenure made secure, and people assisted with the materials for building, the "young cities" can become exciting places of work and promise when the pioneers invent their own communities, build and extend their own homes, plant the trees, build the primary schools, send their children to the government-supported technical schools and training centers, and move easily on foot within their own streets or provide "critical mass" for the bus services to other centers. This is the dream, at least, for the new cities planned for New Bombay and New Bogotá.[10]

Yes, maybe it is a dream, but the only alternative to this environment of commitment, work, and hope is the violence that erupts from the frustrations of the marginated.

In not a few Third World nations, urban planners and those responsible for urban development have taken this road. Dr. O. Fatchurrahman, director of the municipal administration in Jakarta, Indonesia, has voiced the opinion that shantytowns should not simply be done away with as something shameful to house their occupants in new buildings in other parts of the city. It would be better, in his opinion, to mobilize the resources and vitality of shantytowners to make improvements in their part of the city with the means that would be appropriate for them. Shantytown areas would little by little be transformed into a camp of "workyards" for the construction of a community that the "consumer-inhabitants" would feel belonged to them, tailored to their measure.

Plans for the extension of public utilities in Jakarta have been in existence for years but, as the pressure of immigration increases, funding remains inadequate. A sewer system capable of handling the frequent inundations of migrants is nonexistent. Public service projects, despite the enormous effort that they represent, aimed at providing for 16 percent of the city's surface area, which houses 24 percent of the city's population. But now there is agreement that the best way to solve the problem of public services would be to strengthen the shantytown zones. The Jakarta plan envisions a program of community development and self-help that would mobilize shantytowners, in conjunction with a network of training centers, to make improvements in their parts of the city.[11]

The National Household Bank in Brazil found a way to invest in essential urban services. It founded CODESCO, which makes loans to shantytowners for materials for the construction of homes designed by and for them. Loans are repayable over a period of twenty to twenty-five years.[12]

Urban planners also provide communities with what they need for improving the environment around them. An example cited by Lord Holborn is that of a simple system, invented by a team of biologists, chemists, and engineers, for purifying contaminated water. The British relief agency Oxfam has distributed a great number of them, at a cost of about $800 each. Each unit can serve a community of 3,000 persons. The task of an urban planner, in a case such as this, would be to provide instructions for *how* to use such equipment: shantytowners know well *why* they must use it.[13]

The task of urban planners, however, is not only that of improving living conditions and public services. By itself that would not be very much, nor would it be much different from simply moving persons to another location. The real objective is that of convincing them that there is a work place for them in a vital and functional city, and hence there is a possibility for upward social mobility. Planners should try to channel the extraordinary creativity that sociologists have noted in "depressed" shantytown areas. Relocation of their occupants in new apartment buildings would entail the tearing down of the structuring that supports this creativity, that is, their strong interaction within the "natural area" that they want to make more habitable.

The overall aim, in short, is their willing insertion into the life of the city, which carries with it rejection of the idea that they are parasites to be repelled. The aim is that there be diffused among them a feeling of integration, that they feel invited to solidarity with the other city residents, in a joint effort to build and enhance a city for all.

Urban planners, if they take seriously the studies surveyed in chapter 5, do not begin with the whole city; they begin with the "natural areas." Here they find the potential for building up communities on a human scale because they find herein the close and strong networks of support, of creative solidarity and efficacious participation, developed by the collective response of shanty-towners to their immediate needs—a solid base for meeting the exigencies of life together in a city. At bottom, planners strengthen the sense of community already there instead of trying to substitute it in new residential complexes where everything would have to begin from scratch.

The sense of community has to be supported by adequate structures that gradually integrate the life of the community and eventually realize such community "victories" as a school, a church, neighborhood stores, meeting halls, and many other facilities that are tangible expressions of participation in a more open, more rational society. Barbara Ward and René Dubos have written:

> The largest of all modern city builders—the Russians, who constructed the phenomenal total of nine hundred new cities between the wars—embody this principle in their physical plans. In creating their smallest unit, the microdistrict of 8,000 to 12,000 people, Soviet planners try to project the needed number of schools—primary and secondary—the clinics, food stores, repair and dry-cleaning centers, public places, and small gardens appropriate to a community of this size. A cluster of such units making up perhaps a block of 25,000 to 50,000 people would have, in addition, public offices, bigger parks and shopping centers, theaters, restaurants, and other buildings not in continuous use. As size goes up, so, in theory, does the development of services, department stores, hospitals, centers of education and entertainment.[14]

The Russian planners had the advantage of not having to cope with the problems posed by private ownership. But for the cities of the Third World these problems remain a serious obstacle, even if it is only a question of granting shantytowners ownership of their minuscule plot of land. The decision of the Colombian government, mentioned in chapter 5, to legalize their ownership opened the door to a type of solution that augurs well for the future.

And solutions need not be long in coming. Extending this theme to the full range of urban landownership, it can be said with Ward and Dubos that the fate of these cities will certainly be infinitely worse than that of the ugliest, meanest, and most criminal of Western cities if the price of urban building lots would be allowed to increase by letting them be put on the open market. In India, for example, the cost of a building lot in the bigger cities is already three times more than what it is in smaller cities, with the result that the nadir of degradation is found in the *buildings* in the larger cities.

The most urgently needed initiative is that of providing regulations for the use of land, controlling the acquisition of urban land, disallowing—or turning to public use—the speculative profits on increases in the value of land. With an authoritative policy in the field of urban planning, the developing countries could put into effect a certain number of provisions already shown to be effective in developed countries.[15]

Urban planners are therefore trying to withdraw from the open market the mechanisms for allocating urban land and other urban resources. The very nature of a great number of public goods and services such as civil defense, measures taken for the prevention of fires and other hazards, education and health services, imposes some degree of public intervention. And public intervention is on the increase in the more developed countries. It would be foolish to continue to put any hope in the effectiveness of the mechanisms of business transactions. Businesses operate today with the imposition of distorted and artificial prices, with the monopolistic supply of some goods, with a vacuum of information to the consumer, a holding back of the benefits of technological innovation, and no regulatory plans for investments or wages.[16]

A correct use of land and an equitable distribution of public services will not by themselves give to the city a human countenance. More advanced urban planners are now inclined to interpret the "form" of a city not only in terms of efficiency but also in terms of the small pleasures, which, taken together, constitute "experiences" that go well beyond the fact or concept of "physical comfort." The form of a city, besides its physical contours, is understood to include the "sensations" or "feelings" that it generates, and urban planners are called on to interpret this phenomenon. By way of example, a city or a given part of it might generate a "sensation of excitement," a "feeling of security," or an "experience of fear."

With all their confusion and squalor, shantytown zones—"villages" that are forever being built up and torn down—are easier to understand than is the over-schematized plan of Brasilia, says J. Rykert. It is said that the sensation of freedom emerges from the overall configuration of all the elements that go into the composition of a city. But Brasilia is so "efficient" that it precludes the sensation of freedom.[17]

Participation in Urban Planning

Urban planners encourage the participation by all citizens in the life of the city. To live is to participate. Planners encourage participation in the process of city planning. For them it is the best way to attain two objectives at the same time: the formulation of a realistic plan and the mobilization of the real human resources.

Sometimes the attempt to encourage the people to participate is done only to reinforce the values and preferences of the planners. But even when this is not the case, the public may not be prepared to express its true needs and its deepest hopes. Participation must then become education of the public to the projects being drafted by urban planners,[18] and not the acceptance of the choices and preferences of a given urban group.

Viewed in a somewhat different light, participation, instead of stressing the existence of diverse expectations and priorities (a true pluralism, but one that could accentuate the conflicts within the city), can be a means of calming spirits and slowing down the political mobilization of the masses. When this temptation is resisted, participation, for the urban planner, becomes inspiration and support, the raw material of the reconstruction of the city as a community. In practice, the process of participation, community development, and conscientization is channeled.

Community Development

The process of "community development," as understood here, encourages a small-scale "natural area" to express the needs that it perceives. From this a number of proposals are formulated in terms that would elicit collaboration by a number of families on each of the needs. The role of the urban planner, at this stage, is to know how to integrate the various proposals in the overall urban plan in such a way as to be able to obtain the instrumentation and resources (subsidies, funding, loans) with which those concerned would be able to put their own proposals into effect. It will be at the local level and through the catalytic influence of the urban planner that improvements in shantytown zones and other city zones will take concrete form.

The base of this mobilization remains always that "do it yourself" spirit mentioned in chapter 5. Starting with a minimum of community "energy," the urban planner will support and reinforce it, providing the help and advice that seem conducive to the goals. When even this minimum is lacking, planners will try to provoke it directly, basing themselves on analogous situations and their experience with other groups

Conscientization

In the effort to encourage the requisite "minimum of community energy," conscientization techniques are resorted to. In general, immigrants, the jobless, and residents of depressed zones have no "consciousness" of the mechanisms or processes that govern the life of the city. They have even less consciousness of their own capacities and rights. Conscientization, generally conducted in small groups, using nondirective, inductive methods, with explanations and great patience, tries to go beyond the diagnosis of symptoms, where the technique of "community development" often bogs down.

In recent years more advanced urban planners have used conscientization programs in their strategy to prevent the exclusion of the masses from the urban decision-making process, and to promote a deep, if slow, process of participation by the urban base. In some cases—not all too rare—committed urban planners resort to direct politicization of the masses. Ordinarily they will be planners who are not part of the city administration, because their aim is precisely to change the political orientations of the municipality.

In Asia the result of such politicization often takes the form of "popular organizations." Their intention is to "move the waters" with strikes, demonstrations, takeovers, and other forms of public pressure, to modify or make more incisive the actions of those who hold power vis-à-vis the real problems of the city. When this does not work, the "popular organization" moves on to true political struggle with the authorities, to get them replaced. This represents an extreme outreach of urban planning. But such associations must be considered a form of it—an extreme form, indeed, but justified in some cases.

Social Assistance

Participation can also be promoted with individuals. The small local community performs an essential function in support of individual citizens, offering them a "symbolic universe" and ushering them into a complex of roles. Often, however, it does not suffice of itself to integrate the individual into urban life in a concrete manner. For this eventuality urban planners have developed the services of social assistance. Included under this term are all the activities undertaken for the individual in a systematic and personal way. In practice they are the activities performed by "welfare" assistance, which in general operates at the level of the individual person.

We are accustomed to think of social assistance as what is done for persons in extreme need: prisoners, drug addicts, alcoholics, the sick, the delinquent. But here we are speaking of social assistance in terms of the needs of "average" urban immigrants, whose "extreme need" is precisely that of finding their way into the urban framework.

As noted in chapter 5, the city presents the newly arrived immigrants with a serious problem, setting them brusquely before diverse frameworks of reference. The values of their framework—never questioned before, because shared with all their peers—no longer have a social base and they tend to come unhinged. In this situation individuals need all the personal attention possible. The task of introducing them to a climate of pluralism cannot be absolved by impersonal institutions. Each person, at bottom, has his or her own particular framework of reference, to be discovered in patience.

There is an initial social assistance service that normally takes place among groupings of immigrants, and generally is performed by persons who share with the immigrant the same culture of origin. And again we can note the importance of "cushion organizations." Be they ethnic or linguistic, they perform indispensable functions of welcome and incorporation for immigrants. In the atmosphere they cultivate, other forms of social assistance prosper.

Another type of assistance is that of guiding the individual through the labyrinth of the services that the collectivity offers. Perhaps the most valuable help will always be that given to fathers of families during a time of unemployment in order to secure a job.

But help cannot stop there. Once employed, individuals risk finding themselves in a situation of slavery, without social benefits, and at the mercy of their employer. This is especially true in cities under a capitalist regime. Person-to-person contacts will help the individual to be convinced of the necessity of joining a labor union and find in it a support group and participation.

In addition to favoring a good introduction to the production process, social assistance can help the individual to train for the role of consumer. On this, in fact, will depend in large measure the degree of upward social progress of the individual and the family. If they do not know how to evaluate the potentialities and the dangers of urban consumerism, they will always be poor and famished, despite being employed and earning an income. In the city everything is "moneyed." With money all desirable goods and services can be obtained. But not all of them are really useful or suited to all, even if advertising constantly says the opposite. Individuals must form for themselves the criteria of choice and suitability.

A final point: urban mission dare not fail to take urban planning into account, at every level and in all its options. Whatever tends to improve the city must be of interest to urban mission because, when all is said and done, it will affect *persons*. What missionary has never tried to help persons—for example, by trying to find work for someone? And in doing so, what missionary has not stumbled over the iron laws of some urban planners? Missionaries should not be content with tangential and occasional aspects of the planning of "their" city. They must know how to evaluate and absorb it as a whole, as a point of reference, and in their own specific work.

The City as a Sign of the Times

The scope of urban planning can be summed up by saying that at the level furthest removed from the individual person—at the international level—it operates above all on *values*, trying to educate leaders and followers to what modern urban life requires. At the other extreme—at the level of social assistance—it operates on *roles*, helping and encouraging individuals to accept and fill well the urban roles that are theirs. At intermediate levels—national, urban, zonal—it operates through the formation of the *groups* that integrate the individual into a totality of interactions satisfactory to the individual and to society. Urban mission can link its message and its course of activity to each of these levels.

Above all, urban mission will discover the huge discrepancies between the objectives of urban planning and the de facto realizations. Objectives—precisely because they are objectives—are signs of the gulf between the city as it is and the city as it ought to be. They point an accusing finger at the failure of the social construction of the city. The fact that the objectives *remain* unreachable demonstrates the extent of the failure: not only is the city not what it should be, it is also incapable of healing itself.

The negative results of the urban processes treated in chapter 5 reemerge here under a moral light. If urban planning attains a certain insight into the evils of the city, but must then resign itself to expectations of its own failure to furnish a remedy, whose fault is it? The answer comes from the tension between the interests of particular groups and the interests of the whole urban group, and from the predominance of the first-named.

Urban planning is grounded on the principle that some have to give up some things in order to assure the well-being of all. But there are always those who do not want to renounce—and they are in a position to refuse to renounce—what they consider to be their own. The city becomes the arena for a moral struggle between egotism and solidarity.

It is of particular interest to urban mission to know *how* urban planners try to defuse this tension and win the struggle. With their ideas on "participation," they intend to open the egotism of individuals to the fuller spirit of communitarian identification. One school of urban planning tries also to reach, on the basis of participatory roles, other values: service, respect for human dignity, justice and equity, pluralism, interdependence, control, reasonableness, solidarity with the masses.

There will doubtless be other groups of urban planners less interested in the masses and more oriented toward preserving the status quo or even to the instrumentalization of the needs of the citizenry. Their roles signal the values of tradition, competition, private property, and power. Even these groups, however, put solidarity at the pinnacle of their scale of values—with the obvious difference that they have in mind the solidarity of one privileged category, whereas the groups mentioned above have in mind the enlargement of solidarity to embrace the entire populace.

Solidarity, translated into participation, remains the base of all urban planning and the firm orientation of the city-sign. And this orientation will converge with that other orientation expressed in God's plan by the incarnation of the Word.

Part II

The Third World
and
Urban Mission

7

URBAN MISSION:
THE EMERGING RESPONSE

Even though a solution to the urban challenge is not yet in sight, we can even now open ourselves to the hope of salvation for the city.

The concept of "salvation" is not the same as that of "solution." The latter is something human beings arrive at by using their own means; the former is something given to them. If I am in debt, I can go to work, save up money, and pay the debt. This is a solution. But if I am in prison, I cannot get out by my own means: someone else must open the door for me.

Notwithstanding the enormous efforts that have already been exerted by urban planning, the processes set in motion by contemporary urbanization seem out of control. Can people escape their grasp? Are we all in "captivity," prisoners of our own urban creation? If the means at our disposal, as represented by urban planning, do not seem adequate to the challenge, can we not at least hope for some form of salvation?

Religion answers in the affirmative. It helps us go beyond the confines of human experience in order to look for what is transcendent. Christian faith affirms that the transcendent God breaks into human experience to offer salvation—what has been called in this study God's plans. What do these plans have to say about the urban processes surveyed thus far in these pages? For there is divine planning, just as there is human planning, for the city.

To probe this question will be a theological undertaking, but in a very precise and perhaps somewhat unusual sense. Christian theology derives from what is specifically Christian in the history of religions: the intervention of God in human history. Theology is therefore the discipline that accepts the fact of divine intervention and exerts itself to discover ever better its meaning. It is not its concern only to go beyond empirical reality, to discover the transcendent and understand it better. Theology accepts, as kerygma, the intervention of God, in work and in word, in the Word, and concentrates on interpreting it in order to arrive at orthopraxis—that is, at the ways in which

117

human activity should be molded once it has been touched by that intervention.[1]

At this stage of the theological process there will be a linkup with the thread of thought on urban mission: as the orthopraxis of the church, mission is called on to carry ahead the operative presence of God, accepted in an act of faith, as the actuation of the plan of salvation that guides divine intervention in history.

One immediate consequence can be drawn: if there is a plan, there will certainly also be signs of its activation. These signs will be the points of departure for theological interpretation. They are to be found diffused throughout the history of humankind. Each and every "time" of this history yields its own signs—"signs of the times."

Three "times"—the time before Christ, the present time, and the time between—are relevant to this study. For the first time, besides the signs themselves there is a "reading" of them; both are incorporated into the "history of salvation" recounted in the Bible. This reading also gives guidelines for "reading" the signs that we encounter in the two millennia of history that separate us today from the closing of biblical revelation. Both of these "times," then, facilitate the scrutinizing of the signs of our own time.

In the following section three sets of criteria are proposed for a reading of the signs, each set suggested by one of these three times. In their light we shall be able to read the signs revealed by contemporary urbanization.

The Theology of Signs

Not everything that happens around us is a sign of God's active presence. Even if nothing can be without him, many things—primarily sin—are only permitted, not willed. In fact we know from his very Word that there are forces that urge human history toward the rejection of God. The parable of the wheat and the tares opens our eyes to this truth, and John and Paul are both explicit on its significance: "This is the antichrist, he who denies the Father and the Son" (1 Jn. 2:22); "for the mystery of lawlessness is already at work" (2 Thess. 2:7).

If our faith tells us that there are signs of God's work, it tells us too that there are signs of the forces that oppose it. An important question arises: How are we to distinguish the signs of the plan of salvation from those that are in opposition to it?

Revelation of the Plan of Salvation in the Scriptures

Sacred Scripture offers at least two criteria for discerning the signs that come from God. The first criterion is well expressed by John when he writes: "All things were made through him, and without him was not anything made that was made" (Jn. 1:3). Here it is a matter of the Christological bearing of the signs that come from God. Paul reveals the orientation of the entire universe and its history to Christ (Romans and Colossians). The purpose of all created reality has to be attained in Christ. The world as it is today already has this Christological imprint, this underlying impulse toward Christ. God cannot fail in his plan. The ultimate purpose for which the universe was created, embedded like a seed in the heart of the world, will be attained. The whole of history meets in Christ, its alpha and omega.

Another biblical criterion for interpreting history is the eschatological vision. It does not serve only to console during a period of adversity, encouraging one to endure while awaiting a better future. The biblical vision is not a consolation that helps one to avoid the harsh reality of the present. It is not the opium of Christians. The vision is a sign, an *eschaton,* of what God will do—because he has decided to do it. In this sense it reveals what the future will be like, because God most assuredly is doing now what he has decided to do. And so it is neither a utopia nor a condemnation, but the indication of a route already taken, a sign of the orientation already given by God to human history. It is a divine pedagogy that guides people, helping them to obviate the risks that they encounter along the way.

Articulation of God's Plans in the History of the Church

This second criterion will provide the most illuminating insights for a reading of the signs of contemporary urbanization. Besides the point of reference offered by biblical history understood as the Word-Revelation of God, there is also that of the "contemporaneity" of the church with every moment and expression of human existence, which makes it possible for us to scrutinize the signs of the times and interpret them in the light of the Gospel.[2] "By reason of this evangelical penetration from within, it [the church] is in a position to grasp the divine currents present in the phenomena characteristic of each era," writes U. Betti.[3]

The church itself forms part of the history of the two millennia in question, in a special relationship with it, a relationship initiated and modeled by the incarnation. In the incarnation God spoke a definitive Yes to the world and to humankind. In Christ he accepted anew the reality of history, taking it up into himself. Sin too is included in this reality. But where it is, grace abounds. Notwithstanding its overwhelming visibility in the world of today, as in that of yesterday, sin has been conquered by the grace given to humanity in and by Christ.

Such truths govern the church and justify its presence in the world. Its purpose is to discern what is taking place in the world, where God is at work, because he has said his Yes to the world. If God has said Yes to the world in the incarnation, the church is present in the world in order to be able to say, "Here God is saying Yes to the world."

But the church is also in the world to say No where God says No to the world. When egotism, for example, goes contrary to God's plans, the church must say No. And finally the church is in the world to commit itself where it sees grace triumph over sin—precisely to support its victory.

Convergence of the Signs in Contemporary History

It is the Christians' duty to discover what God is doing in the world and to support his work. One particularly effective way to do this is by studying attentively the aspirations of one's contemporaries. If God wishes in fact to move humankind toward a new stage in its trek to salvation, he inspires and gives it the desire for a step forward. This pertains to the anthropological dimension of the theology of the signs of the times,[4] which consists in trying to understand the patterns of history and the centrality of humankind in its continuous evolution. It helps us today to understand that through the aspirations found again and again in our contemporaries we can enter into living contact with God's plans. The fact of common aspirations betokens the presence of the Spirit in contemporary history; faith tells us that the Holy Spirit can speak through present history. He speaks not only from within the Church, but also from within the world. Secular history becomes sacred history inasmuch as it progresses along a projectory of the plan of God. Pope Paul VI, in *Octogesima Adveniens*, pointed out that, despite some false premises, secular movements could give voice to some of the most legitimate aspirations of human nature, as also to some of the profound values of the gospel. Some of these values could reach human beings via a secular movement, retaining their full vigor and truth even though they are present as elements of nonecclesial or antiecclesial currents.

A concrete application of this criterion for reading signs would be to try to see where commonly expressed aspirations and movements converge. If a great number of diverse currents of human life, springing from independent sources and principles, converge in a few basic impulses, such a convergence may well be a sign pointing to an impulse from God. In fact to think that God is not somehow present there would be a mistake. This criterion of convergence, applied to the urban collectivity and the urban church of today, could provide further indications of God's plans for the city.

To recapitulate: once the major impulses of a given time are identified, their interpretation at the level of the Christian faith becomes possible. They must then be viewed in alignment with the following factors: (1) the master plan of salvation as it has been revealed in the Scriptures (the criterion of the coherence of divine activity); (2) the intuitions and orientations of the church in the history of its relationships with the world (the criterion of continuity in the inner life of the church); (3) the convergence of the church's hopes with the aspirations, expectations, and movements of the greater part of humankind (the criterion of convergence).

This is a theology that discerns, or, as Arevalo says, a theology in constant search for where the Yes and the No of the church must be asserted, and where it must carry out its duty. Once a Yes or a No has been asserted, this theology points out the necessity of the Christian's active involvement, because grace is already at work and because it is the duty of the church to be at work with grace.

It is therefore, Arevalo concludes, a theology eminently directed toward action-oriented persons, and especially to laypersons, who have the task of bringing a Christian presence to the world. It is a theology that must be active and activating. It cannot just accept the findings of fifty years ago as valid for today. Every day it must renew its interpretive spirit in prayer, in contemplation, in dialogue, in order to be able to go forward to where God is moving in the human community.[5]

Of every missionary, hence, there is demanded the great qualitative leap forward of faith. "They have eyes but they see not" will also be verified of those in mission today who do not go beyond the processes examined in the preceding chapters. When this first obstacle to the exercise of faith has been overcome, another requirement must be kept in mind: the humility to submit willingly to the judgment of the ecclesial community—a judgment that is generally pronounced by the ecclesiastical magisterium.

In practice, what is needed is a reaching out for love, for unity, for willingness to follow the call of God all the way to the cross, and a greater sensitivity to contemporary history, especially to the particular situation in which each person finds himself or herself.[6]

The Theology of the City

The Biblical Dimension

Almost in line with contemporary urbanization, the Scriptures begin in a garden and end in a city. To understand better the role of the city in the plan of God one has the biblical vision of the New Jerusalem—the renewed city—in the book of Revelation (Rev. 21:2).

This vision seems to indicate the direction in which the progressive activation of the plan of salvation moves and points out the stages needed for its development. In its light, the reality of the contemporary city takes on another aspect, opening itself to new horizons and—ultimately—to salvation.

The New City is presented as the definitive reconciliation of humankind with God. It becomes the ultimate point of the impulse that has long moved humankind, now that God, in Christ, is already definitively present among human beings and accepted by them.

Jerusalem is thus the completion of the history of the city. In the book of Revelation there is another city, Babylon (chaps. 17-18), and John is doubtless thinking also of Babel, symbol of the creative powers of humanity. Babylon, like present-day cities, has its strengths and its weaknesses. As a symbol, its basic weakness seems to be its incapacity to maintain communication among human beings.

To the human failure or the incapacity to find solutions, God responds with a new creative act, the act of salvation: the mystery of the death and resurrection of Christ. If from the viewpoint of the city the New Jerusalem is a goal, from God's viewpoint it is only a beginning. With it begins the presence of God among human beings. In terms of this creative act of God, all that we call history is nothing but prelude and preparation.[7]

What new thing does this city of God offer? It is the dwelling place of God among humans. The city is cohabitation, participation—not, however, that humans reach up to the skies; it is God who reaches down to earth. This is the difference between solution and salvation. At first it was a matter of a divine presence in the desert, because only there was a communion in fellowship created among humans. But now God reconciles the city to himself and there makes his presence transparent.

He does this by means of the church, which is the continuation of the incarnation of his Son and which in turn "incarnates" itself in the city. It has become the people of God, a communion of fellowship, because it is the community of a covenant. This newness was revealed to John. Israel and the city are but a single entity: "Behold, the dwelling of God is with men. He will dwell with them and they shall be his people, and God himself will be with them" (Rev. 21:3-4). These verses sum up the very essence of Israel, the meaning that the Old Testament found in the desert and that the New Testament finds in the Church. The assembly of God takes on the form of a City by realizing in itself what before was only a promise. The Word of God is creative, and it moves toward community.[8]

In the New Jerusalem we witness the final creation. The love of God is manifested in its fullness by producing the effect proper to itself: gathering and uniting human beings together. The book of Revelation reveals the life that permeates the city—a life that comes from the three divine Persons. It is the love of the triune God that makes of humans an Assembly, a People, a restored City.

The Father's love is expressed in the words: "I will be his God and he shall be my son" (Rev. 21:7). It is the paternity of God that generates fellowship among the humans of the city. If men and women become sons and daughters of God, they will also become a community of brothers and sisters.

The Son's love, that of the Lamb, is expressed, instead, in terms of conjugal love. The New Jerusalem is presented as the spouse of the Lamb: "And I saw the holy city, new Jerusalem, coming down out of heaven from God, prepared as a bride adorned for her husband" (Rev. 21:2). According to Paul, the church is an anticipation of this mystery. According to John, the church finds its roots in the mystery of the man and woman of Genesis: the church comes from the opened side of Christ as Eve came from Adam. The new humanity, John is saying, is formed from the substance of the Son of God. And this is why we return so often to the identification of the fellowship and community with the city. The true city is human beings sharing life.

Finally, the Holy Spirit's love is depicted by John as a river that proceeds from the throne of God and the Lamb. Its water is life. Its function is to give life to the city, assuring its existence *qua* humanity. The city of God attains the meaning of humankind as conceived by God. The human being is human because humanity is human persons sharing life.

With this we have arrived at the specific meaning that the master plan of God holds for the city. It is a matter of the passage from "being together" to "living together." The city is community, in contrast to the individualism that has marked some cities in recent times. In this context the vision of the New Jerusalem reveals the meaning of history—a history that pursues communion among humans. The New Jerusalem will be the glory and manifestation of God inasmuch as it is the realization of humankind as God conceived it to be in his plan—as communal. And inasmuch as God made humankind something corporeal, human community is realized in bodily form—and we call it "city."

For their part, when human beings live the love of the triune God in the dimension of city, they manifest God. At the base of everything is the act in which humankind recognizes itself. And individuals will never recognize themselves except by living with all the others in the "human" city.

The New Jerusalem is also the reconciliation of humankind with nature. Nature humanized is the city, a city understood as life shared by humans. The city of God is the reconciliation of humankind with itself, with nature, with God.

At this point the biblical event of Pentecost resolves the contrast between Jerusalem and Babylon. Pentecost is the assembly of the people of God renewed in the nascent church. With the sign of tongues, Pentecost resolves the noncommunicability of Babylon. With the power of the Spirit, it brings salvation. Pentecost incarnates itself in a small group of persons within the city of Jerusalem. It makes itself present to the entire city in the form of a tiny church—to be its sign of salvation.

The Ecclesial Dimension

Western theology was slow to develop in depth the relationship between church and city hinted at in the Bible. But the practical life of the church always took it into account and now we are in a period of recovery. Vatican Council II showed the way with its intuition that the local church is the actualization of the universal church. And it will be the concept of local church that will furnish what we need for a reading of the sign that is the city.

What is a local church? There is some difficulty in determining what dictates its confines, but it seems that these are described by the human social unity in which it works out its mission. Among all such units the most characteristic and best defined is the city. In fact when, at Pentecost, the concept of church began to penetrate the two millennia of Christianity, it always did so in reference to a city. It will be useful to see how the concept of church took shape in the cities.

The New Testament does not provide much information on the structures of the local church. Structures were always present in the life of the church, but juridical terminology was in a state of development at that time. This does not detract from the importance of the local church; even structures of the universal church—papacy and episcopacy—were still in a process of definition.

But the concept of local church was there. It was expressed by the word *ekklesia*, a word applied to local church and universal church in exactly the same way. The sacred authors are not ignorant of distinctions between the two modalities of "being church," but they consider them more as two aspects of the same reality. And so where the Old Testament uses the word *qahal*—the *assembly* of the people of God—the Greek translator puts the word *ekklesia*. The first Christians made use of the same word to describe themselves, well aware that they constituted the eschatological manifestation of the true people of God.

The same word is used to designate the stabilized assemblies or communities in diverse places: the community of Jerusalem, of Antioch, and elsewhere. Here it is important to note the use of the plural—churches. What was begun in Antioch was continued in all the cities where the apostles administered baptism. And thus a new "church" was born in each city, without any break of the overall unity of the church. This can be seen in the epistles of Saint Paul, who was always attentive to the theological implications of the words he used. "Church" does not signify "part" or (ecclesiastical) "division"; it describes those who shared the experience of being the people of God in each locality: the church of God that is in Corinth, in Ephesus, in Rome. Saint John's theology developed that of Saint Paul: the seven letters of the Apocalypse are addressed to seven churches (Rev. 2:3). Each community becomes a personification of the whole church, which is simultaneously universal and local.

Of interest to us is that the local church always coincides with the church of the given city. Paul, who was aware of meetings of Christians in private houses, never refers to them when he speaks of the assembly of the people of God; that always refers to the totality of Christians living in a given city.

It is clear too that Paul knows of another structure still in force at that time, the popular assembly also called *ekklesia*, which was an important element in social life, though it had lost the sovereign power it once had had. In Corinth, Paul presented the church as a *polis*, with its popular assembly, its *ekklesia*. For him, though, the church was not segregated in a ghetto; it was rooted in the urban unity in which it resided and lived.

Paul also refers to the ministry of the churches as a "liturgy"—a term that then referred to the services rendered for the good of the city, as an honor and responsibility, by its wealthier citizens. He speaks of church ministries in the same light.

These New Testament usages were taken up by the Church Fathers in the patristic age. They addressed their letters to "the church that is in . . ." or "the church that is in pilgrimage in . . ." or "that resides at. . . ." This practice became so widespread that it gave rise to use of the expression "residence" or "place" of the church—in Greek, *paroikia:* the place where the church assembled—the *parish.*

What was essential remained fixed: the idea of more than one parish in the same city was unthinkable and was never taken into consideration. It seemed self-evident that all Christians residing in the same city formed a single unit. According to Eusebius, the parish is the church of a city and coincides with the local church. Doctrine and practice remained firm: every city has only one church or parish. In this the practice of the Christians was at variance with parallel situations of the era, such as the synagogues, the schools of philosophy, the mystery religions. The Christians were constrained to develop a new model. For what reason? Because they had to work out a unity at the city level: they understood that their mission was coextensive with the city.

The principle of one parish per city was soon confirmed by legislation: the Council of Chalcedon even made the creation of a new parish conditional upon the unit of a city. And it was corroborated by a corresponding principle: one bishop per city. It was conceivable that a bishop might preside over more than one city, but not that two or more bishops could preside over the same city: that would have been schism. These were deeply rooted principles. In a city there would be various meeting places and diverse groupings of Christians, as the writings of Paul and Ignatius show—but always only one church. In the *Acts of St. Justin* (III. 1. 3) there is even a reference to choosing diverse places for worship—but no reference to more than one church. Irenaeus' letter to Pope Victor on the Eastern controversy is addressed to "the bishop of the church that is in Rome," by someone who was well aware that there were diverse groups of Christians in Rome, each with its own date for celebrating Easter.

The first rural churches emerged only in the third century, in northern Italy. In the fourth and fifth centuries they began to multiply in France as well. They were always founded by the bishop of a very small city (*vicus, pagus, castrum*). A church was organized and clergy assigned to it. The more important centers were presided over by a priest and the others by a deacon. They seem to have been mini-versions of urban parishes and they all followed the principle of one parish per settlement. The unity of the local church, therefore, was not based on the bishop (there were churches without resident bishops) but on the local clergy, called to gather the Christians into unity. In its body of ministers, and in an urban-based framework, the church found its unity and its organizational structure.

If the link between the local church and the city represents authentic tradition, would it not be strange if only the primitive church honored it? Would it be possible for the church to forget for centuries an important element of its nature? In fact in the Middle Ages the church renewed this relationship in an original and informal way.

Toward the eighth century the Carolingians confiscated ecclesiastical property, and church structures began to disintegrate under the pressure of the feudal system. Noblemen demanded chaplains for their own service, and lesser clergy for their dependents. Charlemagne instituted tithing, from which the system of benefices derived. A benefice was assigned to the cleric who took upon himself the care of a residential settlement, which consequently became his "parish." The older structures changed too because under Charlemagne the cities lost the importance they once had. But many cities continued to have only one parish well into the twelfth century, and some few cities as late as the seventeenth century—Bari and Brindisi in Italy, for example. Many cities adopted the Roman practice of station churches as a way to express the unity of the local church.

During the eleventh and twelfth centuries there was a renaissance of urban life in Europe in the guild movement. The bishops felt threatened by the stronger guilds, but the urban clergy, and later the mendicant orders, in general, supported them. The political and social thinking of the Scholastics drew inspiration from the life of the guilds. The church, in consequence, became the animator of the guild movement—thanks to its teaching, not to its structures. It proposed a form of collective life to the urban community and there emerged from it yet another form of the bond between church and city, splendidly symbolized in the cathedral. The cathedral was built by the citizenry, not by the episcopacy, not by the nobility, and it gave expression to the symbiosis of the church and the urban guild movement. Nor was it reserved for worship: it served also as a meeting place where citizens discussed public affairs. The cathedral was not only a testimony of faith but a proof as well of the will to inspire the life of the city to evangelical values. The city would be a bearer of salvation, already prefigured in the reality of the guild movement and in the effort to orient it toward an evangelical vision of humankind.

Christianity also inspired the city through the confraternity. The function of the confraternity in the life of the Christians of the medieval city was crucial. It was not an elitist group; rather, it was supposed to be the Christian people itself, structured and organized for action. In practice all belonged to a confraternity, and it came to form the real structure of the city's laity. It was organized along more existential lines than were the parishes. As in the earliest days of Christianity, ecclesiastical structures were modeled on those of the urban population. But the artificial nature of the parochial structures of the time did not have negative effects on the general population, because the population was also served by this other structure. The confraternities were so in resonance with the social life of the people that often they found themselves in conflict with ecclesiastical authorities.

We must admit, however, that the Council of Trent did not succeed in curbing the medieval erosion of the structures of the primitive church. Taking place four centuries before the era of massive urbanization, its introduction of the division of urban territory into parishes served only to generalize the rural—not the urban—parish model. And this happened in the cities! Then gradually the principle of "noninterference" of the church in public affairs came to be adopted. The church was a "perfect society," and that was enough. The polycentric structure of the urban church was fixed. Not even the religious orders attempted to dismantle the walls thrown up between one internal urban community and another. *From the pastoral point of view, the city was no longer a unity;* it did not have a unified public life. Urban society became provincial. The church took up a position in alignment with the disruptive thrust of the city rather than with a unifying or reconciliatory thrust. When the industrial revolution appeared, the church was too distant and too distracted to accommodate itself to it. Just when everything began to happen in the cities, the church had turned to a path that was decisively rural.

Missionaries in the eastern and southern hemispheres went their own ways and ended with rather different results. In Latin America missions formed part of the new cities that were destined to become the capitals of new states. Unfortunately the innovative experiments of the model cities of Paraguay were not adopted elsewhere; their import was not appreciated, even though the continent called for models of urban development diverse from those of Europe. It can be said, however, that among the cities of the Third World those of Latin America have a strongly Christian cultural matrix.

The same cannot be said of Asia. The inculturation attempts of De Nobili in India and Ricci and Adam Schall in China, after their initial successes, came to nought. Ricci worked in an urban context, conscious of the weight of the city upon Chinese culture. De Nobili too attempted to go beyond the geographic missionary formula in general use, which followed the largely urban-oriented mentality of Western colonial interests (Saint Francis Xavier was one of the best-known examples of this approach), to arrive at a cultural formula. In Asia the culture of the older cities was strong enough to resist the destructive mania that befell the cities of Latin America. Missionaries who were more attentive to the signs of the times wanted to follow the design of the plan of salvation in their attempt to assess and assume cultural heritages in the light of the incarnation, seeing them as bearers of the Word. But those signs were officially and definitively deciphered only by Pius XI and Pius XII, who revoked the prohibitions on Chinese rites—but once again it was too late.

In Africa, as in Latin America, cities south of the Sahara had Western culture imposed on them by Christian colonizers. The arrival of independence, however, coincided with a deeper conscientization on the part of ecclesiastical authorities—partly due to awareness of what had happened in Asia—to the cultural implications of the incarnational bearing of the plan of salvation. Decisions on the modalities of the development of local Christian communities were taken more thoughtfully.

All in all, the church's two millennia have taught it that, within the framework of the plan of salvation, it cannot live on the margin of the city, indifferent to its fate and its aspirations. The church is called and recalled to be in solidarity with the city.

Reading the Sign of the City: A Summary

Reflection on the various processes that explain the city and reveal its function as a sign—undertaken in preceding chapters—confirms the hypothesis
that the contemporary city has a "divided unity." In the cities of the Third
World the complex tension between unity and division is even more accen-
tuated.

The Direction of Urban Processes

Of itself, the demographic process is dispersive: one's capacity to stabilize
relationships with others is limited. The more numerous the others, the
smaller will be the fraction with which one is familiar. On the other hand,
their concentration in a relatively small number of urban centers augments
the capacity to be together. But no sooner are persons concentrated in cities
than they begin to segregate themselves—physically and socially—in "natural areas" and social strata, and they do so in order to be able to "live together." Paradoxically, demographic and geographic processes both increase
and diminish the possibilities for interpersonal relationships.

Migrants flock to the city in search of a more adequate response to their
material and nonmaterial needs. But in most cases they find less of the first.
The city, it is true, offers much—but only to the few who can afford it. It is
always those few who exploit the division of labor that is the keystone of the
economic processes, reducing the city's capacity to bind all citizens together
in a unity of interdependence. The political processes, by reason of their
alliance with economic processes, reinforce the blockage and introduce new
forms of oppression and servitude. No longer do persons live together, the
one *for* the other, but the one lives *from* the other. A vital force is deflected
from its original function of service to unity and liberty, and becomes an
instrument of division between the few who have more and the many who
have less.

Culture, the expression of the inner spirit of urban collectivities, succeeds
to some extent in giving a positive significance to hardships, providing a
certain measure of psychological security, and responding to the more urgent
physical needs. Cultural proccesses aim at cohesion within the "natural
areas" and social strata of the city. But they do so only within each "natural
area" and social stratum, often segregating them from one another and wid-
ening spatial and social distances.

All told, we can perceive a certain progression toward unity, or rather,
toward ever larger groupings: from the dispersion of demographic growth to
the unity of geographic concentration in large cities; from the productive
unity of the family to urban corporate production; from local administrative
unity to that of a vast territory encircling a city; from physical planning to
social planning.

But a regression toward the decomposition of these same unities is also perceivable: geographic concentrations crumble culturally within themselves; economic and political controls are in the hands of a few who use them for their own ends, creating counterpositions—sometimes violent—with the masses; even urban planning is manipulated to the advantage of a minority.

How can direction be given to these contradictory impulses that are responsible for the "divided unity" of the city? Values will tell us. They will indicate where it is that a city's population wants to arrive—even if still in a confused way—in its building of the city. The four predominant values that give rise to these positive impulses seem to be *community* (demographic and geographic processes), *justice* (economic and political processes), *communion* (cultural processes), and *solidarity* (planning processes).

The four underlying values converge in the search for a communitarian life more worthy of the human condition and more expansive. But so far we have spoken only in generalities and have not yet taken up the question of the direction in which the city moves. This can be determined by investigating the significance of each of these values within the framework of the search for urban solutions.

Solidarity is a methodology, or at least urban planners adopt it as one. For them it is also a rich source of motivation. It is of interest to note that it promotes movement toward the *future*, toward a desideratum that is already partially experienced.

Community, on the contrary, is already a solution, in the present. It too is a methodology, but not one elaborated theoretically in the studies of urban planners; it is the spontaneous methodology that springs up in a shantytown.

Justice is both an end and a starting point—namely, that of the distribution of goods and services, power and labor, in an equitable manner among city-dwellers. It has a stabilizing effect and seeks to assure that what there is in the city, even if it is not much, serves all, not just a few.

Communion offers a definitive vision (solution) in which relationships among persons are given higher priority than is the distribution of goods among them. It pays more attention to what the city promises than to what the city now has. It is the alluring goal of cultural processes.

All this tells us a lot about the internal orientation of the city. It tells us what type of solution the city can become for the shared life of its citizens.

But it does not tell us how it fits into God's plans or how it constitutes a sign and instrument of those plans. We shall try to decipher it by applying the criterion of coherence. What type of solution offered by the predominant values in the city is in alignment with the master plan of God? In what way? With what modalities? This brings us to a true and full reading of the city-sign as a point of entrance into God's plans for contemporary urbanization. We must again examine each of the major components (values) of contemporary urbanization, to see if it is coherent with what we already know about that plan of God.

Solidarity immediately makes us think of the theme of "God with us" and —in this study—the incarnation. *Community* is the same value that supported the preparation and development of the plan of God in history, first with the people of Israel and now with the people of the *ekklesia*. *Justice* refers back to the promise of the messianic times and does so in the sense in which it is understood and grasped by the urban masses: "He has filled the hungry with good things, and the rich he has sent empty away" (Lk. 1: 53). *Communion* brings us to the advent of the New Jerusalem and the actualization of the messianic times when God will share his own riches—indeed, his own life—with dwellers in that City.

We *are*, therefore, in alignment. The contemporary city has within it the seeds of the divine plan of salvation. How can the two streams—that of the city and that of the divine plan—be made to converge? We know that the most forceful moments in the history of the city were linked with the progress of technology (see chap. 1). But the conclusions of chapter 6 seem to indicate that the city, set in motion by technological advances, must perfect and "settle" itself by moving forward in *human relations*. Advances in technology solve some problems and create others; the latter seem insoluble except by projecting new relationships among humans. And perhaps this is God's strategy: to make necessary, through the momentous problems of the city, the projection of new relationships and linkages that are a prelude to those of the New Jerusalem.

There are those who stop at this point, hoping that solutions, even if only partial, will eventually come by themselves. There are those who accept the situation as one that is typically human, and therefore intrinsically problematic. And there are those who hope for divine intervention in history. The first remind us of the signs posed by Babel and Babylon; the others remind us of the sign posed by the New Jerusalem, predicted by Isaiah and "seen" by the author of the book of Revelation.

Is it perhaps necessary to remind ourselves that God has already "assumed"—in the incarnation and resurrection of Christ—all human processes and is present in them? In this perspective the sign of the city is also salvation already begun. It is an efficacious sign: *sacramentum urbis*, the sacrament of the people-church for the city and in the city.

Solution and Salvation

The city-sign therefore summons us to deepen, in a theological perspective, the concept of solution in the sense of a preparation for salvation.

The concept of solution incorporated in the city-sign bespeaks liberation from all serious danger—misfortune, sickness, privation, and the like—and thereby prefigures the theological concept of salvation.

Biblical scholars say that in the period after the exile, salvation for the Hebrew people meant something very close to liberation from all evils, personal and communal—total security, in other words. In the Synoptic Gospels the word "salvation" is often used in reference to the healings performed by Jesus; salvation meant the sudden restoration of physical health. But there are other texts in which healing is seen as a visible sign of the salvific power of

Jesus, who confers a salvation that is much broader than that of bodily health. In the first Christian communities there emerged the conviction that salvation in this last sense comes from God through Jesus Christ. Salvation becomes a gratuitous gift, a deed of loving kindness (grace), received through faith. Beginning in this life, salvation comes to its fullness only in the eschatological kingdom.

Theologians today emphasize diverse aspects of salvation. Some of them see it more as a personal reality, whereas others prefer to look at it as a collective reality. Some stress its transcendence—on earth there can be only fleeting experiences of it—whereas others interpret it as a fact of this life, a historical reality. Other theologians say that salvation is at work whenever persons generously come to one another's help.[9]

Salvation, then, even if it is different from the "solution" of urban planners, is not opposed to it. It is not a matter of an either/or, but of a progression—for example, from physical health to the beatific vision; from a solution for the city to salvation of the city. For us, therefore, the salvation that God communicates to the city could be what is manifested in the vision of the New Jerusalem.

Communion and Incarnation

This moves us into the sphere of another concept. God saves because he has made the city his "tent" amid humankind. In the city God communicates with persons and invites them to communicate among themselves. In the city *union* and *communion* become simultaneously a presupposition for and a consequence of salvation. By its very nature salvation consists in a state of fullness, presupposing liberation from a state of privation (illness, pain, and the like).

In John's vision, Christ espouses the city. This is the apex of communion. The city has become "church." And here we find the method par excellence of the missionary: Jesus himself, who became the Son of Man in order to unite himself with humankind, communicating to it the salvation of communion with God. The whole of biblical history converges on the incarnation; it becomes the *method* of salvation.

Ecclesial history continues the incarnation in the life of the church as the spouse of Christ. We called attention above to the more significant moments—for the city—in the urban churches of the first centuries and in the churches of the cities of the Middle Ages. They are moments that converge with the presence of Christ in Jerusalem. Specifically, the more forceful moments of this presence will permit us to see better the goals of the plan of God present amid humankind, God accepted by humankind; persons present to one another, accepting and accepted by one another: union, communion in the freedom of Love.

This constant, vital tension between "finding oneself in the Lord" and "going out to the whole world" in his name constitutes the base of urban mission: the base from which the missionary departs for the city, the base to which converts are directed, the base to which the missionary returns to be reinvigorated with missionary enthusiasm. It coincides with the concept of local church, or better, with the experience of the local church. We know that the church stands at the heart of God's plans because, continuing the work of his Son, it is called to continue his incarnation, to communicate his salvation. The fact of its centrality in urban mission should not surprise us.

Salvation and Church

The relationship between salvation and the church can be understood in various ways. The classical synthesis belongs to Avery Dulles. He identifies five perspectives in current theology. The first stresses the fact that the church is the *means* of salvation—the ferry that transports passengers across the dangers of life. Here the church is viewed as a salvific institution. The second sees salvation more in terms of a communion of the saved. Here the church is more a "space" of salvation than a means of salvation. Communion of life with Christ begins on earth and is consummated in paradise. A third presentation understands the church as the sign of the salvation wrought by God in Christ. As Christ is the original sacrament in which God manifests his redemptive love, so the church is the sacrament in which God's salvific action in Christ shows itself as a sign of his mercy upon humankind in every generation. The fourth perspective is that in which the church is seen as the community that proclaims salvation to the world. Its principal component is the preaching of the gospel. The fifth perspective emphasizes the church's task as an agent in the transformation of the world into the kingdom of God—understanding "kingdom of God" to mean a situation of peace, justice, freedom, fellowship, and abundance.

Dulles continues:

From the first model I accept the idea that the Church should be a means of grace. Through its teaching and other ministries it should help its own members to work out their eternal salvation. From the second model, I adopt the belief that the Church is not a mere means of salvation but a place where divine salvation can be to some extent enjoyed even here on earth. The Church is an anticipation of the final Kingdom. From the third model, I take over the view that the Church is to be, here on earth, a sign or representative of the eternal salvation to which we look forward—a sign admittedly somewhat ambiguous here on earth, but one which in the final Kingdom will be wholly transformed into the reality to which it presently points. From the fourth model I would borrow the idea that the Church proclaims the salvation brought by Jesus Christ, that it heralds the approach of the definitive Kingdom, and that proclamation itself is an eschatological event, in which God's power to save and to condemn is already at work. From the fifth model

finally, I would draw the thesis that the Church has the mission to promote the values of the Kingdom in the larger human society, thus preparing the whole world, insofar as human effort can, for the final
transformation that will occur when God establishes, by his sovereign
intervention, the new heavens and the new earth.[10]

The church, therefore, is simultaneously the means, space, sign, proclamation, and leaven of salvation. In God's plans it is always called to be all this
but in each instance and in an original way, for the cities of the Third World
also. The task of urban mission, consequently, will be that of gathering the
Christians already incarnated and active in the city to make of them the
means, space, sign, proclamation, and leaven of salvation. In other words,
urban mission is called to enable all Christians of the city to feel that *together*
they are bearers of this salvation, in its various modalities, to their specific
city.

An existential question arises at this juncture: How will this be possible?
How can this ideal be made real?

Consequences for Urban Mission

Historically most Christians were trained to concentrate on the first model
of church: our vocation was to board the "ferry" and, on the day of our
death, we would find ourselves on the other shore, that of salvation. It was
not that the other ways of "being church" were not recognized, but they were
considered the responsibility (and privilege) of the hierarchy.

Local Church as Base

Vatican Council II helped to demolish the restricted perspective of what the
church is when it summoned *all* members to "be church," inasmuch as they
are all, together, the people of God. But a change of mentality and of attitude
does not come suddenly. A patient and persistent reeducation is necessary.

Meanwhile, a point of particular interest for urban mission in this change
is the rediscovery and ever greater clarification of the concept of local
church. By its very nature this concept is closer to the existential reality of
believers than is the concept of universal church. The latter is the communion
of all Catholics in the world at the level of values, and of intentional and
institutional membership. It says much, but it is not a concrete communion
of life. No attempt, for example, has ever been made to unite all Catholics to
put through some practical initiative. There will be a universal gathering, but
only on the Last Day.

In the case of the local church, however, in addition to a mystical and
institutional communion, a certain existential experience is both possible and
obligatory. And it is a first step toward translating the concept of church into
the experience of concrete salvation.

The city has had a very special function in the concretization of the concept of local church. Ecclesial history seems to have resolved a delicate problem here: how to delimit the frontiers of the local church. With what criterion can we set the confines of unity? There does not seem to be a criterion internal to the church itself, a doctrinal criterion. For example, participation in the same eucharistic celebration is an insufficient—though of itself valid—criterion. Those who for various reasons do not take part in the eucharistic assembly cannot be considered excluded from the church. On the other hand, the same persons can meet for the Eucharist in diverse places and at diverse times.

In its history the church seems to have adopted a criterion "from outside," in the line of the incarnation. Ecclesial unities are formed from the human unities in which they find themselves. Of particular interest for urban mission is the fact that this external criterion derived—historically, at least—from the city. This is a valuable insight: the city offers to the church an ambient and a model for its local actualization.

The model follows this articulation: the city forms a human unity; the frontiers of the local church, also called to form a human unity, will coincide with those of the city. We are not referring simply to a physical or geographic fact, but to a way of life, a form of communion—possibly the most advanced within the sphere of purely human relations.

Granted that human beings are on the way, now more than ever before, to forming large urban residential settlements, it can be asked whether a greater human unity could be realized in a kind of alliance among cities and in their intercommunion. We do not yet have an answer to this question, but the perspectives are open for a cosmic reconciliation of humankind, a reconciliation that God is even now preparing through the church.

It is more in the cultural than in the geographic sphere that the "localization" of the church is accomplished. It would search to incarnate itself—or better, inculturate itself—globally and loyally in the great citizen community, offering its solidarity in the building up of a more human city. This is the communitarian impulse of evangelization described by Pope Paul VI as "the impact of the gospel on the world in which persons make judgments, establish values, elaborate their thoughts, inspire or construct life patterns . . . evangelizing culture and the cultures . . . beginning always with persons and returning continually to the relationships among them and with God."[11]

It would be an undertaking of an organic pastoral ministry, rather than of an administrative ministry, that will translate this orientation into practice.

Incarnation as Method

Urban mission has no choice: it must espouse the whole culture of the city, incarnating itself in it, as church, in order to save it. Once the problem of its "area"—the concrete boundaries of the local church—has been solved, there remains the question of its internal structuring. Here we must take into account the deep longings of the urban masses for a much stronger sense of communion. We know that communion, in its highest form, is indeed the message of the church. Turning to sociology, to see how human communities give themselves a structure, and keeping in mind that their structuring always depends on the essential functions summarized in chapter 2, conclusions begin to emerge.

The local church must structure itself in such a way that its members project a group manifestation that says the following about them:

1. Having accepted Christ, they gather in the *assembly of believers* to deepen the mystery they share; in this way the church socializes in the faith.

2. Experiencing their union with Christ and among themselves to be of such a nature that it makes them into a single entity, members develop an attitude of *sharing their goods and especially their human talents,* organizing themselves in such a way that no one lacks anything essential, and gifts and tasks are distributed equitably; in this way the church responds lovingly to needs.

3. In order to continue as a single entity, they *accept authority* as a gift and a delicate responsibility, and they recognize it as service to unity, both internally and as regards other communities; in this way the church progresses toward the greater and definitive unity, that of all humankind in the kingdom of the Lord.

4. Living daily life in relation with others, not excluding non-Christians, they *manifest* the *hope* that the Lord will reveal himself again before the Last Day, in events of our time, to give a direction to all that is human; in this way the church realizes its mission, that of discerning the signs of the kingdom of God that is coming.

Salvation as Goal

How are we to translate these structural lines into concrete experience of a group nature? Once again we must apply the three keys of our reading of the sign of the city against the background of biblical and ecclesial history: incarnation as method, salvation as goal, communion as anticipation of the definitive realization of salvation.

On these three lines we can articulate the concrete pastoral consequences of the theology of the city for urban mission in the Third World: incarnation (chap. 8), the offer of salvation (chap. 9), and communion in the church (chap. 10). From the response-solution of urban planners we arrive at the response-salvation of urban missionaries.

8

SOLIDARITY AS GENERIC MISSION

If the method of God's plans for the city is that of the incarnation, mission-aries who seek to implement it can be expected to be called to a high degree of solidarity with the inhabitatnts of the city—indeed, to become themselves "city persons." Following in the footsteps of the Savior, missionaries will offer themselves to God with their own cry of "Here I am, send me!" Convinced that the salvation of humankind today is taking place *there*. Their response will be methodologically similar: *homo factus est.*

For urban mission, *homo* means "urbanite," "city person," creator and creature of the city of today. If the Lord lived his incarnation for thirty years in Nazareth, he did so because he had been sent to Israel, a rural people. Today, continuing his work through his disciples gathered into a church, his incarnation becomes effective also—and perhaps more so—in the city. As U. Betti has observed:

> Because the church has its historical origin in Christ, missionaries who carry it forward know that through it the incarnation of God is the type and cause of its unique relationship with the world. God, making him-self human, entered visibly and irreversibly into the order of his own creation, to recapitulate all things in Christ (Eph. 1:10). In Christ, therefore, who is the presence and realization of the unique and defini-tive salvation, humans reacquire the capacity to be saved—a capacity that was lost with the first sin. And all created things participating in him who is both creator and creature participate in their own way in the capacity of cooperating with God in the salvation of humankind. The church is witness and proclamation of the presence of God among hu-man beings, to offer them salvation where they are and as they are.[1]

It will be the task of Christians, formed by mission, to incarnate in their turn this church in the cities of the Third World. It will be a slow process, as was that of Nazareth, which lasted to the very end of Christ's specific minis-try on earth. But his was the necessary prerequisite to the task of today's

Christians, constituting a generic ministry. Only because he could call himself the Son of man did he render testimony to his message "God is in us." It was not just a matter of "speaking the language," but of feeling himself to be truly "one of them," of knowing that he was accepted as one of them: "Is he not the carpenter's son?"

Becoming a "Person of the City"

To become a "person of the city" means, above all else, to enter into relationships with the inhabitants of the city. If missionaries come from an urban background themselves, they bring with them an experiential knowledge of the quality and quantity of such relationships. But, recalling the definition of the missionary—someone sent to an ambient not his or her own (see chap. 1)—much remains to be done. In fact it will be necessary to get to know even better the inhabitants of the city to which the missionary is sent. They will be of diverse races and diverse cultures, and the missionary will thus have to establish relationships with them that will be diverse from those known previously. The missionary's knowledge of their idiosyncrasies will not grow unless he or she succeeds in establishing a maximum of relationships with them. And it will be precisely these relationships that will permit the missionary to enter ever more deeply into their life and their mentality. On condition that certain laws of nature are observed, a person learns how to swim only by jumping into the water.

As we have seen, all cities have the characteristic of multiplying relationships for the individual inhabitant: there are so many persons around, and so many roles to perform. In addition, the cities of the Third World, because of their enormous tertiary sector, accentuate this characteristic, multiplying yet more these relationships, and deepening them in the sense of making them more like ends in themselves, unlike what obtains in the Western city where relationships dictated by efficiency hold residents in a vise and instrumentalize them. In this respect, immigrants, the unemployed, and the homeless are more disposed than others to communicate.

With Open Arms

The basic attitude of any approach to a Third World urban context is that of not feeling in any way superior. It is the same principle as that of the incarnation: Christ "though he was in the form of God, did not count equality with God a thing to be grasped, but emptied himself, taking the form of a servant, being born in the likeness of men" (Phil. 2:6–7).

The Lord came into the world without expecting to find a place ready for him. There was only the cubbyhole of Bethlehem. The vast majority of city-dwellers in the Third World came to their cities without having a place ready for them. They were overjoyed if relatives or friends offered them a cubbyhole in their house.

In the footsteps of their Master and those of city residents, missionaries will not project the image of having some kind of exclusive claim to what is worthwhile, as if "the best" is what belongs to them and whatever is foreign to them is "inferior."

It should be recalled instead that whatever good thing has been given to them and to the city, has come from one and the same munificence of God, who makes the same sun shine on all, and gives all human beings the same basic human capacity. The missionary must go with open arms. Indeed he or she should go with empty hands.

The missionary attitude must be one of receptivity. The principle at work does not mean that missionaries should despoil themselves of what they have received from the culture of their origin. We realize that every people has its own lifestyle, its own culture that permits it to "function." It is not necessary to jettison this, but only to resist the temptation to export it. The fact that lifestyles of Third World cities differ from those of Western cities does not necessarily make them inferior or alien. We all know that the importation of Western models by non-Western cities has not worked well.

Missionaries must go beyond an attitude of mere adaptation. God is free. Just as he chose certain people without any merit on their part, he could have chosen this or that social group in a particular city to channel to the whole city certain of his blessings, especially in the sphere of religious values—just as he gratuitously chose Israel to channel salvation to all the nations.

It is the principle of the incarnation seen from the other side: Christ continues his incarnation in his church, and, in particular, in the disciple-members of that church. And any person can encounter Christ in them. Pope Paul VI said:

This strong humility will take away from our activity all harshness and sectarianism, and will help us to avoid discouragement when confronted with a task that seems beyond our powers. Christians deepen their hope, knowing that in the first place it is the Lord who is at work in us in the world and that through his Body that is the church—and through it all humankind—he pursues the redemption attained on the cross, the redemption that burst into victory the morning of the resurrection.[2]

As noted in chapter 6, city planning for Third World cities has managed to accomplish much and in diverse ways. Missionaries cannot, therefore, make a pretense of going to the Third World city with their own patented solutions. Nor can they impose their judgment on the futility of the urban planning in progress, and then offer their own solutions. The salvation that Christians hope to bring is the gift of God who is already at work in the city and is bringing his work forward even in the partial solutions worked out by urban planning.

The attitude of "empty hands" means the will to place oneself fully in the currents of urban planning already in place, and thereby express one's solidarity not only with what it has so far achieved but also with what it seeks to achieve. Christians should go to the city humbled and strengthened by the principle of the incarnation: "he . . . did not count equality with God a thing to be grasped" (Phil. 2:6).

The example of the newly arrived immigrant-worker can serve to educate us to this attitude. This is the figure that best characterizes the city of the Third World. The immigrant arrives vibrant with expectations. The city will give so much that was lacking in the rural environment left behind! The immigrant comes with the expectation of receiving rather than giving. But exactly for this reason a quasi-pioneer energy is released driving him or her to live urban days at maximum intensity, to offer services to others in the hope of gaining access to the urban work-system. Laziness finds no place in this mentality; every difficulty and every obstacle is overcome in a spirit of undaunted enthusiasm. Hands are empty, not to beg, but to ask for employment, to dig in. Unfortunately, things soon change. And despite this often repeated experience, the immigrants' rural confreres will continue to besiege the cities, coming from all sides. For our purposes, however, the image of the immigrant-worker remains vivid. Putting themselves in the immigrant-worker's place, missionaries can get a good sense of what it must feel like to be immersed in the flood of urban humanity. They can face urban mission with the immigrants' attitude of open arms, empty hands.

Incarnation in its depth implies the assumption of something more than merely flesh and bones; it includes the assumption of the potentially infinite relationships that sociality, inherent in human existence, carries with it. If Christ took from Mary his hands of flesh, he learned from the culture of his land how to open those hands and how to turn them toward others—to receive from them and to give to them. Incarnation implies inculturation.

Curiosity

Fortified with this humility, missionaries must also have another attitude no less necessary as a kind of preparation for finding their way into the networks of urban relationships: the attitude of unending curiosity.

The Third World city is a dynamic reality in a vibrant tension between change and permanency. There is no way to know where it will lead: it does not follow the patterns of Western urbanization. It is not enough to have studied them once; they must be restudied every day. The major conclusions of contemporary urban research presented in preceding chapters will help missionaries and all Christians only to the extent that they adopt them as instruments and hypotheses to develop their own personal knowledge of this or that particular city. As instruments, they do not suffice of themselves: they must be coupled with an attitude of curiosity. A guitar does not make music by itself; it must be handed to someone who is willing to play it.

Revised and updated knowledge of a particular city will help to prepare one to become a "person of the city," smoothing the road toward assumption of relationships with city residents. And it will educate missionaries to the specifically missionary task: to promote God's plans for the city, plans that will remain hidden unless missionaries make the effort to apprehend the signals that emanate precisely from the urban context. An indispensable condition for reading the signs of the divine plans will therefore be continuous research and, at the same time, objective knowledge of such signals. At that point, however, mission curiosity will be transformed into a profoundly religious attitude—that of contemplation of the divine glory manifested in what is created, including the created urban world.

Intellectual curiosity will spur the missionary on to find out how city-dwellers live and what they do. This by itself is most useful in helping one to enter into relationships with city-dwellers. But one must go further, beyond the barrier of empirical reality, all the way to the spiritual curiosity that will reveal what God is doing when he pitches his tent in the city.

Here again the model can be the immigrant-worker, for whom the city is a vast newness, an unending series of discoveries. Immigrants never stop asking questions. It is an unavoidable requirement for insertion into their new ambience. With tenacity they get support from people who know the city better than they. They make use of every occasion to "try" new experiences, taking the risks they entail. Their success in the city is often in direct relation to the knowledge that they acquire about it. They find work, for example, to the extent that they find out where and from whom to ask for work. They find housing if they gain access to an efficient network of friendly "informers."

Dialogue

Readied by an attitude of humility and curiosity, missionaries can go on to their task of becoming "city persons." The experience of dialogue will be a great help. By its very nature, dialogue implies relationship with another. Partners must be on a basis of parity, in a situation that involves exchange. Humility will assure this basis, and curiosity will spur missionaries on to an exchange of experiences.

Dialogue demands a maximum of openness to others, which means that they must be accepted as they are, and not as the missionary might wish they were. The longer that dialogue continues, the more are relationships reinforced between partners, and there is usually a topical progression from more superficial experiences to the deeper levels of motivations, including religious motivation. We shall take up specifically religious dialogue in the next chapter; here we shall concentrate on generic dialogue.

A prerequisite for this dialogue (and a consequence of it) is acceptance of the idea that the missionary will be changed by the other party. This does not mean, however, that one must accept everything that the dialogue partner gives, without distinguishing between what is valid and what is not. It means, rather, that one must treat the other's convictions with maximum seriousness and, when indicated, alter one's own views accordingly.

The SEDOS Center, in its analysis of the experiences of dialogue made by missionaries, was able to identify three constants of particular interest to urban mission in the Third World.[3] The first constant is presence to the other. Much has been written on this topic, but often it trails off into the abstract. In an urban environment, however, dialogue becomes concrete when one thinks of it as a continuing attitude on one's part, a kind of one-way street leading to the other person. It is possible to be physically present to another person in a city and not feel any relationship with that person. The city, with its predilection for social segmentation, tends to close people up in familiar groups, segregating them from others. Access to apartments is deliberately made difficult; the main door to the building is kept locked and each family defends its privacy even from others in the same building. Missionaries often find themselves caged within the social walls that their hospital, school, or institution erects.

True presence to others, however, is dynamic and always feels an urge to "go out to" the others. To activate this drive, account must be made of two tendencies innate in all of us when we find ourselves in a dialogue situation: we experience a need for complementarity by the humanity present in the other person, and at the same time we experience a need to defend ourselves from the other person. The tendency to open oneself to the other person alternates with the tendency to close oneself off from the other person, in a polarity that explains many aspects of personality. But personality blossoms out precisely in a determinate set of social systems, manifesting roles and values within diverse groups. To live and develop in this context means of necessity to take up multiple relationships of exchange.[4]

The normal content of this presence to others will be one's response to their need to communicate, to be informed, to feel appreciated, supported, accepted.[5] Clearly, an attitude of dialogue will take up much of one's time. To arrive at the openness required, the seriousness and honesty of the other person will have to be probed a number of times.

Besides time, dialogue also demands a good measure of availability, disinterestedness, and tact. In this respect it calls for struggle with the urban "climate" that can induce one to seek protection from unknown persons, to seek refuge in the security and serenity of groups of persons with whom one is familiar, and that makes one think that time spent in long conversations in the true presence of others would be wasteful. But, we must immediately add, this "struggle" is much less severe in Third World cities. In African urban contexts, social networks make long conversations both desirable and natural (see chap. 5). The joie de vivre of a rural atmosphere often holds sway in the city in the protracted gatherings of friends and relatives.

The second constant of dialogue is the need for a better self-definition of the participants. Here again we are on a one-way street, but this time it is directed *toward* us. In a negative vein, it calls for a greater awareness on our part of the extent to which we have not "explained" ourselves to the other person and hence have not reached out to them. We recognize that the other person does not always understand what to us is obvious. In a positive vein, it refers to the evolution of a more acute consciousness of our own identity as "urban persons." And it is from this point that the success of our incarnation in the city begins. We are continually obliged to answer the question: What does it mean to be a "city person" in this particular city? In this way we arrive at a more lucid identification of our "symbolic universes," which furnish us with scales of values that condition our urban life.

The third constant in the attitude of dialogue makes the first two come together in a new relationship with one another. And now we have a two-way street—the appropriate arrangement for dialogue. It will be noticed in fact that, thanks to a better knowledge of one's partner and of oneself, we succeed in explaining ourselves better, with the help of new concepts, even new words. And this is the lesson of language, understood within the context of universal communicability. It is not enough to learn the other person's words; that person's way of putting them together must also be understood. Urban groups have their own jargon and their own understanding of words and phrases in common use by their members. We manage to dialogue with a particular group to the extent that we develop a common language.

Another result of this relationship will be a truer and deeper insertion into the culture of the other person. The fact that, thanks to this relationship, dialogue begins to permeate both the persons involved and their life situation as they live it in the context of the totality of their relationships, means that the two-way traffic (or interaction) will not be limited to an exchange of views on various topics of interest, but will arrive at mutual communication on all aspects of life. In the urban setting, this represents the overcoming of cultural barriers between various social groups (see chap. 5).

And again the urban immigrant-worker can serve as model. Immigrant-workers' socialization in their new environment begins on the basis of dialogue with those who receive them or at least do not shut them out. As noted in chapter 5, they get support from relatives already resident in the city. Relationship smoothes the bumpy road of dialogue. With relatives one is already "friends," and "they know everything." Then too, with them there is less risk of being instrumentalized.

Missionaries can try to visualize city-dwellers as their "relatives." It will help for a good beginning of dialogue with them. And inasmuch as most city residents were once immigrants, dialogue with them will of itself lead to a revision of the missionary's humility and curiosity. When immigrants cannot establish relationships with relatives, they will often approach the urban missionary. The role of the missionary, understood from the rural area of emigration, will give them hope of support in their struggle for admission to the life of the city.

Urban Ministry

The effort to become truly incarnated in the city will make missionaries rise above the urban divisiveness, by multiplying and deepening their stable relationships with residents. If the attitudes discussed just above are necessary for entrance on the appropriate wave of values, the concrete assumption of roles in various groups will integrate missionaries into the urban system. The conceptual framework proposed in chapter 2 will serve here to bring to light the concrete implications of their practical incarnation in the city via the specific roles that they take up there.

In this regard, the essential thing is the assumption of a maximum of roles. As we saw in chapter 2, roles channel and shape one's relationships with other residents, giving those relationships a certain stability and consistency. Every role binds one in a relationship of reciprocity with at least one other person.

Most roles are associated with a particular social group. Taking in another direction the four questions of chapter 2, missionaries can ask themselves the following: In this particular city, what are the social groups that we as missionaries can be members of? What roles can we take up within them? What values will encourage us to enter into these groups and roles? What new knowledge of the urban social system will all this give us?

The last two questions link up again with the theme of urban missionary attitudes, helping one to deepen ever more their practical implications and supporting one's ongoing efforts to become a "person of the city," a "local." This theme has already been treated; here we want to develop the implications of the more concrete and more immediate theme of groups and roles.

A preliminary distinction must be made. There will be ecclesial groups ready to welcome missionaries into the city. It would be easy to give in to the temptation to remain absorbed in them. And so missionaries must remind themselves again and again that, although incarnation can begin in such groups and roles—especially if they have achieved an advanced degree of indigenization—it must not be allowed to become an end in itself. The more fundamental and missionary tension generated by the thrust of incarnation will be toward the groups and roles not yet, or not yet sufficiently reached by the gospel.

In cities where the process of city planning has a certain consistency, the answer to the first question might be found already inscribed in programs of urban development. But it must be given expression in the light of an organic pastoral ministry. The multiple relationships required and the diverse roles that will express it will never fall within the range of what an individual missionary can achieve. The sum total of missionaries—or better, of Christians—will have to divide these roles among themselves via a plan of organic pastoral ministry for the entire city. Thus all missionaries, while developing their own role, will know that other roles are being filled by colleagues and that their own efforts, thanks to the fact that they are "being local church" together with these colleagues, will eventually be part of an urban mission undertaking that has a total impact on the city.

A good point of departure for formulating an organic pastoral ministry of this nature will be reflection on the groups and roles that may serve as entry points to city life, via a study of urban development plans, for such plans will offer the best framework for formulating urban mission projects. In them can be discovered not only the initiatives of various groups for correcting the ills of the city but also indications of groups that are at the root of those ills, or that carry the heaviest burden resulting from them.

Solidarity for Service

Christian commitment in Third World cities has often gone in this direction—namely, solidarity that expresses itself in service to others. The most representative example is perhaps that of Hong Kong. Under extraordinary demographic pressure, the whole city, swollen by the thousands of refugees from mainland China who had fled there in 1958, did the best it could to accommodate them in the little space available and according to the capacities of existing urban services.

Hong Kong created industries to increase employment, using the resources peculiar to its port siting and the industriousness of a huge work force. Its economic planning resulted in a brilliant solution of the problem of unemployment, transforming Hong Kong into a commercial and industrial export center.

Its urban planning aims at the goal of housing for all within a few years— no easy project on a total surface of 400 square miles, largely mountainous and lacking water, on which a population of 4 million has descended. Problems involving human services remained unsolved and it was here that the Christian community stepped in, investing enormous funds and personnel in hospitals, schools, and social-assistance agencies.

For Hong Kong missionaries, answers to the first two questions became clearer: it sufficed to take up roles in groups that the local church had already established. And thus missionaries today are at work largely in the three sectors of medical, educational, and social welfare services.

Before delineating the major lines that seem to orient these three sectors, we should reflect on the missionary attitude that sustains them. It is the attitude of *diakonia*—service in solidarity. In supporting the individual groups that organize them and the roles that carry them forward, this attitude remains intact. Drawing its inspiration from the love of Christ, it sustains the missionaries who spend themselves for those most in need, sowing comfort and hope.

In the perspective of the incarnation, the roles and relationships developed by missionaries will not get far unless motivated by this attitude. But even this will not accomplish much unless it is integrated into the attitude of active solidarity. The new horizons that the city opens to individual sectors clearly show it. It is not a matter of looking for "excuses" to find an opening in a city that is not yet Christian, of looking for available roles in order to have a base for properly missionary roles. This would not be honest, because it would mean twisting such roles to one's own ends, which are often extraneous as such to the urban population. It is, rather, a question of incarnating oneself not simply in the available space (roles) but in the same drive to build a more human city. To be in the city means to be involved in building the city.

Building the city is an undertaking that never ends. Urban services demonstrate it. Take, for example, the problem of hygiene and health. This is something that must be confronted daily, otherwise there will be a proliferation of diseases, with disastrous consequences for a concentrated population. Missionaries have been among the pioneers in this field. But local authorities have long tended to take over citywide responsibility. It is the missionary's place to support them, adhering to the lines of their health planning, in the groups and roles projected by them. The latest ideas developed in this field have come from missionaries at work in the medical, educational, and social-assistance spheres.

Medical Roles: Services in urban hospitals and clinics summon mission workers to keep looking for new goals. It seems that the most important goals come together in the necessity for missionaries to acquaint themselves with the rural ambience from which so many patients come. Health problems are often rooted in the substandard health conditions of village settings. This sets before missionaries a second objective: to learn how to pass beyond medical institutions to strengthen the work of educators. And with this we arrive at a third perspective, which opens up the possibility of collaboration with other disciplines and professions, beginning with education. The final result could be the discovery of new formulas for expressing this service of love. Finally, as for other sectors of urban life, missionaries must never lose sight of the problem of the levels of efficiency. Not everything considered indispensable in a Western clinic would be so in a city such as Calcutta.

Christians must keep on posing certain embarrassing questions, looking beyond the walls of mission hospitals. How many diseases could be eliminated by water purification systems? Or by a campaign for more reasonable prices for agricultural products? Or by health instruction in mission schools, at work places, in private meetings? Or by the participation of local communities in this field of preventive medicine?

In a report to SEDOS, Sister Jane Gates, then superior general of the Medical Missionary Sisters, synthesized urban medical services in these terms: Most of the Sisters run large hospitals located in large cities but they have been expanding their work in other institutions with specific work programs. In Delhi, for instance, there is a program that offers medical services to nine surrounding villages, organized in collaboration with the Don Bosco Technical School, which for its part works with the social studies school of the Islamic University of Jamia. In Patna, Bihar, on the river Ganges, the hospital is responsible for a program of regulation and eradication of tuberculosis in Maner, an area of 80,000 inhabitants dispersed in eighty-eight villages. The new challenge lies in the fact that the hospital as an institution can no longer exist in a vacuum. It must reach out to the population around it, to ascertain its level of health—or of sickness—and then decide how to respond better to the needs. . . . The challenge lies in "how" to proceed. It is immediately obvious that a greater diversification of expertise will be needed than that adequate for a traditional hospital concentrating on the health problems typical of the given area. Health care services today must concern themselves with the whole person—not only with physical illness.[6]

In short, medical roles today orient one toward the urban "natural areas" rather than toward the hospital as a base of services, and the hospital must concern itself not only with the cure of disease but also with its prevention. And this already foresees the collaboration of others not working directly in health services.

Educational Services: Urban educational services are oriented along three projectories: education that continues through the whole of life, is attuned to the needs of the local community, and is committed to social justice. The city, with its manifold needs, opens new horizons for the further development of the already considerable services that missionaries are now offering in their schools—services that result from their educational initiatives.

V. Gottwald of the De La Salle Brothers has observed that there is need to concentrate the Brothers' resources in order to offer more diversified services in urban centers and particularly in their peripheral and emarginated zones: the slums and shantytowns. An honest look at the present distribution of educational undertakings by religious institutes in the major cities in Asia, Latin America, and Africa would reveal that this marginated and "restrained" population has simply been shunted aside.[7] Gottwald then lists the types of educational services in effect: centers for literacy, primary and secondary schools, social centers for community education, residences for students, and youth centers for extracurricular activities.

Of interest here is the reading of the signs of the times as proposed by Father Arrupe, Superior General of the Jesuits. Writing of the 1971 Synod of Bishops, he points out that by scrutinizing them and trying to decipher the meaning of history, participating bishops were, in fact, concerned with God's plans for the salvation of our world. Perceiving the serious injustice that throws around the world of humankind a net of domination, of opposition and abuses that suffocate freedom, and sensing a new awareness that sparks persons to liberate themselves and take charge of their own destiny, the bishops believe that action for justice and participation in the transformation of the world is a constitutive element of the proclamation of the gospel—in other words, of the mission of the church in the redemption of humankind and its liberation from every situation of oppression.[8]

Father Arrupe goes on to draw consequences from this for educational work. Christians cannot separate the proclamation of the Word of God from action for justice and liberation from oppression, he says. Education to justice has become one of the major preoccupations of the church, and its first educational objective must be that of forming "persons for others." Two lines must be followed. The first leads to a deepening of the way of conceiving justice, as this is clarified in the light of the gospel and of the signs of the times. The other promotes a greater understanding of the demands of the person to be educated, as well as the type of person the educator needs to become if he or she intends to serve the evangelical ideal of justice.

Developing this concept of the person for others, Father Arrupe suggests the traits that would typify such a person. Thanks to consciousness, intelligence, and other faculties, this human being would have a centeredness—but a centeredness called to reach out beyond itself to others, in love. Persons who live merely for their own interests not only bring nothing to others but, what is worse, tend to accumulate knowledge, power, and wealth in a way that inevitably deprives others weaker than they of their just share. It is a tragedy, for, living this way, egoists dehumanize themselves. How does one get out of this blind alley, he asks. Is it not suicide to try to live a life of love and justice in a climate of egoism and injustice? Or does it not at least run the risk of setting out on an undertaking bound to end in futility? We all want to be good for others, he points out, and we would be so in a good world. The challenge is to go out to others in an evil world, where the egoism of others and the egoism built into the underlying processes of society assault us all and threaten to annihilate us.[9]

This is exactly what we find in the Third World city. The missionary response to it cannot be other than that of Saint Paul: "Do not be overcome by evil, but overcome evil with good" (Rom. 12:21). The educators who want to be involved in forming "persons for others" will do what they can to have them aim at a simpler lifestyle, at not deriving profit from unjust situations, at becoming agents of change with a view to greater social justice. This will mean abandoning certain time-honored practices.

An example along these lines was singled out in a circular issued by the International Bureau of Education (Geneva). Where educational systems reinforce the dehumanization of the unemployed, it becomes necessary to stimulate and support a radical critique. This could take the form of championing models of a de-institutionalized, or humanized, type of education, leading to refusal to participate in existing systems as long as they remain unchanged. In such situations voluntary organizations, including the churches, could function as catalysts for the community. For participation in reform of the system, they would unite those who are more closely attuned to the situation: political authorities, educators, researchers, union officials, employers, and community groups.[10]

It is evident that the Third World offers an abundance of opportunities for involvement for education for justice. Work in the schools—whether mission schools or other schools—must remain a high-priority service in the social and human construction of the city. The important thing is to know how to perceive the new exigencies of urban life in order to review ceaselessly one's own orientations. The concept of social justice offers the guiding criterion for such revision.

Social-Assistance Roles: The social-assistance sector of the missionary urban commitment extends in practice to all mission undertakings that are not medical or educational. It is, accordingly, very heterogeneous, covering the entire gamut of traditional works of charity (in orphanages, homes for the elderly, the care of the disabled and handicapped) as well as more modern work in vocational training centers, agrarian cooperatives, credit unions, rehabilitation centers for drug addicts, centers involved in women's liberation, and the like.

It should be noted that the spatial concentration of the city makes all this possible. In fact the most highly specialized services cannot be put to use outside the urban context. A religious Sister who is a specialist in the care of spastics can hardly expect to employ her expertise fully in a village: in all likelihood, there would not be that many spastics there, and the need for institutionalized care would be less obvious, because rural family groupings take greater interest in their disadvantaged members.

There is no need here to go into the various types of social-assistance services. We shall only emphasize a point made above: mission work should not be undertaken exclusively in projects directed by church organizations. Today—and this applies also to medical and educational services—many missionaries take up roles in social-assistance agencies run by governmental or other public bodies. In terms of the incarnational purposes of urban mission, results are often the same, or even better.

Among the various categories of social-assistance work, the area of family services merits special attention. The city frequently confronts one with instances where a husband has left his wife and children behind in their village, or a young couple has married without family approval, or a married man is living with a "second" wife. Relatives are almost always too distant to be able to offer financial, physical, moral, and psychological help when crises arise. In this context the ministry of family counseling demands a good knowledge of the customs of the people involved. The church, which has always defended and upheld the family, is called on to provide such a ministry.

Another form of social assistance that has attracted the special concern of urban missionaries in recent years is community development (see chap. 6), which has a prominent place in the planning of urban development. This is a role that missionaries take up in a communitarian effort begun by others, or in which missionaries act as catalysts of the dynamic forces of neighborhoods or other city subdivisions, by "helping them to help themselves."

Solidarity for Conscientization

There is no doubt that the service to others performed in medical, educational, and social-assistance roles puts one on the path of the incarnation. But that is not enough. This service must extend beyond the confines of these spheres of service, to void the danger of missionaries' withholding themselves from broader urban processes and creating "a city within the city." The full weight of missionary involvement must be thrown up against the divisive poles that are ever present in the social dynamism of the city.

Both within and beyond ecclesial groups, mission workers must take on the work of conscientization, keeping in mind the ancient Chinese adage given wider currency in recent years by the cooperative movement of Antigonish, Nova Scotia: "If you give a hungry man a fish, he will be hungry again the next day; but if you teach him how to be a fisherman, he'll not hunger again."

The missionary endeavor must be to go beyond the limits of services that operate at the level of symptoms, in order to penetrate to the level of the processes that are at the roots of symptoms. This is the more compelling aspect of education to justice!

According to the ecumenical consultation on urban mission held in Kyoto in August 1970, Christians must question ministry that is devoted exclusively to social service. Emphasis should be given to ministry that seeks to help urban groups and urban communities to organize themselves for action. A paternalistic approach in this must be avoided; it should be done in such a way that the urban groups become conscious of the oppression they are subjected to and become capable of expressing their challenge to the power structures in place. In this way Christian mission will come closer to being participation: it will mean helping the people to take a step forward, helping the poor to become their own advocates. This approach will also bring on a creative conflict, because it must reject sugar-coated solutions that do not remove the real causes of oppression."

Conscientization makes missionaries renounce the attempt and the temptation to put things in order by themselves. It leads them to prefer the longer path of letting others do things their own way. And its validity can be seen too in the fact that it permits others to shoulder their own responsibilities, not trusting solely in missionaries but in themselves and their own means. This is the thrust of education for justice and liberation that goes beyond the limitations of the school and the educational work mentioned earlier. Again, this is the path of the incarnation.

Urban development planning can certainly furnish insights for the work of conscientization, by making missionaries aware of the groups that are at the origin of the processes that give shape to the city. Two of these groups often in alliance with each other belong to the economic and the political spheres (see chap. 4). Another group that assumes major importance in the Third World is that of the "social communicators," who of necessity choose the city for their base of operations.

Economic groups: Among economic groups, we single out the labor unions; in Western cities they have accomplished much for workers, but in Asian, Latin American, and African cities they still have a long way to go.

The conscientization of groups of workers will consequently merit greater efforts on the part of urban mission. It could begin by giving more encouragement to the few missionaries who are already active in this sphere. Finding themselves side by side with groups of diverse or even hostile inspiration need not discourage missionaries. They have valuable directives in this matter from *Pacem in Terris* and *Octogesima Adveniens*: distinctions can be made between ideologies and practical initiatives.

In ecumenical circles in Geneva, urban mission is often equated with industrial mission. The city is viewed as the base of the major industries that dominate worldwide economic processes. The Third World city also belongs in this framework because it, too, is often the base of large multinational corporations that condition the local economy (see chap. 4). In his 1973 annual report, H. Daniel, from India, then secretary of Urban and Industrial Mission, of the World Council of Churches, touched on urban mission with regard to the economic sphere. In its contacts with approximately five hundred local projects in sixty countries, the Urban and Industrial Mission found that concrete approaches were different, but fell into certain generic categories, including educational concerns for the promotion of better industrial relations. This includes work with management and union groups, worker training programs, response to other training needs within factories and industrial installations, and concern for ways of improving the lot of those who are weaker—the powerless, the voiceless. This entails organizing communities and groups to confront their own needs and resolve their own problems with the appropriate means.[12]

In this area there is no lack of new ideas and new initiatives, especially in the search for an answer to the problem of unemployment. In the list of projects sponsored by CIDSE, there are such headings as credit union, workshops, small businesses, energy sources, professional training, transportation, and technical assistance. And what is always stressed is the aim of "helping others to help themselves."

The important thing is to observe and to encourage cooperation among Christians of all churches in the priority assigned to working on the underlying processes—not merely on their symptoms—that affect the economically disadvantaged. Such cooperation will reveal how important the economic sector is for urban mission. Economic processes most often have their propulsive centers in cities. In the final analysis, action taken on them—in the city—will be the most effective.

Political Groups: The economic sphere has long been conditioned by politics. In *Octogesima Adveniens* Pope Paul VI stated:

Economic processes—an essential part of contemporary life—can be a source of fraternity and a sign of divine providence if they serve the needs of humanity. They provide occasions for concrete exchanges among individuals, for the recognition of rights, for the recognition of services rendered, for the affirmation of dignity in work. Although economics is often the terrain of confrontation and domination, it can inaugurate dialogue and favor cooperation. But if it assumes an exaggerated importance, there is a risk that it will captivate human energies and human freedom. This explains the necessary passage from economics to politics. . . .

Everyone is aware that in the social and economic spheres . . . ultimate decisions pertain to political power. . . . To take politics seriously means to affirm the duty of humankind, and every individual human being, to acknowledge concrete reality and the freedom of choice offered to work jointly for the good of the city. Politics is a necessary way—though not the only one—for Christians to live a Christian commitment.[13]

The goal will be a wider participation in decision-making, making it possible for all to be informed, to express themselves, and to commit themselves in a shared sense of responsibility. This is the all-important road of responsibility recommended by urban planning (see chap. 6). Conscientization aims at precisely this. And for this reason it is often called politicization or animation, or simply participation. These are diverse nuances of the same fundamental drive to liberate others from the obstacles of ignorance, pressure, and inertia, to "help them to help themselves" by activating their own potentialities and responsibilities.

If for the urban poor conscientization means guidance to an awareness of their own political weight and of the portion of the political power that is rightfully theirs, for the rich it means guidance to make them better conscious of the harmful consequences to the common good (and hence also to their own good) of the processes now going on, which favor them in the short run. For political authorities it means heightened awareness of the danger of the abuse—even if unintentional—of political power when it favors a distorted and unjust, because oppressive and divisive, status quo.

There remains a basic question implicit in the analysis of political processes detailed in chapter 4: From what angle should missionaries seek a presence in the roles of urban power? With those in power or with those in opposition to them? The answer will depend not only on the objective conditions in which a given city finds itself, but also on the subjective dispositions of the individual who raises the question. The gospel defers an answer to conscience because it refuses to separate the good from the evil in the wheat field sown with tares that is the city. All we can do here is spell out the basic requirements of political incarnation, first in the established order and then in an opposition stance.

Taking up a point made in the discussion on culture (see chap. 5), it must be said that attitudes depend to some extent on the position that individuals have in the political "pecking order" or outside it. From these attitudes flow the ideologies that justify or criticize the hierarchies of power in place, in a particular urban situation. History shows that the Christian church is perfectly capable of doing either the one or the other. It has at times developed an integrist function, justifying the existent political and economic order. But it has also exercised a critical function, exhorting the beneficiaries of an existent order to opt for a superior order, and igniting in the hearts of the weak and the poor a sense of their own dignity and their own rights.

To say that all persons who have power are corrupt is an oversimplification. There are among them some who use their power to "direct" others, not to dominate them. The missionary's task in their regard will be to augment their influence. In this vision, to "direct" is not the same thing as to "position" every citizen in an ideal city, in an integrist vision, but to recognize all citizens as important persons, awakening them to a higher level of awareness and freedom.

This reawakening will always be conditioned by the given historical urban context. But it must not be "systematized" into an ideology. If it is, the search for awareness and freedom comes to an end. The extent to which missionaries hold themselves open to the diversity of options will be the measure of the quality of their incarnation in roles of political power. Such an openness will also make allowance for the conflicts between individuals and the various exigencies of urban planning (described in chap. 6).

Power is necessary to ensure the common good of the city. But it is not necessary that those who hold it at a given moment keep it forever. On the contrary, an essential condition of missionary incarnation in political-power roles is that missionaries consider such incarnation as temporary. Equally important for those who are already exercising a role in political power is that they remain critical of their own use of power. The best judges of this will be citizens, especially those among them who have ever been, in one way or another, victims of the abuse of power.

Another path of conscientization is the taking up of roles in contestation. This brings us to the question of violence. The gospel rejects the use of violence.[14] The Lord bases his appeal on the conscience and freedom of individual persons. The role of the urban guerrilla is not an acceptable one for the missionary's political incarnation in the city. The fact that in the past violence was sometimes used in "evangelization" cannot serve as a precedent; it must be condemned absolutely.

But the question of the use of nonviolent force remains. From the viewpoint of values, two currents appear in contemporary thinking within the church. The political theology being developed in Germany insists that the Christian should not and must not reject a critical role vis-à-vis the established order or a denunciatory role vis-à-vis relationships of force that stifle individual freedoms. A second current, coming from Latin American liberation theology, accepts this thesis and adds another to it: revolution—and hence subversion of the established order—can be considered a legitimate vehicle of values, even evangelical values.

From the viewpoint of the roles already assumed by committed Christians in this sector—often called "leftist"—it is said that only by embracing the cause of an oppressed class can the gospel be proclaimed. Everything else, in consequence, is viewed as an aspect of the struggle between a dominant class and an oppressed class—the struggle that characterizes, in the Marxist vision, the whole of human society. Leftist Christians go so far as to contest the social doctrine of the church inasmuch as it is an ideology that can be used to reinforce the status quo.

Without siding with either of these positions, one can nonetheless admit that there is always a certain internal logic in political processes that expose some enthusiasts to the temptation of using force (as also ideas and values) to impose the established order. This is the cultural violence of power. To sacrifice human lives and ideas is part of the inner logic of domination, even when the ideas and values are "borrowed" from the gospel.

All in all, it must be said that missionaries cannot absolutely abandon to others the roles of power. It would be the privatization of Christianity. Private life would become their comfortable niche, assigned by the holders of power, to neutralize Christian action. When all is said and done, Christianity is of interest to the holders of power to the extent to which they obtain support from it. When that is not the case, they try to contain it—in the private sphere. This must be pointed out because the charismatic movement, which has already spread to Third World cities, could be tempted to make urban mission something exclusively "private." With the excuse of making their lives "spiritual," Christians would leave the door open for the political processes that justify the existent economic order.

Cultural Groups: On the theme of power, those in control of social communications merit special attention. Although their power is more subtle than political power, it is sometimes more effective: "The media of social communication, by their very nature, constitute a new power. . . and have a grave responsibility in relation to the veracity of the information they diffuse, in relation to the needs and occasions that they give rise to, and to the values that they support," states *Octogesima Adveniens.*[15] The persons who exercise this power are in the cities. The urban missionary will have to establish relationships with them.

The alliance of economic and political powers is effectively contested by cultural processes, which question their legitimacy (see chap. 4). At stake is the process of the formation of public opinion. This is often what defines, in pragmatic and operative terms, the "symbolic universes" that constitute the culture and the cultures of the cities. As such it becomes a powerful force, a true sign of our times, because it creates a reaction, shared by many, to contemporary events and situations. If it is a characteristic of our times, it is so in a special way in today's cities. The reaction is bound up with the rapid expansion and development of the social communication media, with the movement for mass education, with a growing social and democratic consciousness, and with a greater awareness of the right to information—all of which are more discernible in the urban environment.

The two decisive factors in the formation of real public opinion are an information system that effectively circulates knowledge of facts, and the values, with their symbolic universes, that condition the perception of the reality of one's own historical situation. There can be no doubt that the mass media are among the most effective means for informing and forming public opinion. In fact—and this underlines anew the negative convergences of urban processes—the mass media, due to the concentrations that the city makes possible, are often controlled by economic and political interests, and the information they diffuse is truncated, filtered, and slanted, if not simply falsified.

The incarnation of missionaries in the groups that give shape to this sector of urban life is, consequently, of capital importance for urban "life together." The larger agencies and major organs of information are the ones that form public opinion. When the economic and political motivations of small groups manage to direct their services to *all* groups and the *whole* city, affiliation with them becomes even more important, albeit more difficult. Here it is better to do something small than resign oneself to doing nothing at all. Convinced that complete and impartial information is an essential—if not the only—element of public education, and also a necessary condition for mission, missionaries, within the limits imposed on them, must do what they can to see that those who receive information are protected from prejudice.

Difficulties can also come from those who are part of this sector. The role of a social communicator is played out under the triple tyranny of the sensationalism, general interest, and originality of the news they are expected to communicate. Once these obstacles are overcome, a communicator must be sincere and open, and willing to accept criticism.[16]

Participation

The import of urban mission, in its generic, incarnational makeup, can be summed up in the attitudes of humility, curiosity, and dialogue, in the roles of health services, education, and social assistance, and in participation in groups for conscientization. As a whole these elements will guide the mission way progressively from intellectual acceptance of the city, at the level of knowledge, to its vital acceptance, at the level of commitment—from knowledge of the city to urban participation.

This participation has its base in the ecclesial groups and roles already in situ, but it does not give all its energy to them. Participation implies a turning toward other groups as well, inviting the individual missionary to take up roles of active service and conscientization with them.

The communitarian aspect of this participation will work itself out in an organic plan of urban pastoral and missionary ministry that will bind together the various groupings and roles proposed for Christians, and align them with the city's planning for development.

The individual aspect—to be worked out by each missionary—will find expression in the expertise that their assumption of diverse roles will demand. Everyone realizes that in order to perform the roles we have been discussing, the missionary must also become a professional. Medical missionary Sisters cannot act in that capacity without a background in medical studies. Missionary educators cannot teach without the certification that studies in pedagogy lead to. Professional expertise is a necessary—if by itself incomplete—part of what is required for the assumption of urban roles by Christian missionaries.

We must, however, make reference again to the admonition in the early part of this chapter: to participate does not mean to dominate or to impose; incarnation does not mean to put oneself at the center of the stage. Expertise must not be allowed to become a new form of power.

Although incarnation does not let Christians remain at the level of attitudes but urges them on to concrete commitment in active services and the work of conscientization for city residents, it does so in respect to the particular conditions of the given city. Among them the first thing that a missionary must discover—in order to honor it—is its urban planning, that is, the modality of growth that the city wants to give itself. Incarnation, like solidarity, will not try to start from zero, ignoring this effort at future planning; it invites one to enter into those plans—to participate.

What better way to sum up this chapter than with the words of the spiritual pastor of a major Third World city:

> Radicating ourselves in the Word of God and in the life of the church, we try to show that we shall realize the desire of Christ only by taking up his work and participating in it where it is more difficult, not sidestepping but committing ourselves to every task that comes to light from a given social situation and that leads us to bring Christ to life there. No one should be considered excluded from participation in human and ecclesial life. There the individual will find the meaning of life and the perpetual source of renewal and joy. Christians of today want total participation. If participation effectively expresses the freedom of the offspring of God and at the same time makes cohabitation on this earth more agreeable, it becomes a necessity for us to make of it our ideal . . . and to have the strength to commit ourselves to humankind and its great ideals, offering our collaboration at all levels and committing to it all our potentialities.[17]

These are the words of Cardinal Arns, archbishop of São Paulo, Brazil. They recapitulate the various modalities of urban incarnation in the particular situation of his great city, where the overwhelming majority of residents claim to be Christians. But, as we shall hear from Cardinal Arns in the following chapter, urban mission does not stop here. From the generic ministry of participation it is called to progress to the specific ministry of proclamation.

The vision of urban mission that would result from the ever fuller activation of the incarnational impulse of God's plans described in this chapter would be that of a multitude of Christians, all in their own work places in the great worksite of the social construction of the Third World city.

It is a thought-provoking vision: all Christians—not simply the "professional" missionaries—have a place in it. Nor is it merely a place of *presence,* assured by their attitudes of humility, curiosity, and dialogue; it is above all else a place of *responsibility,* demanded by the roles that everyone is called to develop within the multiplicity of groups that together form the urban social system.

It is a vision of solidarity with each "segment" of the city and with its "whole." The incarnational thrust does not select this or that aspect, more or less strategic, of the city, but takes in the whole city—the collectivity and the individual components—just as the Lord has taken up our humanity, in its totality and in each one of us.

It is a beautiful vision but, as we have noted, one not yet complete. The Lord assumed human reality in order to save it, to liberate it from its sinful component, which he did not assume.

We must therefore look into the implications of the actualization of the redemptive aspect of the plan of God for the city via the communication of salvation.

9

EVANGELIZATION
AS SPECIFIC MISSION

The triumphant moment for mission comes when an individual discovers or rediscovers Jesus Christ. This is the moment of evangelization. It is mandated by the very nature of the proclamation that we shall now examine in its urban modalities.

If the theological concept of incarnation leads missionaries to blend with the masses, in order to share with them the struggle for a more human city, the theological concept of evangelization guides missionaries to distinguish themselves from the masses, in order to take up their specific task in the process of urban liberation and reconciliation.

Incarnation remains the generic, essential aspect of mission. But it is not sufficient of itself, because there remains its specific aspect, no less necessary, the dynamic process of "teaching" the individual the "Jesus event." With all persons missionaries share the expectations and efforts for a city more worthy of all, but they also bring the good news of salvation already effected and offered by God for the city, in Christ.

The Process of Evangelization

Pope Paul VI defined evangelization as

A complex process, composed of multiple elements: the renewal of humankind, testimony, explicit proclamation, heartfelt adherence, entrance into the community, initiatives of discipleship, the gathering and interpretation of signs, . . . elements that are complementary and mutually enriching. All these elements must be paid attention to, and each one of them integrated with the others.[1]

Giving priority to the element of testimony—that is, witness—and examining it within the framework of the relationship between two persons is the intent of this chapter. The working definition of evangelization will therefore be formulated in terms of a process of interaction between one person committed to Christ and another person who does not know him, or does not know him well enough. When this second person, thanks to the relationship between them, learns that the first person "has a relationship with Christ," the process of interaction lays bare its evangelical power-content: it leads to the discovery, or rediscovery, of Christ. It is distinguished from other relationships precisely by this, that it leads to Christ.

From another perspective, this can be seen as an angular relationship. Christ is the end-point of the angle, the Christian is the center-point, and the non-Christian is the other end-point. By faith, Christ and the Christian are "in relationship." By incarnation, the Christian and the non-Christian are also "in relationship." At the moment when the non-Christian becomes aware, thanks to the familiarity nurtured by interaction, that the Christian is in relationship with Christ, evangelization takes place.

We must immediately add a clarification: evangelization is *not* conversion. The non-Christian is not yet committed to Christ. Furthermore, conversion does not depend on the Christian, but on Christ. Only he can call someone to the faith; only he can offer this gift. And the non-Christian can refuse it. But when the non-Christian accepts it, the angle becomes a triangle: the new Christian enters into a direct "relationship of faith" with Christ, the apex of the triangle.

If the essence of evangelization can be envisioned in a triangular relationship, its connection with the incarnational impetus of urban mission (treated in the preceding chapter) is immediately clarified further. To become incarnate means to establish relationships with others. But these relationships are the "genus," the "prime matter," from which the "species" of evangelization is elicited. Simple relationships become faith relationships. When Christians introduce into the relationships that they already have with others—thanks to their roles in society—the liberative, redemptive, and salvific impetus that derives from their faith relationship with Christ the Liberator, Redeemer, and Savior, at that moment they begin to evangelize.

This is universally valid, and it is of particular interest for the Third World city. Relationships abound in the city. Opportunities for Christians to enter into relationships are everywhere. And the city's need for a liberative "gust of fresh air" is acute. There are myriads of persons who have the time, the wish, and the need to "enter into relationships" with others, because of unemployment, oppression, and margination. The opportunities for incarnation are so evident as to constitute an unmistakable sign of the urgency of the need for evangelization.

Urban mission, accordingly, will consist in establishing relationships where they did not exist before (generic mission) and in transforming already existent relationships into relationships of evangelization (specific mission). Every relationship established by Christians with other city-dwellers will thus have the potential to become a relationship of evangelization.

The World Council of Churches concretizes this quintessentially Christian thrust in its motto "To confess Christ today." In the preparatory documents for the fifth assembly of the World Council of Churches, in Nairobi, November 1975, the concept of relationship is emphasized. Throughout the whole world, declared assembly delegates, Christians are learning that they cannot and should not live in isolation. Christian individuals, groups, and congregations are discovering more and more that they have a mission to implement toward the poor of the city slums, the oppressed in racist societies, and those exploited in factories and on farmlands; and also toward the unconcerned—the bored and the smug—in rich countries. And in all the places where Christians are rousing themselves to help their fellow humans, they find themselves at the side of persons of other faiths, Marxists, humanists, nationalists, philanthropists. What distinguishes Christians from their allies and friends—and even their enemies—is certainly not what they *do* in a given situation. What distinguishes them is that they *confess Christ*.[2]

But there is an enormous obstacle blocking the work of evangelization: not all who call themselves Christians truly "confess Christ." Not all "Christians" let the light of Christ pass through them in their relationships with others, even though they are called to do so in a summons issued by Pope Paul VI, in which he seems to have had in mind the situation of the cities of the Third World:

> Today more than ever before, the Word of God cannot be proclaimed and heard unless it is accompanied by the witness to the power of the Holy Spirit that is at work in the deeds that Christians perform in the service of their fellow humans, especially where their life and their future are at stake. . . . In concrete situations, and taking into account the variety of ways in which individuals are in solidarity with others, a legitimate variety of possible options must be acknowledged. One and the same Christian faith can lead to diverse commitments. The church invites all Christians to the twofold task of animation and innovation in the creation and adaptation of structures to provide for the real needs of today.[3]

This is a "summons" because the urgency of urban evangelization does not derive only from the multitudinous new opportunities that the city offers us, nor only from the enrichment that specific mission contribution can make in the search for answers to its needs, but also, and most of all, from the underlying impulse of the divine plan of salvation.

Salvation must penetrate the city precisely by being "incarnated" in the multiplicity of roles that city life involves. This will take place through the mediation of the Christians who live there. The "methodology" of this mediation is both communitarian and personal.

The close contact that the urban context facilitates with persons of other religions and other ideologies obliges Christians to ask themselves how this salvation will pass through them to the others. In the light of Vatican II, the answer is that all humans who find salvation do so by the power of Christ, even if without a formal adherence to him. But then there arises a practical and bewildering question that threatens to erode the evangelical motivation of many Christians: If this is so, is the explicit proclamation of the gospel still necessary?

In his address on Asia at the 1974 Synod of Bishops, Cardinal Cordeiro stressed the affirmative nature of the answer to this question:

> Although Christians have in the past studied and discovered values in the major religions of Asia, the church has never experienced this need more than it does today. . . . All the [episcopal] conferences affirm that neither the positive elements in these major religions, nor the truth contained in them, nor the place that they occupy in the plan of salvation diminishes in any way the necessity and obligation of preaching Christ.[4]

The same synod, in a text approved by a wide majority, amplified this response, relating it to the ideologies of today:

> Persons attain salvation to the extent that, even unconsciously, they come to be moved by the spirit of Christ and participate in his fullness. . . . Although we must continue to hold that the Holy Spirit gives to everyone the possibility of being incorporated into the paschal mystery in a way that is known only by the Lord, it differs greatly from the way of those who in the worship of Christ see the Father (cf. Jn. 14:9), in the words of Christ comprehend the goodness and humanity of the divine Savior, and in the institutions founded by him enjoy the abundance of his grace. It is especially in the crucified and risen Christ—in whose power evangelization takes place—that the Father is glorified, his salvific plan is fully manifested, the sacrifice acceptable to him is offered up, and the image of the new person, to which we are called, is shown.[5]

Must we not see the impulse of the plan of salvation in the fact that the city of the Third World makes us realize with greater incisiveness the personal need of all for salvation (see chap. 4)? And must we not see it also in the fact that the Third World city opens up the possibility of other "symbolic universes" that can reveal the meaning of this salvation? Is not this convergence a call for liberation from the slavery of ignorance and error? The desire for a fuller life? City residents will remain in their slavery and in their incomplete life until it is given to them to know the true name of him who first calls them by name. They must come to know him in whose name they are to be saved.

We should now take a closer look at how the obstacle mentioned earlier can be surmounted—the fact that not all Christians in fact accept the duty of "confessing Christ." What seems needed is to develop the three attitudes of faith, dialogue, and openness to others. Urban missionaries will often be called on to strengthen these attitudes in themselves and in all Christians.

Maturation of the Urban Christian

Living the Faith

The attitude of faith must be deepened; Christians must seek to be always more conscious of their relationship with Christ. This is a sine qua non for the work of evangelization, because it assures communication between Christ and the evangelizer. Exposing themselves, by faith, to the light of Christ, missionaries will be flooded with it and, by that very fact, will become capable of illuminating others. Like Moses, who came down from the mountain with his face radiant after having conversed with the Lord, this exposure will equip them for the work of evangelization.

Urban missionaries must know how to find the time for retreat from the city in order to renew themselves, their energies, and their motivation for their work in it. The attitude of faith will carry them on to contemplation, to the experience of God. Such times of retreat are moments of pure waiting and searching for him. At the opportune moment—which can never be calculated in advance or planned—God will come into their solitude, thus breaking his own silence. The mountain will become Tabor; the desert will become the place of covenant. The moments will be brief and probably rare, but they will suffice to illuminate the remainder of one's life with their refulgent light.

The four evangelists dwell on analogous moments in the life of Jesus, who prayed in the desert before his active ministry, prayed through the night, when he could hardly extricate himself from the crowds. The city will offer many crowds and much to be done. But missionaries must not let this keep them from constantly reinforcing their relationship with Him who sends them to the city. Only this contemplative experience, which is the experience of God, can keep mission's true visage intact. And the evangelists speak more often about faith than about charity. Evidently there cannot be authentic love of God without experience of God, and the only access to it is an attitude of faith.

In such moments of light missionaries will understand better the impulse and the details of God's plans for their particular city. If they bring to the desert and the mountain of their contemplative prayer the experiences "passed" to them through the network of their new urban relationships, they will see those experiences in a new light. This will be the moment for discerning deepest meanings, and missionaries will be enabled to put those meanings together as so many elements in the mosaic of God's plans. The meaning and import of mission will thus be illuminated. The fact that the Third World city offers such a diversity of experiences must become for missionaries a further and urgent motive for turning to God, for God to decipher for them the complex realities that they would never manage to understand by themselves.

In addition, missionaries will experience what it means to be *sent*. This is the most beautiful moment in the whole mission experience. It is the moment when missionaries understand that they are not the ones who bring salvation to the city, that they are not the only ones who take an interest in it. There is Someone else who loves it, and who has the power and the will to save it. It is then that missionaries truly discover themselves, in solidarity with the initiative and the planning of the one who sends them, and they surrender the idea that they hold everything in their hands alone.

The great urban missionary Saint Paul, after long months in the desert, could bring his experience of salvation to the first ecclesial communities. Paul's profound experience was an experience of faith, not only in the sense of an intellectual assent to the ensemble of truths communicated by the Word of God, but also and especially in the sense of *pistis*: unconditional confidence in Christ, the Lord and Savior. Again, it is the experience of covenant, but now at its apex, in the person of Christ. By baptism the believer is ontologically incorporated into Christ; by faith the believer is psychologically conscious that he is borne by Christ and in Christ. "I know whom I have believed" (2 Tim. 1:12).

For Saint John the attitude of faith that characterizes one's relationship with Christ is made even more specific: the Christian "believes in love." To believe in Christ means to believe that Christ loves humankind, that in him God loves humankind. The relationship with Christ becomes a relationship of love. But this is not to be understood as if the initiative came from the human being; it comes from God himself. And this means that it cannot be diminished. Even if human beings do not always accept it, the current of love toward them does not slacken, because it does not depend on their response but on his definitive decision to love humanity, even when it sins, even when humans do not know or recognize their sinfulness.

The attitude of faith inclines humans to "expose" themselves fully to the essential values of the plan of salvation. It inclines them to make themselves always more explicitly conscious of what they already are in fact—namely, human beings in communion with God the creator, in Christ.

This "self-exposure" can be called awareness, contemplation, meditation, prayer. The label does not matter. What is crucial here for missionaries is to experience salvation within themselves because only after having experienced it can they communicate it to others via their relationships. In other words, after having experienced the process of evangelization and its fruition, missionaries can lead others to experience it. It is improbable that the salvific Word could pass through a missionary without causing a change in the person.

To strengthen this attitude of faith, the catechumenate, according to the findings of missionaries, particularly in Africa, represents a very valuable instrument. It should no longer be conceived of as simply the preparation of adult converts for baptism, but as a form of continuing education, a permanent formation of the baptized in the faith received and embraced by them. The catechumenate becomes in practice

> the catechetical service of the church that deepens the faith of converts, educates them to Christian practices, awakens in them evangelical attitudes with motives that come from the faith, and introduces them to participation in and co-responsibility with the ecclesial community, and the reception of the sacraments of initiation, in successive stages.[6]

It is a matter of providing support for the difficult pilgrimage of the faith. The supportive structure will be the catechumenal group itself. Beginning with the experiences of its members and the realities of its urban context, it will receive a basic orientation from the Word of God, to which it will give its response in prayer, especially liturgical prayer. True religious instruction will be articulated along the course of the history of salvation and interiorized by a "conversion of heart."

Building Bridges

As the attitude of faith opens Christians ever more to the Lord, that of religious dialogue opens them to their fellow humans and gives them the opportunity to witness to the gospel. It is an opening that supports the base of the triangle that exemplifies evangelization. Nor is it of itself different from the simple dialogue touched on in the preceding chapter, except in its intention to go beyond the confines of the empirical order to arrive at the religious. On this base the attitude of faith will bring into effect an orientation recommended by Vatican II:

> The Catholic Church regards with sincere reverence those ways of conduct and of life, those precepts and teachings that . . . often reflect a ray of that truth that enlightens all persons. . . . The church therefore exhorts its members, through dialogue and collaboration with the followers of other religions, carried out with prudence and love, and witnessing always to the Christian faith and life, to recognize, preserve, and promote the spiritual and moral good, as well as the socio-cultural values, found among them.[7]

In doing so, the first constant of simple dialogue is realized—presence to the other—while giving priority to religious experience. The religious Sisters of a mission among Muslims have described their work as trying to get to know the Muslims as they are, to see and hear what they see and hear in their own daily lives, to discover what it is that nourishes their thinking, to experience with them what is true, what is good, what is beautiful. This means that the Sisters are learning how to consider Islam as a faith, to discover in their Muslim friends the religious values that animate them, to consider these non-

Christian believers as brothers and sisters, and to open the door to authentic dialogue.[x]

It is clear that here a process has begun that opens these religious Sisters to the presence of God in other religions, thus realizing the second constant of dialogue—namely, a deeper knowledge of their own identity. This goes well beyond the simplistic attitude of Christians who think that they have a monopoly on God's truth. A group of missionaries in Bangkok, for instance, are orienting themselves to a more serious acceptance of the local Buddhism, no longer considering it simply as something very interesting though destined to evanesce before the light of Christ, but as a possible vehicle of further light on the way in which God comes to humans in one and the same Christ. As one consequence, a missionary from that group, after having served as the secretary to a *bonze*, became a professor at a Buddhist seminary and underwent a series of spiritual retreats under the supervision of Buddhist masters. He has made the observation that the primary beneficiaries of dialogue are the missionaries themselves, saying that now he understood better the Christian message, in the sense of a deeper awareness of God, a closer encounter with Christ, and a clearer distinction between religion and faith, between theology and truth.[9]

Such self-knowledge is of extreme value in the urban ambience, where no framework of reference is accepted as absolute by all, and where confrontation between diverse "universes of religious symbols" becomes a daily occurrence. It alone can provide the cultural anchorage necessary for choosing the particular elements needed for putting together one's own life project.

The life project of a Christian must take into account that of others. And here we arrive at the third constant of dialogue, the two-way street that will transform the relationship between two partners, enriching it with new and unexpected contents. Crisis cannot be precluded, especially in the early stages of such dialogue, as a study document prepared by Father Marcello Zago for the Episcopal Conference of Laos shows well:

> In the Buddhist context we meet with a typical case of the noncomprehension of the Christian message when presented in catechetical or biblical categories. The problem of language becomes truly acute and fundamental. . . . The salvation given by Christ appears to them to involve a religious alienation, a disengagement of personal effort. . . . The teaching of Christ seems to be a good thing in itself, but as one slowly advances in perfection [understood in the Buddhist tradition], it seems to Buddhists that one would have to depend less and less on Christ. But in Christianity the contrary is true. To receive life from him, to participate always more and more in his life, seems to them in a certain way a foundering in the eddy of rebirths. . . . The [Christian] path to perfection seems to them only the first steps toward spiritual progress. The precepts and sacraments seem to them only external instruments, or the bark as distinguished from the sap of a tree. Even charity seems to them something external.[10]

And there are extremely unfortunate historical precedents. In the past practically all religions—Christianity included—distrusted dialogue with others, in the undisguised intention of safeguarding the beliefs of their own members. To that was added the burden of a complex of historical suspicions, antipathies, and even condemnations of entire peoples of diverse religious convictions. Today things are moving in a different direction. The cities of the Third World, where the world's major religions often find themselves on common territory, offer missionaries splendid occasions for moving in the new direction. It is a duty that derives from Christian faith in universal fellowship under God the Father in Christ. And it is especially a consequence of faith in Christ, the keystone of God the Father's plan of salvation. When initial crises are overcome, both dialogue partners will be clearer in their own minds as to their own path to the Transcendent.

Missionaries must therefore make use of all possible occasions to enter into dialogue. The urban context itself provides such occasions in abundance. City officials in Singapore, for example, in 1972 invited the representatives of religious groups (and there were many of them) to a dialogue among themselves on the contribution that religion could make to city life. In Third World cities the social dimensions of religion could offer a solid platform for religious dialogue. Themes of common interest, that touch on religious elements at times, could take people beyond the phase of mutual tolerance, where they could arrive at relationships of reciprocal understanding, of collaboration and communion.

This does not necessarily imply conversation or discussion. There can be dialogue without formal discussion, as when two religious groups meet together for prayer or to share some spiritual experience. Dialogue is not simply an exercise in reasoning, but an activity that emanates from hearts full of love and understanding. Dialogue will be truly religious only when the participants, notwithstanding diversities in their immediate objectives, share a preoccupation with the Transcendent, an attitude of total respect for the convictions of others, and an opening of mind and heart in fellowship.

Prospects are very encouraging as has been expressed by the general chapter of the Oblates of Mary Immaculate. Their task of evangelization includes, as an integral component, joint search for the truth with adherents of other faiths. And this is done by means of dialogue and the joint discovery of the foreshadowings of the gospel hidden in other religions. They want to share with the others the best thing that they possess: they want to make a gift to others of themselves.[11]

To make a gift of oneself means to carry dialogue all the way to love and to take the risks that this involves. When Christians expose themselves completely to another, manifesting their most intimate secrets—including, therefore, their commitment-faith in Christ—they make themselves vulnerable. The other person or group can take advantage of this extreme openness, and even "infect" Christians, penetrating to their innermost self. And in the dialogue partner there may be hidden an exploiter, or even someone diametrically opposed to the Christian religion.

This is a risk that must be taken—but only if one's attitude of faith is as strong as it should be. And Christians will never have such an attitude until they become convinced that their only security in mission is in Him who "knows what is in the human being" and who never abandons them.

Spreading the Nets

The attitude of dialogue deepens one's relationships with city residents; the attitude of "spreading the nets" invites one to multiply them to the maximum. Dialogue looks to the quality of relationships; "expansion" of dialogue looks to their quantity.

Even if opportunities are plentiful in the city, actually to reach out to another person is not easy. Even in rural contexts, where everyone knows everyone else, in-depth relationships are very difficult to establish beyond a certain limit. The individual always remains within the circle of his or her own family and near relatives. In the city, where most persons do not know one another, the difficulties are multiplied. There are so many persons, and they come and go so rapidly, that it may seem futile to try to establish serious relationships with anyone.

Generally, city residents know in the abstract the major categories of other residents: those who live in certain parts of the city, landlords, merchants, and the others, as we saw in chapter 2. But city life tends to restrict close relationships to a very limited circle. The door to the house is always closed, unlike the open door in the countryside. The city person thinks of other persons in categorical terms; the country person stands in personal relationship with other persons.

In the Catholic schools in the city of Hong Kong, there are five members of other religions or ideologies for each Catholic pupil. Missionaries at work there wonder about the validity of their educational work. Should the schools be closed in order to send missionaries elsewhere, to evangelize? On the other hand, might it not be better to educate the Catholic pupils to a missionary relationship with their five counterparts who do not know Christ? The educational program could be reshaped to make provision for educating Catholic pupils to become committed missionaries in their own schools. Such an openness to others could certainly be inculcated in Catholic students if they are urged and prepared to adopt this attitude.

In the city of Hong Kong the ratio of Christians to non-Christians is 1 to 11. For Asia, this is rather high. Yet the witness of Christians does not "pass" through them to the others. The non-Catholic Chinese population acknowledges their contribution in regard to hospitals, schools, and social services. But they tend to classify Catholics in the category of the wealthy and powerful, aligned with the government (and therefore protagonists of the status quo) and aligned with the past (and therefore with the West). In addition, seen from outside, Catholics as a group do not seem important. Even if they constitute a visible group, it is only one of many religions, which, taken together, occupy only a marginal position in the busy urban society. When non-Catholics come to individuate Catholics as a distinct group, they do so as "God's group" (thus distinguishing them from "Christ's group," the Protestants).

One particular aspect of the problem is linked with that identification. Catholics who evangelize do so in the context of other evangelizers. This is standard in Third World cities. The hearers of "the Catholics' gospel" cannot but see Catholics as one of at least five groups or types of evangelizers. The other four would be the ecumenists (who, for the most part, belong to the World Council of Churches), the evangelicals (other Protestants), the Orthodox, and, in Africa, the new independent churches, of local origin. Catholic evangelizers dare not ignore this perception on the part of the person to whom their evangelization is directed.

Perhaps the best approach to this situation would be that of an opening of oneself to each of these other groups of fellow Christians. An opening to non-Christians, if it is authentic, would thus also be a reaching out to those who are closer.

The central problem of the attitude of "spreading the nets" seems to remain that of the apparent dichotomy between quality and quantity. Given the limitations, how can missionaries aim at quality (dialogue) and quantity (extension) simultaneously?

The demographic dimension of the city imposes the latter attitude on us, in convergence with the always valid mandate to "go to all peoples." Hence it is not a question of having to make a choice: a few but good, or many but mediocre. There is only one missionary mandate: it sends missionaries to *all* to give them *everything*.

By itself, the city resolves part of this problem. The apparent dichotomy begins to dissolve when we recall its geographic dimension. The diverse peoples of the world are not dispersed evenly over the planet's surface: they are concentrated in cities. The burden of long missionary journeys, without means and without roads, vanishes. Entire communities are found settled along three or four city streets. What is more, networks of social communication prepare the way for urban missionaries, disposing minds to personal encounter with the living witness of the Lord. The various urban groups, furthermore, will become centers of communication, if one knows how to mobilize them. Missionaries must, accordingly, make use of this opportunity that the city offers.

The dichotomy is fully resolved, however, only when the duty of evangelization is understood as a responsibility incumbent on every Christian. To arrive at this, the whole church will have to be "missionized" as a precondition to the possibility of evangelizing the world. The extension of the missionary radius of activity implies, therefore, the transposition of the concept of "the whole church is missionary" from that of ideals (where it has long been rooted) to that of the concrete attitudes of urban Christians.

In this sphere the most radical and most painful "conversions" will be those of "professional" missionaries. If the task of evangelization were to be delegated exclusively to them, the "spreading of nets" would never be realized to the measure demanded by the missionary mandate. They must be called on to renounce the monopolistic attitude that the church, at a certain stage in its history, imposed on them. No longer shall they maintain that they are the "exclusive bearers" of evangelical charisms. Conversion from a monopolistic attitude to one of sharing will not be easy. But it is necessary, especially in Third World cities, where the ratio of "professional missionaries" to the local population is dwindling—to their disadvantage. But this does not mean that veteran missionaries will not be able to exercise a ministry. In the cities, as we shall see, new ministries will emerge for the education and animation of Christians to a missionary attitude. Indeed, missionaries themselves would be the best missionary animators.

Activity of the Urban Christian

Urban mission demands of Christians that they pursue and relate their roles in city life to the function of evangelization. Urban mission thus urges on them, as a prime value, fidelity to the missionary mandate to "go to all peoples" of the city, to confess Christ to them. This is the operative consequence of the attitude of faith just discussed. It is a goal that will transform their unity based on the profession of faith into a dynamic reality capable of orienting the city toward the unity of shared life inculcated by the plan of God.

Catholics generally do not live this mandate. It is therefore urgent that there be introduced into Christian communities active ministries to awaken in them a growing consciousness of their missionary responsibilities. The goal will be that of transforming a group of Christians into a small church, and then into an urban mission (chap. 10).

Here we can catalogue the types of ministry that those who are more mission-animated could assume immediately. The point of convergence of the citywide activity of these ministries will be education to the attitudes demanded by urban mission. Their cumulative impact will be that of transforming the entire urban Christian community into a citywide missionary school.

What is already taking place in a major Third World city shows us that this is not just a dream. F. Ricci writes:

> The diocese of São Paulo has become a gigantic school in which the entire people learns of its own Christian roots in a complex articulation at various levels, from catechesis for the young to the "scientific" study of biblical theology. These are things that are being done throughout the world, but here the climate is different: the whole church is a huge populist and universalist school, such as the church knew how to be only in certain epochs in the past: a great learning workshop for the people.[12]

Cardinal Arns, missionary pastor of São Paulo, one of the largest and most vivacious cities of Latin America, in his express intention to animate his flock to the mission of the church faced with the challenge of the modern world, has proposed ten ministries, some new, some old.[13] His list incorporates other lists very well, and we shall adopt it here, since São Paulo excels in its popular Christian dynamism as much as it does in its human heterogeneity.

Of the ten ministries that Cardinal Arns lists, five concern more the incarnational impetus of urban mission. They are the direct ministries of (1) caring for the sick, (2) teaching, (3) family services, (4) worker liaison, and (5) communication. These ministries were mentioned in the preceding chapter. There the competencies that they require were discussed; here the spirit that they should diffuse will be the main concern.

Ministries are not, at bottom, simply roles that permit persons to gain entry into the ecclesial community and, in the final analysis, into the urban community; they are also vehicles of values and experiences that transform a person more and more into a "confessor" of Christ. It is precisely this dynamism that the other five ministries express—ministries that deal more directly with the conscientization of Christians, to awaken them to their evangelical duties. These are the ministries of (1) catechesis, (2) community animation, (3) religious vocations, (4) priesthood, and (5) continuing education.

Ministry of Catechesis

The ministry of catechesis looks to the essential contents and the existential stages of the pilgrimage of faith that constitutes "in Christ" the life of every Christian. As such it helps individuals to construct their own lives on the base of the Word of God and to take nourishment from it, reading it as a liberative and inspiring message.

Christian formation, the organization of the catechumenate (sketched above), and initiation to the Christian life in the Spirit are radicated—thanks to the ministry of catechesis—in the concrete life lived in the urban environment. Christians are oriented to the eucharistic celebration, understood as the assembly convoked by the risen Savior, where koinonia draws its origins and where the missions of diakonia have their beginning. In this way the catechist becomes the support of individual Christians and of the groups they form.

Ministry of Community Animation

The ministry of community animation aims at the formation of small ecclesial groups oriented toward the development of fellowship, of faith in the Word of Christ, and of true worship. In the words of Cardinal Arns:

All nascent communities need persons trained in the spirit of Moses. They need guides who know how to listen to the Word of God and to lead the people to Sinai, the definitive covenant—men and women gifted with great faith, great patience, a spirit of prayer, and of absolute docility to the designs of God revealed by him and by his church.[14]

The capacity of a guide to build bridges between "the concrete particular" and "the reality of the universal" assumes paramount importance. It will be for this ministry to integrate fully the small group into the larger urban church. It will also be its task to encourage various types of groups, and at the same time to know how to relate them to the overarching oneness of ecclesial life, as Ricci explains:

> Everything is done in the line of evangelization. There are concrete programs. . . . The articulation of the structures of the organic unity of the diocese [São Paulo, Brazil] is surprisingly minute and detailed— "surprisingly" at least in comparison with the more conventional image of Brazil, which is one of unbridled spontaneity and an almost total lack of regulation, and of a church in a retarded state of evolution. On the contrary, São Paulo is a mature church: in some way and at some moment, a qualitative leap forward must have taken place because there is more seriousness than improvisation, and this is evident. Spontaneity is aligned with an undertaking pursued with intelligence; the motivations for it are explicit and are often reformulated; consensus is not the result of authoritarian imposition, but the result of a search joined in by all and a continuous confrontation.[15]

Ministry of Religious Vocations

The ministry of religious vocations is intended as a support for the consecrated religious life. This life, stabilized by the vows of religion, is a precious facet of the Christian legacy shared by all. Its potential for urban mission has not yet been fully realized. During the phases of the study on this theme conducted by SEDOS, it was found that, notwithstanding the fact that a great number of religious missionaries have long been at work in Third World cities, and notwithstanding the sensitivity to the problem evidenced by their superiors, the road to the full urban use of their talents is still far from completion.[16]

Meanwhile it should be noted that, in view of the specifically urban need to deal simultaneously with citywide mission and with the formation of small groups, the focal point of the religious life—that is, the communal life—can serve as a model for the urban ecclesial group.

Ministry of Priesthood

The ministry of the priesthood concentrates on the sacramental services of the church and on the responsibility for the unity of the urban church.

Father G. S. Gorgulho has commented on this ministry as practiced in the diocese of São Paulo:

> Just as the people, so too the clergy show great talents and great potential. There are fifteen hundred priests in the diocese, of the most varied nationalities. They see in their bishop-pastor an effective pole of unity and hope. In the past they lived in the routine of a parochial ministry, without concerning themselves much about renewal or the specifically urban dimensions of the pastoral ministry, but now they look always to the unity and the missionary dimension of an organic group activity. Although not shirking responsibility for this or that individual person, they are primarily committed to a joint responsibility for the evangelization of the city and to giving an example of fraternal communion, necessary and adequate to the healing of secular life.[17]

With the development of other ministries and the "declericalization" of the church, the sacerdotal ministry is recovering its original charism. The urban ambience, which offers it opportunities for specialization, constitutes a further impulse in this direction: besides its collective responsibility to unite the entire community of Christians at the level of the local urban church, there remains that of grouping Christians into smaller assemblies in the various zones of the city, around the risen Savior, to dispense there his Word and his eucharistic food.

Ministry of Continuing Education

The ministry of continuing education is directed to all persons charged with one or more of the ministries described above. It does not stop with technical or intellectual training, although it recognizes their irreplaceable necessity. It aims also at creating enthusiasm and participation, introducing the biblical, liturgical, and spiritual riches of the Christian patrimony to ecclesial ministers. Beyond an initial period, longer or shorter, when new ministers are also introduced to methods of self-education, continuing education demands periodic sessions of aggiornamento in the form of meetings, workshops, demonstrations of new techniques and ideas, and training courses.

The content of this education is not restricted to the evangelical sphere, but also embraces various aspects of human life. In the present study it always includes a deepened analysis of the particular city in question, a renewal of the motivations behind urban mission, and training in the techniques required by individual ministries. Personal and ever ready help between periods of aggiornamento is part of any continuing education program. In this way the danger of excessive improvisation and isolation is averted.

The vision growing out of this outline of the implications of the "maturation of the urban Christian" is that of an assembly of individuals, each in close relationship with Christ, who gives them the experience of salvation, and with other city-dwellers, who permit them to let this experience "pass" through them to the multitude of those who have not known Christ.

It is an exhilarating vision. Inviting Christians to multiply their presence in the myriads of roles generated by urban life, according to the methodology of the incarnation, the vision urges them on to disperse themselves in the city, in order that each one may concentrate his or her efforts in one particular social grouping. Missionaries engrossed in a shantytown settlement will have difficulty finding the time, or the heart, to commit themselves elsewhere as well. On the contrary, the very fact of being committed to shantytowners blocks their way to other groups segregated from them by the holding power of geographic, economic, political, and cultural processes.

This same vision summons missionaries to take their place in the current of the redemption. That is, in their proclamation to so many groups and across so many diverse roles, they will bring about a convergence at a higher level, and will contribute to the dissolution of the divisions caused by geographic, economic, political, and cultural segmentations imposed by the city. Missionaries are dispersed, incarnating themselves in diverse groups, to relate all of them to the oneness of their condition and their calling. And it will not be only at the level of values—the values of salvation. The vision recalls also the physical meeting of all Christians, even though separated because of their localized incarnation, in the grouping that calls itself "church." The vision carries an appeal for all Christians to reunite in assembly around Christ, in his church, the central, constant and integrating component of God's plans for the city, to teach there the difficult art of living together, of being sons and daughters of one and the same Father.

10

CHURCH AS MISSION

The touchstone of the validity of our reading of the signs of God's plans for the city will be the actualization of the attitudes of solidarity and evangelization on the part of Christians in their everyday lives.

The task of urban mission, accordingly, will be that of ushering Christians not, as in the past, into merely juridical and impersonal structures, but into the vital experiences of the local church. These experiences are at the very heart of the same divine plans. Just as the city succeeds in giving form to many human experiences, anchoring them in a well-defined site, so too urban mission must know how to make its own impulses converge in a life-space where believers will feel united around the risen Lord.

Of capital importance in this perspective is the attempt to identify the conditions that will lead to "the experience of church." As long as Christians remain at the level of hope only, or even that of individual accomplishments, they can, to be sure, *preach* the church, but they will never arrive at *making it experienced* by others. The fact remains that the Lord has called Christians to *be a church*, and not merely to do research in or teach ecclesiology.

The Experience of Church

The distinction between the mystery of the church and the experience of church will be a preliminary step toward translating the essential and structural lines of the local church (see chap. 7) into the experience of incarnated solidarity and evangelical salvation.

The distinction between church and experience of church will permit us to make the transition from the essential to the existential. "Church" encompasses the whole mystery of the people of God, the mystical body of Christ, existing independently of us. The experience of church is our vital and conscious inclusion in this mystery, which brings with it a sense of communion with a group of fellow believers at whose center is Christ the Lord. The most useful biblical illustration is that of the two disciples on the road to Emmaus with the risen Savior, an encounter that made them say: "Did not our hearts burn within us while he talked to us on the road, while he opened to us the scriptures?" (Lk. 24:32).

We can now formulate the fundamental question of urban mission in more precise terms: How is a group of Christians to be prepared for the experience of church that the Lord will certainly grant them?

It is, first of all, a matter of experiencing the communion between God and human beings, and that of human beings among themselves. This will be the realization of the model of the church as the site of the experience of salvation, concretized in the feeling of being together, liberated from sin, united around the risen Lord.

The qualitative leap from "groups of Christians" to "the experience of church" becomes possible to the extent that members of the group open themselves to the other members, and especially to Christ present in the group by faith. This opening implies a conscious and deliberate acceptance of the transcendent God who reveals himself in Jesus.

To make this opening possible, certain sociological conditions (beyond the attitudes treated in chaps. 8 and 9) must be met. Groups do not have to be large. Relationships of openness can hardly be cultivated and deepened except in restricted circles. To pave the way to the experience of church, it is therefore necessary to break up large groups into smaller units. The Emmaus group was composed of the minimum number: two, plus the Lord. Our ecclesial groups should not exceed about fifteen members. In this regard missionaries will easily be reminded of the experience of family-type groups and of movements such as the Legion of Mary, and of the "cell" or "cadre" principle. This is a necessary prerequisite for "being together," and it must be respected.

It seems, therefore, that the contemporary ecclesial phenomenon known as the "base community" is the privileged place where the conditions for the maturation of the experience of church are best ensured. Another reason for this choice is based on a reading of the signs of the city. The achievements of these small Christian communities in Asia, Latin America, and Africa are impressive, achievements that give evidence of being convergent indications of the way in which the Lord is pursuing his plans in human history.

Voices from the Third World are in agreement with this interpretation. A first one comes from Asia: "For effective evangelization and the participation of our people, the formation of small, basic communities is indispensable. . . . The most important and central need of Catholics in Malaysia is the formation of basic Christian communities."[1] Bishop Pironio, delegate of the Latin American episcopacy to the 1974 Synod of Bishops, stated there that base communities are "the primary cell-groups of the entire ecclesial edifice, centers of evangelization and the most important factor in human promotion."[2] The bishops of Eastern Africa have expressed their agreement, saying that they believe that the Christian communities at this base level will be the best adapted to promote an intense and authentic vitality, and to become witnesses in their own milieus.[3]

These communities will serve as a basis for the fusion of the secular roles of Christians with their ministries in the church. Roles and ministries will be carefully studied in these communities, under the close and interested scrutiny of fellow members. Fusion will lead to a dynamic synthesis of life and faith.

The two major contexts for their activity will be the "natural areas" of the city and the social classes delineated in chapter 2. Members of base communities that are implanted in these contexts will be able to share fully in their ongoing life and will bring to them the dynamism of the faith. The small communities are better able to respond to real needs, and therefore better qualified to experiment with new ways of relating faith and life. They will in this way learn for themselves the urgency of detecting the voice of God in the comings and goings of daily events, of practicing discernment of spirits, and of calling upon other communities for help. As the general meeting of base communities in Vitoria, Brazil (1975), brought out, this flexibility permits them greater accessibility to students and to the poor than other ecclesial structures enjoy.[4]

These communities will also inject new life into parishes and already existent Christian associations and movements. In particular they will permit the parish to delineate better and pursue its own functions, probably in the directions of coordination, inspiration, and lifelong education. "These communities will be a sphere of evangelization, of benefit to larger communities, and will be a help for the church universal" (Pope Paul VI).[5]

These communities will sometimes put more emphasis on secular life than on the faith, and vice versa. There are two basic types of experience in this regard: that which predominates in the person of action, and that which predominates in the person more inclined to contemplation. In fact, however, both of them are expressions of the same fundamental characteristic of the Christian life: the dynamic tension between being with God and being sent by him into the world.

The element of spontaneity that their size makes possible will restore to the urban church the creative function that seems to have characterized the first Christian communities. At bottom, what joins members together is not the mere fact of the same juridical territory, but the fact that they share a "natural area" of the city or a particular category of life or work, and the fact that they promote the maturation of all other members by their interpersonal commitments, their work in the world, and the enrichment they bring to the culture of the city.

We must also be aware of the limitations of ecclesial base communities. They are not qualified to assume pastoral responsibilities for matters that affect wider areas of human life. Persons do not live only at the level of interpersonal relationships; they are also caught up in mass social systems. They are conditioned by the state, by the social communication media, by the schools, by the industrial world, and by other structures of contemporary urban life.

It is here that the tension between smallness and bigness becomes critical. It is not a question of choosing between alternatives; we must choose both of them, precisely in order to be able to live in an always more human way. Smallness favors the synthesis of harmony and creativity; it favors interpersonal interaction. Bigness keeps people from shutting themselves up in themselves; it helps to widen their horizons, and offers pillars of support invaluable for sustaining the innate fragility of what is small.

Nor does the base community pretend to offer a solution for all the urban problems of our time. It represents a point of departure from which a "nobody" can begin again to become a "somebody."[6] This new departure is nothing other than the historical development—the becoming—of the church, a dynamic experience that involves the total profundity of the mystery of the incarnation, of the body of Christ that is born, grows, and acts. Nothing essential has been changed. The seventh congress of the Italian Theological Association (1977) expressed this essential function of the church very well when it stated:

> The nucleus around which is formed and manifested the awareness of the mission of the church in its historical evolution has always demanded both proclamation (kerygma) and its actualization in the life of the church, as the following of Christ and the proclaiming of the risen Lord, present and active in his historical community.[7]

And thus the goal of the new departure will be that of rediscovering—precisely in the new experiences with, through, and in fellow believers—the dimensions of the church, the unique body of Christ. This is a meaningful analogy, applicable to urban churches. The Christian family is another analogy. Vatican II referred to it anew as a "domestic church," where, according to Pope Paul VI,

> the diverse aspects of the integral church [can be encountered in such a way that they become] a place where the gospel is transmitted and from which it radiates. . . . In the intimacy of a family conscious of this mission, all members evangelize and are themselves evangelized. Parents do not only communicate the gospel to their children, but can receive from them that same gospel lived in depth. Such a family becomes evangelical for other families and for the whole ambience in which it lives.[8]

For purposes of this study, however, the base community, rather than the family, is the appropriate model for the experience of church. It is better suited for bringing out certain responsibilities incumbent on the church, that is, its sacramentality, its service to the world, and its vital tensions: cross/resurrection, assembly/mission, history/eschatology. The supportive structure of the experience of urban church will therefore be the small group.

The Small Group

On the analogy of Emmaus, every small group of Christians—already existent or yet to be created—has in itself the potentiality to generate the experience of church. Small groups of Christians abound in the metropolis. Our apostolate has learned much from the efficiency of the urban context about the formation of groups, the division of labor among them, as pointed out in chapter 2. In addition, the large numbers of the faithful have often obligated pastors to divide their flocks into smaller groupings.

By "small group" is meant a limited number of persons that come together because of their being Christian. Here the concept of group embraces the whole gamut of groupings, from the community of three religious Sisters to the team that directs the Sunday liturgy. Urban pluralism will not admit of formula restrictions.

Interest in small groups was stressed by the 1974 Synod of Bishops, which spoke of the characteristics of its members as persons bound by relationships of fellowship and animated by the intention of practicing the Christian life by way of forming a living organism; persons who live by the spirit of Christ, nourishing their life by prayer in common, meditation on the Word of God and the eucharistic celebration, and who are open to the world by the joint testimony of their apostolic and evangelical life and by their joint activity.[9]

Characteristics of persons who join small groups have been delineated by Father C. Koser, then Franciscan Superior General. They include

> the need for more intense interpersonal relationships; for a more vital and less formal practice of religion; for a more efficacious involvement in the life of fellow humans, of the poor, of marginal groups; for an active participation of all members in the life of the group, especially in the decision-making process; for complete equality (and therefore in the elimination of hierarchical formulations); for a spontaneous and direct evangelical life; for a flexibility that bypasses preestablished programming and organization; for listening to the world and its development; for cooperation in secular life; for a paschal, charismatic, prophetic life. . . . [The small groups have] an average life of about five years.[10]

Ecclesial interest converges with secular interest. Chapter 6 stressed the importance that urban planners attach to participation at the base of an urban population. Their community development projects often depend on the quality of the small groups that are involved in them. The Coventry world conference on urban life (1968) made the apt statement that the most original contribution that Christians can give to the metropolis would be the formation of small groups, work- or neighborhood-related, animated by the dynamism of the faith.[11] For urban mission the all-important factor is the potentiality for experiencing the church. We must therefore return to the fundamental question: What are the necessary and sufficient conditions for a small group to become a church?

How Group Becomes Church

Openness to the Lord

It appears now that the conditions for making a small group become a church can be synthesized in the highest degree of openness to others. Among these "others," the first is the Other par excellence, the risen Lord, present "where two or three are gathered together in my name."

Openness to the Lord coincides with the attitude of faith treated in the preceding chapter. The only thing to be added here is the communitarian dimension of the faith. Here the liturgy becomes a confession of Christ and finds again its whole missionary impulse.

Professor I. Bria, commenting on an Orthodox consultation on confessing Christ today, focuses on the horizons of such openness to God. The proclamation of the gospel contains an element of scandal (*skandalion*), he says, because human wisdom can never comprehend the transcendent wisdom of God. The paradox of mission becomes apparent when the church is understood as the end of mission, and not as a means of mission. Mission points to the advent of the communion that God offers the world in the form of the body of Christ, the church—the historical community that reflects the communion of life with God. Mission confirms the centrality of the Logos of all creation. It is realized in a context of resistance to evil and to sin. The cross is the ineluctable context of mission that can lead to a foretaste of the kingdom but not to its construction by means of social and historical elements.[12]

Openness to Other Members

Extended openness is built on preexistent openness, that is, the openness of each member to other members of the group. But it should not be presumed. It develops little by little as interaction among members increases. Nor is it wise to underestimate the positive function of conflict in the promotion of openness. Sometimes contrast is of greater value than apparent agreement of the varying points of view that inevitably punctuate the life of every group: under the pretense of charity and union there is often hidden an actually closed attitude toward others. In this regard, a knowledge of the elements of group dynamics can serve to ease the way to greater openness.

In the urban context, clarity on the various processes of social segregation and its class conflicts seems of capital importance. We need not be afraid of mixing small groups within the limits of the practicable, putting side by side the rich and the poor, old and young. But on the other hand, it is also well to respect the homogeneity of natural or spontaneous groups already in existence. The important thing is mutual education to respect and appreciate others "as they are," that is, with all the baggage of class, age, race, education, and ideology that they carry into the group. This will be a true school of the attitude of openness to the others who are outside the group.

Openness to Outsiders

By "outsiders" is meant the various categories of persons who are not small-group members; they are present throughout the city and are often found in the circles close to the small group. The degree of openness to them will signal the readiness of the group to compose a church rather than a sect. The distinction between sect and church developed by sociologists of religion can help us to appreciate better the importance of structural openness.

According to sociologists, a group is built on the good equilibrium that its members have established among themselves, not without effort. The arrival of an outsider represents a threat to that equilibrium. The first reaction of a group is that of closing itself up within itself, as if to defend its precious equilibrium. We have all lived through the experience of feeling comfortable with friends until the moment the doorbell rang and the unexpected visitor entered—and ruined everything! We had to start all over from the beginning!

This normal group experience, viewed now in a religious perspective, explains the origin of a sect, which can here be defined as a group that has discovered something of great value to its members in the sphere of religion. It then separates itself from the world around it, defending itself from the possible and probable contagion that would mean the loss of what it has found. The sect closes in on itself in order to continue to be religious "against" a milieu that it judges to be irreligious.

This model (but without its label) could be useful in the evaluation of certain urban religious groups that have a high degree of internal cohesion but that pattern themselves "apart" from other groups and "in exclusion from" all the problems of the city. Perhaps it is precisely its dense cohesion that inclines the group to close itself off: it fears it has too much to lose, too much to risk.

There is one particular type of "other" that the small Christian group will always be called on to hold itself open to: the person who seeks to become part of it. In an urban situation, it will most often be city newcomers who will seek admission—though they may not openly say so—because they seek to escape anonymity and to find support in any type of group. To the extent that the group knows how to overcome itself (and its instinct for self-preservation) and to risk admitting others in the name of Christ who urges it to be hospitable to outsiders, it will be ready to become a church.

For the group, as for the individual Christian, the paradox of the gospel remains: "unless a grain of wheat falls into the earth and dies, it remains alone; but if it dies, it bears much fruit" (Jn. 12:24). To the extent to which the group knows how to die as a sociological unit, it will rise again as church.

To accept the other one "who comes," and to accept the subsequent "death" of the precarious equilibrium of a group that "feels comfortable" with itself, is perhaps the greatest proof of the maturity of the small ecclesial group. Only thus, through Christians themselves, does the church become the means and the theater of salvation. But this is only the first test. It is also necessary that the group know how to open itself to the others who do *not* come. For them too the church must become kingdom and proclamation. Once again the instinctive impulse of the group must be resisted, and this time more radically. This is the necessary and sufficient condition for urban church to become urban mission.

Openness to others who are not members and do not want to become members of the small group will follow at the communitarian level the lines traced at the individual level by the attitudes of secular and religious dialogue (see chaps. 8 and 9). Here we need only examine the structural implications for the group as such.

Nonmembers of the Group-Church

There are two major categories of these "others." The first includes all the Christians who belong to the same urban church. The second includes all the other city inhabitants. How is the group-church to orient itself toward these two categories? With the first category, it will establish diverse relationships of a strictly structural nature, which we shall examine briefly here, following a multilevel curve, according as the social distance between the group and the urban structure increases. These two categories meet in a third relationship, namely, organic or joint pastoral ministry.

The Parish

The first and closest type of relationship will be the one taken up with the parish. It is a relationship of complementarity. The small group can facilitate interaction with members, but cannot turn itself into a self-sufficient "mini-parish." A small group, for example, will seldom have a biblical scholar to guide its collective study of the Bible. But it can ask for one, as the occasion requires, from the parish. A small group will easily become discouraged as it gradually becomes aware of the enormous range of urban problems. But, thanks to its relationship with the parish, it can find other small groups and align itself with their projects.

For its part, the parish, if it lacks the life-space offered by small groups for the deepening of ecclesial life, risks becoming simply a religious service station. In addition it risks losing vital contact with the population base if it does not have the link represented by small groups residing in the streets and neighborhoods of the city.

The parish of Ghilenje, in Lusaka, Zambia, is divided into 117 sections, with fifty to sixty houses in each section. A central team composed of a priest, two religious Sisters, and a catechist works at animating the various sections. It begins by organizing "reflection meetings" where the values of the particular clan and those of the church are discussed and compared. The place taken by the clan's ancestors is compared with that taken by Christ in the church. The whole process of catechesis is then worked out along the lines suggested by these values: baptism becomes the rite of initiation, the Eucharist becomes the rite of a sacrificial meal.

As soon as the meetings begin to show a pattern of consistency, a leader is chosen. That person is assisted by a council formed by others who take an interest in such activities as visiting the sick, collecting money and provisions for the needy, teaching Christian doctrine, and helping with family problems. The divisional council is then encouraged by the central team to assume responsibility for baptisms, marriages, other celebrations, and the worship assemblies of the particular section.

Difficulties are not conspicuous by their absence. Efforts are concentrated on areas where progress seems slower than it should be and on the insidious nature of discouragement. Positive results have been seen in the fact of a Christian renewal of life, the working out of the value of unity within pluralism, the shouldering of responsibilities by the laity, and the emergence of new ministries.[13]

Interparochial Groups

The second category covers the relationship established by the groups that operate beyond parish confines with other small groups of a similar orientation. This approach also helps to overcome the danger of isolation and the discouragement that comes with it, and simultaneously ensures the small group of the nourishment of "positive content" in the person and work of specialists who are qualified to assist small groups, on request, and in the reinforcing support of larger, more mature groups.

In Asia, the ecumenical Asian Committee for People's Organizations (ACPO) provides support for this type of interparochial relationship. Its principal function is that of recruiting and training specialists to help small groups overcome their recurrent difficulties and bolster their efforts in the city. It also promotes an exchange of information based on their experiences, and it raises funds for projects of special interests.[14]

Joint Pastoral Ministry

A third type of relationship is needed to make these first two types of territorial and functional relationships converge within a unified and organic framework of activity vis-à-vis the totality represented by the city. This is the structure of the joint pastoral ministry long since accepted by many urban pastors. It is a structure that generally embraces one or more dioceses and seems qualified to recover the unity of urban ecclesial activity that was in effect in the first ages of the church.

The principle of organic pastoral ministry coincides with conclusions on cultural processes reached in this study (see chap. 5). Besides the realities of the "natural areas," there are also those of the urban totality and those of the mutual conditioning between them. Urban mission must take account of them and, in consequence, reinforce the structures set up to channel their activity at this level also.

The small group, thanks to its ties with the local parish and with other intermediate bodies, has its contribution to make in substantiating the universal dimension of the church.

A Zairean Joint Pastoral Ministry Experiment: In his planning for the city of Kinshasa, Zaire, Cardinal Malula invited a group of laypersons to take a three-year training course in pastoral and missionary animation. In September 1974 he recalled the priests from some urban parishes and put these lay graduates in their place. These laypersons, in addition to their professional duties and their parochial responsibilities, assumed other responsibilities at the diocesan and intermediate levels, thus participating at all levels of pastoral planning.

This is a vision that allows for a different "use" of presbyterial ministries. In Cardinal Malula's plans, priests are reassigned to reinforce the urban sacerdotal ministry and that of lay animation.[15]

Extrapastoral Work: Joint pastoral ministry can also extend to work areas that are not directly pastoral. The various federations of hospital workers, teaching Sisters, and Christian welfare-type workers contribute more if they find their rightful place in it. Their regrouping not only permits each category of service personnel to reinforce its own work—via an exchange of what has been learned from various experiments—but also its involvement in secular urban planning.

It is clear that here the structure of joint pastoral ministry coincides with the secular structure of urban planning. As such, it provides an answer to the problem of how to make the dispersed resources of an entire city focus on objectives considered to be of high priority.

The Sacramental Impact

The multidimensional openness of the members of small groups will help them to come to the experience of church, only if the basic facets of its life are given the emphasis they merit. Among these the sacramental life, epitomized in the eucharistic celebration, comes first. Here the Lord makes himself present "in communion" with them, renewing "his hour" with them, inviting them to "eat and drink" with him in the postresurrection era. He makes himself "seen" in the breaking of bread, "opening their eyes," as he once did for the disciples on the road to Emmaus. *Objectively* this is the high point of group life, and it is normal that sometimes it is the strongest moment *subjectively* as well. When so, it becomes the most significant experience of church for group members. In the urban context, it is the moment when those dispersed in the anonymous masses recognize one another, united around him who has "visited the world."

The Eucharist is the center of all sacraments. In the intimacy of the interpersonal relationships of the small group, it becomes a standing invitation to the sacrament of reconciliation, in which Christ passes into their midst via his peace, a peace that, once received from him, will be shared by all members in gratitude and joy. It is the restorative sacrament so necessary for those who, day after day, struggle with the anomalies and injustices of the metropolis. It is the sign that will one day make more manifest the kingdom of him who, having reconciled us with the Father, wants us to be reconciled among ourselves, and thereby strengthened for life together in the city.

The other sacraments are not received with the same regularity as the Eucharist and reconciliation, and are rarely received within the small group as such. But their lives are touched by them, due to the impulse of faith that they radiate. These other sacraments bolster, in an ever more incisive way, the potentiality for personal, vital contacts with the Lord, precisely via the relationships that group members establish with other baptized persons, other confirmed persons, other sick persons, other priests, and other married Christians.

Recent liturgical changes in the Catholic Church have enriched all the sacraments with rites that reinforce their communitarian dimension. In fact the initial evaluations of liturgical renewal showed that its purposes seemed to be realized only in the setting of small groups. In the urban context, where interpersonal intimacy is less appreciated, they can reacquire their original significance in making psychologically present, within the small grouping of Christians, the Lord who "calls them by name," loving them and saving them, and making of them, thanks to baptism, one body and one heart.

The Eucharist, besides "forming the church," according to the famous expression of Henri de Lubac, calls the group back to the specifically salvific activity of the Lord, that is, to his paschal cycle, to his death and resurrection, which, continuing within the group, engenders both his love and our salvation. In this way it opens the group to the vital tension that is the touchstone of every experience of church.

In the Synoptic Gospels the proclamation of the cross and resurrection is put in close association with the transfiguration experience. If it is "good for us to be here," it is also necessary to "suffer much" in order to be readied for resurrection. The group opens itself not only to the sufferings and daily death of each of its members, but also to the suffering and death of those who, together with them, share urban life, opening their "inculturation" to its ultimate redemptive and salvific finality.

If the Eucharist gives life, in the new experiences it generates, to the paschal model of the history of salvation that day after day continues its course among the urban masses, it also stimulates the small group to new deepenings of the Word of God. The Eucharist becomes the complement of the Word, and the two together become the principle of its course through the history of humankind. Word and sacrament become one. Word and sacrament, pasch and mission, coalesce into a single life-giving current. Disciples, close to the Lord, will sense ever more insistently their missionary mandate: it is the tension that transforms church into mission. On the one hand there is the "come to me," and on the other hand the "go to all peoples." Christians live between two poles: when they are among the urban masses, the Lord calls them to himself, in the small group; but as soon as they respond, he sends them back to the city. It is the same tension that animates Christ as true Son of God and, simultaneously, true Son of man, always reaching out more to the Father, and always more receptive to the pleas of human yearnings.

How does this second pole of God's plans for the city take expression? It is essential for urban mission to identify the conditions that make of the small group not only an experience of church but also of mission.

How Group-Church Becomes Urban Mission

Christians are first of all sent to the persons who populate the ambients where they live, work, and spend the other moments of their daily lives (see chaps. 8 and 9). In this regard the Third World city has a clear advantage over the First World city and over the rural world: it offers more occasions for entering into relationships with others and hence for missionaries to immerse themselves in the heart of the social system. In the Third World city, relationships are more personalized, less bent on the demands of efficiency, and they abound, not only because there are more persons there but also because they have more time for others. The preponderance of the informal sector in economic processes is the most evident sign of it.

Urban mission, in this context, becomes more present and effective to the extent to which the small group succeeds in making the evangelical attitudes treated in the preceding chapter pass into the urban system via its members. Without the warmth and encouragement of the base that the small group represents, individual Christians will hardly be able to implant these attitudes in the field, ready for sowing, that their family and work relationships constitute.

A small group can feel itself sent, as such, to a particular "people," according to the discernment it itself makes of the specific intentions of the Lord. Each group should figure out for itself what it should do as a group. The perspectives here extend to the entire range of opportunities provided by the urban system.

Toward Special Urban Ambients

Certain "types" of persons are to be found only in cities, because it is only there that they find the context in which life is possible for them. University students are an example. A small group of Christians could well feel called to the university world, to help with the particular challenges that young Christians encounter there. It is estimated that there are millions of college-level students in Asia; a half-million of them are concentrated in the city of Tokyo. Not only is this a key population sector, often it is also one that is in search of help.

The experience of missionaries seems to suggest the formation of groups of students who would work, pray, and spend leisure time together, with a vision of the totality of God's plans, performing precise tasks within the university context. In Zaire committed Christian students visit indifferent Christians dispersed throughout the city.

Another ambient that is found only in cities is that of social communications. Usually we think immediately of the media that social communicators make available to society, as in fact we are doing in this chapter. But we should also think about the persons in that sphere, who often must work in very special circumstances and who are sometimes made the object of extreme pressures by other groups. It is only logical that an ecclesial group dedicate itself to them, not thinking of them as "media monarchs" but as fellow humans to be loved and appreciated.

Other groups should address themselves to the very complicated world of labor. The networks of relationships that this sphere of life tends to construct in the informal economic sectors of Third World cities could offer undreamed-of openings. But there are also openings in the labor union movement, employment agencies, distribution centers, and many other organized centers of activity, pulsing with stimuli for the creativity of Christians who are committed and active at the small-group level.

In many cities small groups are particularly attracted to minorities that are generally left out of the central concerns of urban life. They are groupings that tend to be resistant to dialogue because they are inclined to see others as a threat to their precarious status. But they have great need of hearts that will understand them, of hands that reach out to help them. In the exodus to the cities these groups discover many needs that they never experienced before.

Minorities attract attention because they speak their own language, or come from a particular ethnic background, or profess a religion different from that of the majority. Those who come to the cities as immigrants or refugees deserve special attention: perhaps at no other time in their lives are they so receptive to the Gospel. This gives small ecclesial groups the opportunity to take an interest in them. Experience has shown that after a certain period of time—that is, once a certain degree of urbanization is reached—their openness disappears.

The district of Ramos Millan in Mexico City, for example, was flooded with newcomers in the decade from 1950 to 1960. Pentecostal groups suddenly experienced extraordinary success with them, but other church groups did not. Later, when the other church groups began to reach out to them, the streets in Ramos Millan were already paved, the houses renovated, the residents employed, and they did not respond to these church approaches with the same enthusiasm as they had to the Pentecostals. Who knows what might have taken place several years earlier? One of the goals of urban mission is that of "planting" a local church in every new neighborhood, helping all residents to confront the isolation, insecurity, and frustrations of the new way of life.

Immigrant communities sometimes form a bridge for the evangelization of the countryside surrounding a city. The comings and goings of persons between big cities and rural villages help circulate evangelical values, extending missionary frontiers. The Mayan village of Komchen, not far from Merida (Yucatan, Mexico), was closed to the gospel until 1970. Then the local henequen industry collapsed and Komchen men had to look for work in the factories of Merida. When they went back home they brought new ideas with them. Today Komchen has its own form of Christian presence.

In this perspective, interesting ideas for transforming an urban church into a missionary base for rural zones have come from Africa, where the ties between city and country are especially close. Arrangements were made, in a particular area, for rural clergy to spend periods of time with urban parishes. But a report to SEDOS noted a problem. There was reluctance to leave small rural parishes without a resident clergy. This no doubt resulted from the emphasis put on the necessity of the sacraments, as if they were the only way that the Christian life could be nourished. Often those in charge of urban parishes did not understand their own parishioners very well because they could not speak the language and they did not know how the people had lived in their previous, rural environment. For their part, rural priests frequently hindered their own work because they had no exposure to the new dimensions of the apostolate in urban areas.[16]

Toward Ordinary Urban Ambients

Besides the missionary impulse that takes the form of reaching out to special urban ambients, the orientation of small ecclesial groups toward "ordinary" ambients should not be overlooked. In Latin America, for example, there are many experiments going on with direct forms of evangelization already translated into concrete terms. One example, mentioned by Father Gorgulho, may serve as an indication:

> After a period of preparation, *favela*-dwellers are encouraged to form a group that will go to proclaim the gospel to another group, in an ever growing progression. They try to reach others at the roots of their daily life, and acclimate them to the idea of forming small Christian communities.[17]

Protestants have developed a number of models for implementing the missionary mandate to "go to the peoples" of the Third World city. The International Congress for World Evangelization (1974) studied five of them.

The first consists in "planting" a chapel or a small place of worship, entrusting it to a small group already formed, and giving them the assignment of developing it into a "church." This method entails ever growing difficulties, because its costs are prohibitive.

The second method is more practical and more in line with what has been suggested above: a group already formed and active in a given neighborhood encourages the formation of "daughter groups" in new neighborhoods where its members go to live. It begins with meetings—including liturgical—in private houses. The "mother church" helps with moral and financial support.

The third method entails the founding of Bible schools. Participants are urged to become animators of other groups, whether already formed or to be formed. This follows the path of the transition from personal witness to communal testimony and the formation of new "local churches." These schools pursue a very down-to-earth approach, sending their "students" out to sell bibles and, when doors are opened, to organize Scripture study meetings.

The fourth method takes on the "modern frontier of the church's mission," the huge apartment-building complexes. In San Juan, Puerto Rico, Sunday schools have been developed precisely for—and within—the maxi-apartment-building context. Missionaries must know how to distinguish between the tenants of luxury apartments, who want only to be left in peace, and those of the population base who, as a rule, are very suspicious of strangers but feel themselves isolated from the community. An initial approach to them is made all the more difficult in apartment complexes where entrance gates and doors are kept locked.

This type of missionary experience has been easier to implement in Singapore. Practically 75 percent of the urban population lives in immense apartment complexes that contain as many as 200,000 housing units. Soon after the "housing revolution," which made of Singapore a model for the solution of housing problems, Christian missionaries learned that a group is more open to religious change when it is going through territorial or social displacement. A study in 1972 revealed that residents were more open to the gospel during the first months of maxi-apartment residence than later on.

James W. K. Wong, director of the Church Growth Study Center in Singapore, responded to the challenge by working out an approach tailored specifically to it. Small groups of Christians enter into dialogue with apartment tenants. Keeping abreast of plans for new building projects, they do what they can to prevent the repetition of mistakes and omissions in earlier projects—for example, the absence of a general meeting room for each apartment building. Then the more committed and gifted are trained for the specialized ministries that dialogue and the formation of new Christian groups demand. Christian families already living in an apartment complex become the basis for the formation of a type of "domestic church." The parish becomes a center for the formation and support of the ministries that the domestic churches need.[18]

The fifth method, like the others, bases itself on the principle that the local church is not a place but a group of persons. It too begins with Bible schools, a third of which become transformed into "domestic churches," "family churches," which then visit other families. It is interesting to note that, in one report to the 1974 congress, it was stated that twenty or more persons must be invited to a meeting in order to ensure that five of them will come. The groups have about twenty members each; to survive they need the help of and linkage with other groups.[19]

For this linkage, the structures of a joint, organic pastoral ministry, as sketched above, are needed. Once it is in existence, how does a joint ministry reach out toward those who do not yet have a vital relationship with Christ?

Toward Those Who Do Not Know Christ

Here again the Protestant experience has been extensive, especially through one of their "campaign strategies," the citywide crusade, a type of "internal" mission, aimed at an entire city, within the course of a few days, by as large a group of Christians as possible. The word "crusade" suggests an organized mobilization to "win over" as many residents as possible to the person and message of Christ. It is justified by the bimillennial Christian experience of the recurrent appearance of great evangelizer saints attracting the attention of the masses. But the contemporary urban context makes it more interesting; it enlarges the audience and offers original channels of communication.

Crusades often succeed in "waking up" an entire city, particularly those in control of economic and political processes. They also reach the "famished in spirit," as happened to Cornelius (cf. Acts 10), who was searching for the definitive divine Word in an anonymous God. Crusades also attract the young, even those who generally have no contact with Christian groups. Besides the obvious opportunity to have themselves seen as a unified body that extends to all parts of the city, crusades give these ecclesial groups the opportunity to reevaluate the degree of their accessibility.

A crusade usually takes place in an atmosphere of jubilation, with songs, cheers, prayers, and other manifestations of festivity. It can indeed be a moment of renewal and of renewed commitment for Christians, stimulating them to create new groups and to explore new roads for the evangelization of the city.

According to Luis Palau, who has organized this type of mission in virtually all major Latin American cities, it is not just a publicity campaign but the confluence of a number of diverse urban ministries in a "moment of grace." A crusade also runs some serious risks, among them that of creating false expectations, especially when there is no active follow-up in depth and over a long period of time. Palau's formula, however, foresees and confronts these risks. His procedure involves the three elements of preparation, penetration, and preservation.

Preparation begins with study sessions for the missionaries and continues with the conscientization of the faithful and their orientation for mission in the true and full sense of the term. Interesting is the training to make "god-fathers" of those who respond to the crusade's call, the holding of Bible study sessions in private homes, the formation of new groups, the dialoguing with diverse categories of city residents, and many other techniques.

Penetration consists in a series of mass meetings and study sessions that attract the attention of the mass media, in personal appearances and public "testimonies" of the faithful, in spot consultations throughout the city to assess the reactions of residents, in working breakfasts for officials, in morning Bible classes, and in an extensive use of audiovisual and communications media.

Preservation, the most difficult aspect, begins with moving along the roads opened by the crusade. It often includes the inauguration of "godfather ministries" in private homes, the organization of Bible weeks in every church the week after the mission, the daily (if possible) use of the radio, or at least of the press and audiovisual media, and the "day of welcome" for newcomers.[20]

Structures for Reaching Out to the City

The essential function that the type of initiatives just described accords to the media of social communication illustrates and emphasizes the role of structures in the transformation of urban church into urban mission.

What is done on television, by way of example, is not only something of value in itself—bringing the Christian message through the walls of urban apartment buildings to the everyday life of families, believing and non-believing—but is also of value as a support to the evangelical thrust of the church, in the dialoguing and evangelization done by various ecclesial groups, at the base level of the small groups and at the intermediate level of the bishop and his immediate collaborators.

In Japan statisticians had estimated the number of Christians to be about 1 million. But then in a government census an additional million stated that they were Christians. There have always been more persons who identify themselves as Christians than those who have actually been baptized. Still, explanations of the Japanese phenomenon are elusive. Certainly one of the major factors has been that of the communication of the evangelical message by the mass media. In Tokyo the Good Shepherd movement has been very successful; it is an initiative of Maryknoll Missioners who have learned how to make use of the enormous potentials offered by the metropolis. There is no way of knowing how many persons they have reached. Then too there is the fact that a high percentage of the most popular Japanese writers are Christians.

Only an urban church, across its central, intermediate, and peripheral structures, coordinated by a joint pastoral ministry, can fashion and maintain the structuring of evangelical activity needed today. And when it does so, it becomes urban mission. Opportunities are plentiful. The sector of social communications is only one of the many that constitute and condition urban life. It will be up to a joint pastoral ministry to see to it that each sector is touched by one or more church structures.

In general, urban mission must develop structures for ecumenism, for dialogue, and for ecclesial service. Ecumenical commissions, dialogue groups, justice and peace commissions have long been in existence, and on a wide scale. But they will remain lifeless if they are not a help to the small groups at the base of the urban population. It will be the task of urban mission to vivify these groups, continually searching for ways to give support to the population base, in the small groups.

The same applies, at a more controllable level, to the structures—whether existent or yet to be instituted—of ecumenism, dialogue, and ecclesial service within parochial confines or those of specific groupings (such as hospitals, schools, urban social services). In a certain sense they are even more necessary, inasmuch as the distance between them and the small groups is more manageable.

These structures support the centrifugal impulse of the small basic communities. Once again the sector of social communications can illustrate the point. When a Christian meets an unknown person, the latter could recall: "You are one of the people I saw on TV the other day." In other words, the terrain is prepared. Again, it is not that evangelization is to be pictured as a publicity campaign following the lead of television commercials, selling products in viewers' homes. The example is meant only to illustrate the link, always there, between what is taking place at the "impersonal," central levels and the dynamic life of the population base. This link is important enough to warrant the careful attention of those involved in drawing up the plans for a joint pastoral ministry: it is not rare for what is done at the population base to be contradicted by what is done at other levels.

The City as a Sign of the Times

Only when the signals emanating from the urban church become intelligible to the masses of the city can we say that urban mission is proclaiming the Word of God. This is the terminal point, the final goal. There are two convergent lines—direct proclamation and interpretation—to be traced in substantiating this theme.

First is the line of direct proclamation. "Go to preach" is an obligation, a mandate. The question of language comes up here once again. The support of the city will be decisive in answering it. In the Third World the city is becoming the meeting place of "all the languages" of a given nation, and consequently the laboratory of a common language.

It is a serious problem. Cardinal Arns wagered everything on *biblical language* in his concern to "give a tongue" to the heterogeneity of the ecclesial groups in São Paulo. And he succeeded. But, as we have seen, what goes well in Latin America may not go well in Buddhist Asia, for example. At any rate, the problem of language must be gone into, it is a problem considered by the 1974 Synod of Bishops:

> Preachers must expound the deposit of faith in such a way that the Word of God is made clear to human intelligence, as if incarnated in human conditions. To do this preachers must try to discover, by dialogue, how traditions and social order are related to divine truths.[21]

The discovery of these interrelations is essential for urban mission. They represent the points of convergence between the plan of God as contained in revelation and the plan of God as actualized in the city. They make the teaching of faith concretely meaningful. That is, they make the act of preaching *true,* not illusive:

> Preaching occupies a central place in evangelization. By it the divine plan of salvation is made manifest. By it especially the faith—without which it is impossible to please God (Heb. 11:16)—is aroused and developed. By faith human beings surrender themselves freely to God, paying the homage of their intellects and their wills to the God who reveals himself, and freely assenting to his reveleation (*Dei Verbum*, no. 5). The faith, although it permeates the whole of human life, cannot exist unless the human person accepts as true the deeds and words of God. Because the assent to revelation presupposes the preaching of the Word, so it is that the whole dynamism of the Christian life, in its origination and its evolution, depends on preaching. Faith comes from hearing—hearing the Word of Christ (Rom. 10:18). This explains why the principal function of the church is the preaching of the gospel. . . . [We must] be able to say that we have not omitted anything necessary for the faith in our Lord Jesus Christ to be proclaimed publicly, and from house to house (Acts 20:20).[22]

Today direct, *public* proclamation is the responsibility of the urban church as such, rather than that of any one of its members dispersed throughout the city.

Second is the line of interpretation. The *public* interpretation of what these members do, in their small or large groups, is the prerogative of the urban church, understood as a unitary structure. Only via this interpretation can the sign already constituted by the Christian commitment of these members become truly decipherable and intelligible.

If missionaries wish to give testimony, they must make sure that the conditions are present for it to be understood by those to whom it is directed. It is not seldom that city-dwellers, bombarded by all kinds of "messages," take the message in the sense that was not intended. The city then becomes a sign of incommunicability, another Babel.

In this sense, missionaries can never do enough to make sure that the concrete efforts they make to incarnate themselves in the city will be understood in their true meaning, as expressions of solidarity in the planning for a more human city. The need to explain themselves can also be an occasion for reviewing their own positions.

Besides explaining the "external" deeds of ecclesial groups, it is also necessary to explain the meaning of what they do "internally." It is easy to say that others will be evangelized when they see that missionaries "love one another." But love is not all that visible, especially in the city, where there is a strong inclination to defend one's own privacy and to respect that of others. True love is centrifugal; it includes the effort to help others to understand the meaning of what we do.

In brief: it would be a mistake to presume that everything missionaries do will be understood correctly. Clarity may typify the rural ambient, but it certainly does not typify the urban. Pluralism necessitates an explanation of deeds and decisions.

Conclusion

In these reflections on Third World urban life we have uncovered an ambivalent city, in which demography and geography first concentrate great numbers of persons and then segregate them into groups closed off from one another. We have disentangled economic and political processes that, in close alliance, generate situations of extreme hardship, injustice, and oppression for the urban majorities, to the advantage of a small minority. On the other hand, we have also uncovered a positive response—in the cultural process relating to the masses, and in the process of urban planning relating to the elites—in the efforts to give the Third World city a more human countenance.

Unfortunately the negative outweighs the positive. Solutions presently being implemented do not seem adequate to the urban problematic. Therapy may cure some few of the social ills, but far-reaching, long-range, constructive objectives are being transformed into reality at a snail's pace. At the empirical, experimental level, no way out of this situation has been charted for us. We can only maintain an attitude of openness to the transcendent level—not immediately experiential—of divine intervention into the entirety of human history, and therefore into contemporary urban history.

What goals do God's plans envisage for the Third World city, as they move towards the integral salvation of the urban humanity of our time? We have found the answer in the church. And we have found there the challenge to incorporate this answer into urban mission.

Adhering to the initial purposes of this study we have remained at the general level of the major orientations offered by the reading of the plan of God in the light of the scriptures, of Christian experience, and of contemporary urban history. Even at this level we experience an urge to accept, in a spirit of what we take to be realism, the ambivalence of urban processes in order to go quickly to work reinforcing what is positive and blocking what is negative.

Both the Bible and ecclesial history furnish the same criterion for distinguishing the one from the other: God is *for* the city, but he wills it as a union, a communion of integrally liberated persons. He wills it as the "tent" of his reconciliation with humankind, and of humankind with itself. Everything that is division, segregation, slavery, is negative. Everything that is union, communion, liberation is positive. Thanks to its communitarian thrust, the Third World city is a magnificent workshop-laboratory for the construction of the kingdom of the Lord.

193

God's plans point out the methodology for fostering the positive impulses: to become incarnate in the city and communicate to it the salvation received individually and collectively. Urban mission therefore becomes everything that can facilitate this incarnation and this communication. And it will be the experience of church—*local* church—that will "convey" all this.

Incarnation takes place, above all, at the level of relationships. It is from them that the communication of salvation in evangelization passes to others. And it is here that Third World cities have advantages over other cities. Third World cities seem to offer more openings than First World cities. And this is *the* opportunity, the "opportune" point of access, for urban mission.

But urban mission is not to be a substitute or an alternative for what is already being done in these cities in the "human" response of urban planning. True to its incarnational inspiration, urban mission will take its place *within* the work of urban planning, in an attitude of solidarity. Nor will it take over directive roles; that would be nothing other than a new form of domination, and it would be presumptuous as well. Its contribution—which cannot come from any other source—will be that of complementing the "human" response with the divine response of the plan of salvation. In this plan the church—and it alone—is called to be the sign and sacrament of salvation.

The church will become the sacrament of the city—*sacramentum urbis*— only to the extent that it transforms itself into urban mission, and that means to the extent that it succeeds in instilling in its members the incarnational attitudes of humility, curiosity, and dialogue, and succeeds in inspiring them to take up roles of ecclesial service and to form groups that undertake conscientization and evangelization.

This is exactly the place that seems to be assigned to urban mission in God's plans for the salvation of the Third World city: to translate into experiential reality the ontological reality of the church as the sacrament for the city. This is the age-old missionary challenge, but in a modality suited to our generation characterized as it is by the urbanization of the Third World. "Go, . . . preach the gospel" to the peoples concentrated in the metropolises. "I am with you . . . signs will accompany those who believe" (Mk. 16:15; Mt. 28:20; and Mk. 16:17).

At this point the challenge of mission becomes an act of faith. The Eleven "went forth and preached everywhere, while the Lord worked with them and confirmed the message by the signs that attended it" (Mk. 16:20). It is an act of faith that there is a plan of grace for the cities of the Third World, and that the Lord is carrying it out in their socioeconomic processes, in urban planning, and in the local church.

If this is the base for Christian missionaries, where they can meet Christ, then the city is the field, where they meet him again. The tension between "base" and "field" is the very life of urban mission. And it is a life of faith, because only in faith does urban mission find motivation and assurance.

NOTES

1. Mission to the Cities of the Third World

1. See Walter M. Abbott, ed., *The Documents of Vatican II* (New York: Association Press, 1974), *Lumen Gentium*, no. 11.
2. See G. P. Murdoch, *Outline of World Cultures* (New Haven: Human Resources Area Files, Yale University Press, 1963).
3. See International Congress for World Evangelization, *Unreached Peoples* (Monrovia, Liberia Mission Advanced Research Center, 1974).
4. *Osservatore Romano*, Oct 6, 1974, p. 5.
5. See Gideon Sjoberg, "The Rural-Urban Dimension," in Robert L. Faris, ed., *Handbook of Modern Sociology* (Chicago: Rand-McNally, 1966), pp. 138-41.
6. See Sjoberg, "The Rural-Urban Dimension," pp. 149-55.
7. See *The Growth of World Population: Urban and Rural* (New York: United Nations, 1970).
8. Statistics taken from *Demographic Yearbook, 1971* (New York: United Nations, 1972); V. Showers, *World Facts and Figures* (New York: Wiley, 1979); J. Paxton, ed., *The Statesman's Year-Book 1979-1980* (New York: St. Martin's Press, 1979).
9. *Report on the World Social Situation* (New York: United Nations, 1971), passim.
10. See Barbara Ward and René Dubos, *Only One Earth* (New York: Norton, 1972), chap. 8.
11. *Report on the World Social Situation*, p. 185.
12. See Paul Bairoch, *Le chômage urbain dans les pays en voie de développement* (BIT—Bureau International du Travail, International Labour Organisation, Geneva, 1973).
13. Ibid.
14. See "The World Employment Program," in *BIT Informations* (Geneva, 1973), p. 7.
15. See *Report on the World Social Situation*, p. 39.
16. Ibid., p. 51.
17. See *World Housing Conditions* (New York: United Nations, 1965) p. 65 and IV, 8.
18. See *Report on the World Social Situation*, p. 186.
19. Ibid., p. 3.
20. See P. K. Sen, in *The Exploding Cities* (London: Oyez, 1974), p. 50.
21. See *Sunday Times* (London), March 31, 1974.
22. See *Report on the World Social Situation*, p. 26.
23. Ibid., p. 62.
24. See R. Gbadamosi, in *The Exploding Cities*, p. 39.
25. Barbara Ward, *The Home of Man* (New York: Norton, 1976), p. 125.
26. See *Sunday Times*, London, March 31, 1974.
27. See J. Clyde Mitchell, ed., *Social Networks in Urban Situations* (Atlantic Highlands, N.J.: Humanities Press, 1969).
28. Carolina Maria de Jesus, "Child of the Dark," *Impact*, Manila, August 1972; published as a New American Library Paperback as *Child of the Dark: The Diary of Carolina Maria de Jesus*, 1974.

2. A System to Be Understood

1. See Ferdinand Tönnies, *Community and Society* (New York: Harper & Row Torchbook, 1977).
2. See Emile Durkheim, *The Division of Labor in Society* (New York: Free Press, 1968).
3. See R. Redfield, *Peasant Society and Culture* (Chicago: University of Chicago Press, 1956).

4. See W. Christaller, *A Critique and Translation of* Die zentralen Orte, trans. C. W. Baskin (Ann Arbor, Mich.: University Microfilms, 1957).

5. See R.E. Park, *Human Communities* (Chicago: University of Chicago Press, 1952).

6. See J.H. Fichter, *Sociology,* 2nd ed. (Chicago: University of Chicago Press, 1971).

7. See Karl Marx and Friedrich Engels, *Manifesto of the Communist Party* (San Francisco: China Books, 1965).

8. See Max Weber, *Theory of Social and Economic Organization* (New York: Free Press, 1947); *The City* (New York: Free Press, 1966).

9. See J. Beshers, *Urban Social Structure* (New York: Free Press, 1962).

10. See SEDOS Documentation 73/333.

11. See Max Weber, *Economy and Society,* 3 vols. (Totowa, N.J.: Bedminster, 1968).

12. Ibid.

13. See R.E. Park, et al., *City* (Chicago: University of Chicago Press, 1968).

14. See L. Wirth, "Urbanism as a Way of Life," *American Journal of Sociology* 44 (1938).

15. G. Bettin, "Elementi per una teoria della città," *Working Papers sulla società contemporanea* (Milan-Bologna, 1974), p. 105.

16. See Gideon Sjoberg, *The Pre-Industrial City Past and Present* (New York: Free Press, 1965).

17. T.G.McGee, *The Urbanization Process in the Third World* (London: Bell, 1971), p 50. Quotation within McGee quotation from Redfield–Singer, "The Cultural Role of Cities," *Economic Development and Cultural Change* 3, no. 1 (1954): 59.

18. Interview in *Dimensioni Nuove* (Turin, 1977), no. 5, p. 36.

19. See J. Abu Lughod, "Migrant Adjustment to City Life," *American Journal of Sociology* 67 (1961): 23.

20. *Octogesima Adveniens,* no. 9–12 (Eng. trans. from *The Pope Speaks* 16, no. 2, Summer 1971, p. 142).

3. More Persons in Less Space

1. Statistics taken from *Demographic Yearbook 1971* (New York: United Nations, 1972); A. McCormack, *The Population Problem* (New York: Crowell, 1970).

2. Cited in A. Ronchey, *Atlante ideologico* (Milan: Garzanti, 1973), p. 9.

3. A. McCormack, *L'esplosione demografica—Un problema cristiano* (Bologna: Editrice Missionaria Italiana, 1974).

4. See *Report on the World Social Situation* (New York: United Nations, 1971), p. 15.

5. See H. Cole, in *The Exploding Cities* (London: Oyez), p. 110.

6. See SEDOS Documentation 72/43.

7. See W. Christaller, *A Critique and Translation of* Die zentralen Orte, trans. C. W. Baskin (Ann Arbor, Mich.: University Microfilms, 1957).

8. See J. H. Von Thunen, *Isolated State* (London: Pergamon, 1966).

9. See E. W. Burgess, *The City* (Chicago: University of Chicago Press, 1925).

10. See *Report on the World Social Situation.*

4. Orderly Response to Needs

1. See G. Breese, ed., *The City in Newly Developing Countries* (Englewood Cliffs, N. J.: Prentice-Hall, 1968), p. 11.

2. E. Jelin, in SEDOS Documentation 77/1.

3. See A. G. Frank, "Sociology of Development," *Catalyst* 3 (1967): 20-73.

4. C. Geertz, *Peddlers and Princes* (1963), cited in T.G. McGee, *The Urbanization Process in the Third World* (London: Bell, 1971), p. 90.

5. See SEDOS Documentation 77/11.

6. See E. Jelin, in *The Exploding Cities* (London: Oyez, 1974).

7. See "Declaration of Principles for a New Economic Order," 2229, Plenary Session of May 1, 1974, United Nations World Population Conference (Bucharest).

8. See "Vancouver Declaration," in SEDOS Documentation 77/1.

9. M. Candito, "L'alibi demografico," *La Stampa* (Turin), Sept. 3, 1974, p. 3.

10. See M. Castells, *Imperialismo e urbanizzazione in America Latina* (Milan: Mazzotta, 1972), p. 13.

11. See *Octogesima Adveniens,* no. 10.

12. See *Report on the World Social Situation* (New York: United Nations, 1971).
13. See M. Stewart, *The City* (Middlesex, England: Penguin, 1972).
14. See John Kenneth Galbraith, in *The Exploding Cities*, p. 162.
15. See McGee, *The Urbanization Process*, p. 64.
16. See P. K. Sen, in *The Exploding Cities*.

5. The Meaning of Urban Life

1. See H. E. Nottridge, *The Sociology of Urban Living* (London: Routledge, 1972), p. 92.
2. See G. D. Suttles, *The Social Order of the Slum* (Chicago: University of Chicago Press, 1968).
3. See Nottridge, *Sociology*, p. 98.
4. See M. Castells, *Imperialismo e urbanizzazione in America Latina* (Milan: Mazzotta, 1972), p. 22.
5. See R. M. Solzbacher, in *Papers on Urban Industrial Issues in Africa* (Somerset: All Africa Conference of Churches, 1970).
6. See *Report on the Seminar on Uncontrolled Settlements* (New York: United Nations, 1971).
7. See H. Dunkerley in *The Exploding Cities* (London: Oyez, 1974), p. 125.
8. See Oscar Lewis, *La Vida* (New York: Random, 1966), Introduction.
9. See R. Wade, "A Culture in Poverty?" in *IDS* [Institute of Development Studies] *Bulletin*, Sussex University, no. 5 (1973): 4–30.
10. See E. Jelin, in *The Exploding Cities*, p. 159.
11. See Frantz Fanon, *The Wretched of the Earth* (New York: Grove, 1965).
12. See J. Clyde Mitchell, ed., *Social Networks in Urban Situations* (Atlantic Highlands, N.J.: Humanities Press, 1969).
13. See Elizabeth Bott, *Family and Social Network*, 2nd ed. (New York: Free Press, 1972.)
14. See Thomas Luckmann, *Invisible Religion* (New York: Macmillan, 1967), p. 43.
15. See Peter Berger, *The Social Reality of Religion* (London: Faber, 1969).
16. See M. Hill, *The Sociology of Religion* (New York: Basic Books, 1973).

6. Urban Planning

1. See M. Stewart, ed., *The City: Problems of Planning* (Middlesex, England: Penguin, 1972), pp. 11–24.
2. See INTER Documentation, Zurich, for development plans; available also at SEDOS, Rome.
3. See Barbara Ward and René Dubos, *Only One Earth* (New York: Norton, 1972).
4. See P.L. Vathavikul, *Regional Planning as Tool for Development*, Symposium on Regional Development, Tokyo, 1969.
5. See A. A. Laquian, in *The Exploding Cities* (London: Oyez, 1974), p. 140.
6. See N. Maxwell, in *The Exploding Cities*.
7. See H. J. Gans, in Stewart, ed., *The City: Problems of Planning*.
8. See *Report on the World Social Situation* (New York: United Nations, 1971).
9. C. Correa, quoted in *Sunday Times* (London: March 31, 1974).
10. Barbara Ward, *The Home of Man* (New York: Norton, 1976), p. 233.
11. See O. Fatchurrahman, in *The Exploding Cities*, p. 133.
12. See J. A. Rios, in *The Exploding Cities*, p. 48.
13. See Lord Holborn, in *The Exploding Cities*, p. 99.
14. Ward and Dubos, *Only One Earth*, p. 94.
15. See Ward and Dubos, *Only One Earth*.
16. See M. Stewart, ed., *The City: Problems of Planning*, p. 44.
17. See J. Rykert, in *The Exploding Cities*, p. 95.
18. See S. Damer and C. Hague, "Public Participation in Planning," *Town Planning Review* 42 (1971): 217.

7. Urban Mission: The Emerging Response

1. See I. Mancini, *Teologia ideologia utopia* (Brescia: Queriniana, 1974).
2. See *Gaudium et Spes*, no. 4, 11.

3. U. Betti, "La Chiesa a servizio dell' umanità," *Osservatore Romano,* March 2, 1975, p. 3.
4. See L.-G Arevalo, *Theology in Action* (Manila: Urban-Industrial Mission, 1972), pp. 51-60.
5. See Arevalo, *Theology in Action.*
6. See J. Policarpo, *Sinais dos Tiempos* (Lisbon: Sampedro, 1971).
7. See A. Bundervoet, *La théologie de la ville,* SEDOS Documentation 73/27.
8. See José Comblin, *Teologia della città* (Assisi: Cittadella, 1971).
9. See Avery Dulles, "The Church and Salvation," *Missiology* 2 (1973).
10. Dulles, "The Church and Salvation," pp. 79–80.
11. *Evangelii Nuntiandi,* no. 19–20

8. Solidarity as Generic Mission

1. U. Betti, "La Chiesa a servizio dell' umanità," *Osservatore Romano,* March 2, 1975, p. 3.
2. *Octogesima Adveniens,* no. 48.
3. SEDOS Documentation 74/557.
4. See C. Mina et al., *L'io e il gruppo nella psicologia* (Rome: Città Nuova, 1968), p. 14.
5. See L. Debarge, *Psychologie et pastorale* (Paris: Desclée, 1968), p. 127.
6. See J. Gates, cited in SEDOS *Joint Venture,* no. 11 (Rome, 1973): 34.
7. V. Gottwald, in SEDOS Documentation 73/261.
8. See 1971 Synod of Bishops, "Justice in the World," no. 6.
9. See P. Arrupe, *A Planet to Heal* (Rome: Ignatian Center for Spirituality, 1975), p. 37.
10. Cited in SEDOS *Joint Venture,* no. 11, p. 37.
11. See *Thrusts,* Urban and Industrial Mission (Geneva: World Council of Churches, 1970).
12. See *Report,* Urban and Industrial Mission (Geneva: World Council of Churches, 1973).
13. *Octogesima Adveniens,* no. 46.
14. See René Girard, *Violence and the Sacred* (Baltimore: Johns Hopkins University Press, 1977).
15. *Octogesima Adveniens,* no. 20.
16. See P. Arrupe, *A Planet to Heal,* p. 91.
17. See P. E. Arns, ed., *Pastorale per un'unità di Chiesa e di Popolo* (Milan: Jaca Book, 1975), pp. 28–40.

9. Evangelization as Specific Mission

1. *Evangelii Nuntiandi,* no. 24.
2. See World Council of Churches, Fifth Assembly Documentation, section 1 (Geneva, 1974).
3. *Octogesima Adveniens,* no. 50.
4. J. Cordeiro, "Relazione sull'evangelizzazione in Asia," in *Sinodo 1974, I Semi del Vangelo. Studi e Interventi dei Vescovi d'Asia* (Bologna: Editrice Missionaria Italiana, 1975), p. 73.
5. See 1974 Synod, *Suffragia,* no. 8.
6. C. Floristan Samanes, *Il Catecumenato* (Rome: Paoline, 1974), p. 13.
7. *Nostra Aetate,* no. 2.
8. See SEDOS Documentation 74/562.
9. See SEDOS Documentation 73/78.
10. M. Zago, "L'evangelizzazione ai Buddhisti," *Communio* 15 (May–June 1974): 54.
11. See *La visée missionnaire* (Rome: Oblates of Mary Immaculate, 1972), p. 25.
12. F. Ricci, in P. E. Arns, ed., *Pastorale per un'unità di Chiesa e di Popolo* (Milan: Jaca Book, 1975), p. 13
13. See P. E. Arns, ed., *Pastorale.*
14. Ibid., p. 75.
15. F. Ricci, in Arns, ed., *Pastorale,* p. 15.
16. See SEDOS Documentation 73/33.
17. G. S. Gorgulho, in Arns, ed., *Pastorale,* p. 24.

10. Church as Mission

1. *I Semi del Vangelo. Studi e Interventi dei Vescovi d'Asia* (Bologna: Editrice Missionaria Italiana, 1975), p. 115.

2. *L'evangelizzazione nel Mondo* (Turin: LDC, 1974), p. 46.

3. See *Guidelines of the 1973 Plenary* (Nairobi: Association of Member Episcopal Conferences in Eastern Africa, 1973), no. 2, 10.

4. *Pro Mundi Vita* (Brussels), 1976, no. 68, p. 8.

5. *Evangelii Nuntiandi*, no. 58.

6. See José Comblin, "Les communautés de base," *Concilium,* French ed., no. 104, p. 93.

7. G. Marchesi, "La Coscienza che la Chiesa ha della sua missione," *Civiltà Cattolica*, no. 3041 (March 5, 1977), p. 477.

8. *Evangelii Nuntiandi*, no. 71.

9. See SEDOS Documentation 74/793.

10. C. Koser, Union of Superiors General, Rome, Circular 32/74.

11. See Stephen Verney, *People and Cities* (Old Tappan, N. J.: Revell, 1971).

12. See I. Bria, "An Orthodox Consultation," *International Review of Mission*, January 1975, p. 67.

13. Kinshasa (Zaire), *Documentation et Information Africaines,* April 22, 1974.

14. See SEDOS Documentation 72/53.

15. See *Fides*, Sept. 25, 1974, p. 513.

16. See SEDOS *Joint Venture* II (Rome, 1973): 32.

17. C. S. Gorgulho, in P. E. Arns, ed., *Pastorale per un'unità di Chiesa e di Popolo* (Milan: Jaca Book, 1975), p. 26.

18. See J.W.K. Wong, in J. D. Douglas, ed., *Let the Earth Hear His Voice* (Minneapolis: World Wide Publications, 1975), p. 93.

19. See R. S. Greenway, in Douglas, ed., *Let the Earth Hear His Voice*, p. 917.

20. See L. Palau, in Douglas, ed., *Let the Earth Hear His Voice*, p. 601.

21. *Suffragia*, no. 18 (1974 Synod of Bishops).

22. *Suffragia*, no. 16 (1974 Synod of Bishops).

Index

201